JUL 2002

HIDDEN HISTORIES
OF WOMEN
IN THE
NEW SOUTH

Southern Women

A series of books developed from the Southern Conference on Women's History sponsored by the Southern Association for Women Historians.

edited by

Virginia Bernhard

Betty Brandon

Elizabeth Fox-Genovese

Theda Perdue

HIDDEN HISTORIES
OF WOMEN
IN THE
NEW SOUTH

EDITED BY

VIRGINIA BERNHARD

BETTY BRANDON

ELIZABETH FOX-GENOVESE

THEDA PERDUE

ELIZABETH HAYES TURNER

University of Missouri Press
COLUMBIA AND LONDON

Copyright © 1994 by
The Curators of the University of Missouri
University of Missouri Press, Columbia, Missouri 65201
Printed and bound in the United States of America
5 4 3 2 1   98 97 96 95 94

Library of Congress Cataloging-in-Publication Data

Hidden histories of women in the New South / edited by Virginia
    Bernhard . . . [et al.].
        p.   cm.
    Includes bibliographical references (p.   ) and index.
    ISBN 0-8262-0958-0 (acid-free paper)
    1. Women—Southern States—History.   2. Afro-American
women—Southern States—History.   3. Women in politics—Southern
States—History.   4. Women social reformers—Southern States—
History.   I. Bernhard, Virginia, 1937–
HQ1438.S63H53   1994
305.4'0975—dc20   94-9978
                                                                      CIP

⊗™ This paper meets the requirements of the
American National Standard for Permanence of Paper
for Printed Library Materials, Z39.48, 1984.

Designer: Elizabeth K. Fett
Typesetter: Connell-Zeko Type & Graphics
Printer and Binder: Rose Printing Company, Inc.
Typefaces: ITC Garamond Light and Garamond Book

CONTENTS

RACIAL COOPERATION
AND REFORM MOVEMENTS

HIDDEN HISTORIES
OF WOMEN
IN THE
NEW SOUTH

EDITORS' INTRODUCTION

A generation ago, "women's history" meant the history of a handful of individuals, mostly white and mostly middle or upper class. Among them were women like Abigail Adams, whose prominence stemmed from their marriages to famous men, or Elizabeth Cady Stanton and Susan B. Anthony, whose militance in the cause of women's rights entitled them to a small place in the mainstream of American history. There might have been a token nod to a Phillis Wheatley or a Harriet Tubman, but women of color, regardless of their accomplishments, were generally disregarded. In recent years, however, the mainstream has grown wider, its currents diffused by racial and ethnic studies as well as women's studies, reshaping the terrain of America's past. Part of that emerging landscape is the experience of not just a few women but of many: slaves, immigrants, Native Americans, factory workers, housewives, reformers—all part of the diverse group that comprises at least one-half the country's population. Women's history has come into its own, and scholars of both sexes have begun to appreciate its power to enrich—and sometimes to alter—the course of traditional history.

The essays in this volume, whose subjects range from the 1870s to the 1960s, are "hidden histories" in the sense that they explore the experiences of women whose lives have gone largely unnoticed by historians. Women in prison, in mental institutions, in isolated rural areas, and women activists for temperance, suffrage, birth control, and civil rights offer new perspectives, not only on the history of women but on the South. These essays were first presented as papers at the second Southern Conference on Women's History at the Duke University–University of North Carolina Center for Research on Women, June 7 and 8, 1991.[1] The authors—some

1. Selected papers from the first Southern Conference on Women's History in 1988 were published in Virginia Bernhard et al., eds., *Southern Women: Histories and Identities* (Columbia: University of Missouri Press, 1992).

1

established scholars, some new-minted Ph.D.'s—are as diverse as their subjects. Their work, like that of many of their colleagues, has been shaped by present concerns about race and class as well as gender; each essay in its own way addresses the challenge of multiculturalism.

At the 1991 conference, Mary Frederickson, one of the participants on a panel devoted to multiculturalism, defined its meaning for women's history:

> For those who work in the field of women's history, the theory of multiculturalism, considered apart from the political tempest of the early 1990s, presents a special challenge. Women's history must focus on multiple identities, understand the theory and practice of overlapping allegiances, and deal with diversity, while at the same time attempting to move beyond simple pluralism. The problem is to acknowledge difference in the past and affirm it in the present, while not fracturing the political and social unity that is crucial to the nation's survival. . . .
>
> The complexity of the southern past, the interwoven histories of a bi-racial people, means that some important keys to understanding the historical construction of gender, of identity, perspective, and multiple voices are hidden within southern culture. Gender-specific ideologies, behaviors, organizations, style, rhetoric, and institutions have defined the lives of all southern women to a greater or lesser degree. Gender has circumscribed their actions and delineated their dreams.
>
> At times race has been a more powerful determinant than gender. One can argue, for example, that the dominant white society in the South often has worked to obliterate gender as a category for non-white southerners. De-feminization and de-masculinization have proved powerful tools for imposing dominance and control. In these contexts, femininity and masculinity have become concepts charged with political meaning, and self-defined gender prescriptions emerge as forms of defiance and resistance for non-whites. Gender has often worked in different ways for white women and men. White society has been bifurcated by male and female gender identification; at the same time black society has been perceived by whites as free of gender prescriptions. Narrowly defined conceptions of femininity and masculinity for white southerners limited behavior, language, ideology, education, social networks and family roles. While African American southerners defied the dominant society by adopting their own gendered prescriptions

for behavior, their refusal to comply with white-imposed prescriptions can be interpreted as a challenge to the social system.[2]

Multiculturalism and women's history intersect at the crucial connections between gender and race, ideology and identity, work and life. The essays presented here explore southern women's history from three perspectives: institutions of social control, gender prescriptions and government programs, and racial cooperation in the pursuit of social change. In the 1880s, southern prisons, and in the early 1900s, asylums and birth control clinics, all sought various means of subduing or setting apart women whose race, deviant behavior, and class might threaten white, middle-class society. The ideal southern woman was apolitical, submissive, and virtuous, and woe to the woman who deviated without middle-class status to protect her. On the other hand, sometimes the "ideal" women turned gender prescriptions to their advantage, campaigning for civic improvement under the banner of home and motherhood; antisuffragists raised that same banner to argue against votes for women. Government agents for the Department of Agriculture worked for change while reinforcing time-honored notions about farm women's work—but only white women's work. On occasion, work for the betterment of society crossed racial lines in organizations as diverse as the Woman's Christian Temperance Union, the Southern Student Organizing Committee, and the Student Nonviolent Coordinating Committee. In each instance, the post-Reconstruction South, with its burdensome legacy of slavery, its hallowed codes of honor, and its exalted view of planter aristocracy, served as the inescapable, unalterable backdrop for the interplay of ideas and actions.

In Mary Ellen Curtin's "The 'Human World' of Black Women in Alabama Prisons, 1870–1900," the harsh legalities of the black codes, the South's answer to emancipation, put black women behind bars and on work gangs. Drawing from largely untapped sources of state and county prison records, Curtin has found numbers of these "hidden" women, many whose only offense was to trade in an illicit market or argue with an employer. Others were incarcerated for public disorder, an offense too often defined by whites whose views of race, political allegiance, and gender roles differed from

2. Mary Frederickson, "Back to the Crossroads: The Challenges of a Multicultural History" (paper presented at the second Southern Conference on Women's History, Chapel Hill, N.C., June 7, 1991).

those of the newly freed blacks. Once in prison, black women were often at the mercy of white male officials, who put them to work on convict lease gangs in mines or on farms and subjected them to verbal and physical abuse. Despite unjust and brutal treatment, black female prisoners found ways to resist and to create their own world within prison walls. The story of these women reveals as much about justice and freedom in the New South as about the inmates of its prisons.

Women in asylums have a history as little known as that of women in prisons, and one that demands a closer look at southern society's views of women's nature. Steven Noll's essay, "'A Far Greater Menace': Feebleminded Females in the South, 1900–1940," delves into the archives of mental institutions and the history of mental retardation to explore the mentality that prescribed institutionalization for women whose behavior did not conform to prevailing gender prescriptions. Since early-twentieth-century mental institutions were almost exclusively administered by men, male perceptions of female behavior and of what constituted deviant behavior played a crucial role in determining which women were labeled "feebleminded." Southern notions of gentility, propriety, and sexuality combined powerfully with male ideas of women as helpless, hysterical, and often lustful creatures who, if they were lower class, were in need of confinement for their own good and the good of society. Noll's study offers a fresh perspective on gender and class stereotypes and on the ways that such stereotypes affect the development of social institutions.

Birth control clinics, or "centers for contraceptive advice," as they were called in the 1930s, until now have received little attention from historians. Marianne Leung's study of birth control in Arkansas points to a need for similar studies in other regions and suggests that birth control activists drew upon differing ideologies in constructing their agendas. In "'Better Babies': Birth Control in Arkansas during the 1930s," Leung finds that the confluence of the economic hardships of the Great Depression with the spread of Margaret Sanger's ideas on birth control inspired the Little Rock clinic to focus on poor women. Said one of its founders, a banker's wife with six children: "We love a big family. When you cannot take care of a big family, I try to help you." Leung explores the complex motives and rationales of the early birth control movement and, in so doing, reveals much about middle-class mores and the double-edged nature of population control. Poor women grate-fully accepted contraceptive advice, and reformers rejoiced at the limitation of the class most likely to become a burden to society.

Motherhood in general was so smiled upon, however, that a group of determined, reform-minded women might march safely under its banner, as did a coalition of affluent Dallas matrons in the 1890s. Campaigning demurely at first, declaring they only wanted better schools and parks for their children, they perfected their techniques of applying pressure to a male power structure, ex-panded their sphere of influence, and by the early 1900s were transferring their tactics to politics and the suffrage movement. It is well known that early suffragists linked women's desire to protect home and family with the need to vote, but Elizabeth York En-stam's carefully detailed study, "They Called It 'Motherhood': Dallas Women and Public Life, 1895–1918," reveals precisely how one group of dedicated women moved gracefully and skillfully from home and hearth to the arena of public policy.

As Enstam has shown, images of motherhood and domesticity were powerful weapons in political debates, and their use was not limited to one side. Across the South, people who opposed suf-frage for women rallied their forces around traditional notions of women and family life. Elna Green's essay, "'Ideals of Government, of Home, and of Women': The Ideology of Southern White Anti-suffragism," analyzes the beliefs of the antisuffragists in the con-text of the South's nostalgia for plantation society and a world in which rich and poor, women and blacks, all knew their place. In so doing, she sheds new light on the ideas of the southern suffragists, who were willing to accept blacks as a voting minority. Green also explores the little-known world of black antisuffragists, whose views, sometimes based on fear of white reprisals, differed markedly from those of their white counterparts. For both races, images of home, motherhood, and family and a desire to protect the status quo framed their antisuffrage arguments.

Woman's place was in the home: there was no question about that from any sector in the South, but when it came to gender prescriptions for white women's work and black women's work, opinions differed noticeably. Two essays, one on rural women by Lynne A. Rieff, and the other on the programs of the United States Department of Agriculture by Kathleen C. Hilton, complement each other. While Hilton's study, "'Both in the Field, Each with a Plow':

Race and Gender in USDA Policy, 1907–1929," ranges across the South, Rieff's essay, "'Go Ahead and Do All You Can': Southern Progressives and Alabama Home Demonstration Clubs, 1914–1940," turns a microscope on Progressive ideology and USDA programs in Alabama. Hilton finds that government agents carefully distinguished agriculture (men's work) from home economics (women's sphere) for white farm families but not for rural blacks. The South's African Americans, as usual, found discrimination in both USDA and Progressive Era reform policies. Rieff's study examines the efforts of progressive reformers, who remained bound by their traditional views of race, class, and gender while nourishing hopes of revitalizing the rural South. Studies of southern progressivism, not to mention populism, should benefit from these findings.

As one group of Dallas women bent gender prescriptions to suit its own activist purposes, other groups across the South bravely crossed racial boundaries to further their reform interests. In "'A Melting Time': Black Women, White Women, and the WCTU in North Carolina, 1880–1900," Glenda Elizabeth Gilmore examines how the Woman's Christian Temperance Union briefly united white and black women in an extraordinary experiment in interracial cooperation. To be praised more for its aims than for its accomplishments, the cooperative effort was short-lived and ultimately unsuccessful, leaving African Americans again disappointed by white attitudes. It was nonetheless, as Gilmore puts it, a time when "racial boundaries 'melted' ever so slightly."

In the 1960s, southern whites tried to enlist blacks in another cooperative effort with better results. Stunned by the racial violence spreading across the South in the early civil rights movement, a small number of white college students formed the Southern Student Organizing Committee, daring to speak out against the bigotry and injustice they saw around them. Christina Greene's essay, "'We'll Take Our Stand': Race, Class, and Gender in the Southern Student Organizing Committee, 1964–1969," describes the formation of this little-known civil rights organization. SSOC actively sought the aid of young blacks and worked closely with the Student Nonviolent Coordinating Committee, initiating the White Folks Project as part of the larger Freedom Summer effort in 1964 in Mississippi. Greene notes the complications of SNCC's black power movement and the problems of gender as well as race within SOCC. Along the way, she uncovered some early links between the civil rights movement and the "women's liberation" movement of the 1960s.

Gender prescriptions allowed no room for women's activism regardless of race. Cynthia Griggs Fleming's moving portrait of one young black woman who struggled with her own identity as executive secretary of SNCC and as wife and mother illustrates the tensions between men and women and between work and family that troubled women of both races. As Fleming points out in "'More Than a Lady': Ruby Doris Smith Robinson and Black Women's Leadership in the Student Nonviolent Coordinating Committee," Robinson fought fiercely for the cause of racial justice and just as fiercely against the cancer that took her life at the age of twenty-five. Both Green and Fleming draw extensively on oral history for these studies, and their work—especially the reminiscences of some key figures in SSOC and SNCC—offer fresh perspectives on the civil rights movement.

The "hidden histories" in this volume do in many ways what women's history is meant to do: they use fresh evidence to add to the store of knowledge about women. They also mark new points where gender has combined with race, class, and ideology to shape the mainstream of American history.

INSTITUTIONS OF
SOCIAL CONTROL

The "Human World" of Black Women in Alabama Prisons, 1870-1900

MARY ELLEN CURTIN

The reaction of black women to the convict leasing system, a new form of forced labor that followed quickly on the heels of slavery, raises many important questions about the meaning of freedom and of slavery to black people in the postemancipation era. Black women constituted a significant part of the prison population compelled to work under Alabama's postbellum convict leasing system; they too were exploited by convict leasing (as were men) and suffered under it.[1] Focusing on the economic exploitation alone, however, misses the "human world" of black women—misses, that is, their place within their communities and their various means of self-assertion, resistance, and survival.[2] Asking why these women

This essay was written while I was a fellow at the Carter G. Woodson Institute, which I thank for its financial support. Ray Gavins introduced me to the work of Hans Medick and thoughtfully suggested the title for this essay. I would also like to thank Kirsten Fischer, Ann Farnsworth, Leslie Rowland, Tera Hunter, Nancy Hewitt, and Ray Gavins for their encouragement, comments, and suggestions.

1. None of the published work on convict leasing in Alabama mentions the existence of women prisoners or the fact that women worked in mining camps. For example, see Robert David Ward and William Warren Rogers, *Convicts, Coal, and the Banner Mine Tragedy* (Tuscaloosa: University of Alabama Press, 1987), chap. 2; and A. J. Going, *Bourbon Democracy in Alabama, 1874–1898* (Tuscaloosa: University of Alabama Press, 1951), chap. 11.

2. Hans Medick, "'Missionaries in the Row Boat'? Ethnological Ways of Knowing as a Challenge to Social History," *Comparative Studies in Society and History* 29 (January 1987): 76–98. Medick's term "human world" does not refer only or simply to the realm of emotion or relationships; rather, he is frustrated with the inability of social science language to incorporate human

11

were in prison and how they survived, and tracing their actions upon release, provide a perspective that goes beyond prison history. The story of black women prisoners gives insights into the world, work, and personal struggles of rural black women during and after Reconstruction.

Prisoners in Alabama were designated as either state or county convicts depending on the type of offense and length of sentence. The system of serving hard labor for the county emerged from the black codes of 1866. These laws, designed to reinstate white racial control, curtailed basic black freedoms. African Americans could be arrested for vagrancy and fined. If they could not pay, they were hired out to employers who held them in slavery-like conditions for the terms of their sentences. In principle, county convicts were those convicted of misdemeanors and "minor" felonies; no county convict could be sentenced for more than two years. In practice, however, a total sentence included additional days to cover court costs, usually calculated at thirty cents a day, so county convicts served prison terms months longer than their actual sentences. At one time the county system was nearly abolished, but local governments had a financial incentive to fight for its continuance, since all income derived from leasing county convicts went to the counties. During Reconstruction the black codes were repealed, but serving at hard labor for the county as punishment for trivial offenses persisted well into the twentieth century.[3]

Since no records for county prisoners were kept until 1883, information on women and crime during the 1870s comes from records on women who were state prisoners, all of whom were incarcerated for more than two years on felony charges. The state paid for the court costs of such prisoners and received the income from leasing out their labor, so the state Department of Corrections

---

experience and agency into theories of social change. To that end, this essay is an attempt to place the history of women prisoners within the changing context of political struggle and their community life in postbellum Alabama.

3. County camps clearly were for blacks only. During the 1880s Bullock, Dallas, Greene, Hale, Lowndes, Marengo, Perry, and Sumter—all Black Belt counties—did not imprison or lease a single white prisoner. *First Biennial Report of the Inspectors of Convicts to the Governor, from October 1, 1884, to October 1, 1886* (Montgomery: Barrett and Co., 1886), 186–228; *Third Biennial Report of the Inspectors of Convicts to the Governor, from October 1, 1888, to September 30, 1890* (Montgomery: Brown Printing Co., 1890), 198–220.

kept track of prisoners, money, and contractors by issuing annual reports. These reports begin in 1869 and list the prisoner's name, race, former occupation, age, sex, and county of origin.[4] Between 1869 and 1883, approximately 111 women were incarcerated as state prisoners, and of these, only 4 were white.[5] These reports also list the contractors who leased prisoners and show that African American women prisoners worked in lumber camps, in mining camps, on farms, and in rock quarries.

An overwhelmingly black prison population working on farms and in mines under unmitigated white authority smacked of slavery, and the leasing of black prisoners for profit held poignant implications for all black people. Jesse Duke, the black editor of the *Montgomery Herald,* spoke in outrage against "prejudiced grand and petit juries" whose actions "fill up the coal mines and public works" with black citizens. He called the leasing system "the curse of the present age" and pointed out that blacks were prosecuted "more for spite and revenge than anything else."[6] Recent studies of the convict leasing system and of crime in the late nineteenth century echo the links Duke made between racism, profiteering, and incarceration.

Convict leasing in the postbellum South has generally been situated within the context of continuing antebellum racism and postwar debt. New South approaches to understanding the phenomenon of convict labor for profit point to the hard times faced

4. These records show that African Americans constituted the vast majority of the state's prison population. In antebellum Alabama 99 percent of the penitentiary population was white; in 1870, however, whites represented less than one quarter of all prisoners. Edward L. Ayers, *Vengeance and Justice: Crime and Punishment in the Nineteenth-Century American South* (New York: Oxford University Press, 1984), 295 n. 57; *Annual Report of the Inspectors of the Alabama Penitentiary, from October 1, 1869, to October 1, 1870* (Montgomery: John G. Stokes & Co., 1870), 20.

5. See the following annual reports of the penitentiary inspectors, all published in Montgomery: *Annual Report of the Inspectors of the Alabama Penitentiary, Oct. 1, 1869, to Oct. 1, 1870* (John G. Stokes & Co., 1870); . . . *from March 1 to Sept. 30, 1873* (Arthur Bingham, 1873); . . . *from Oct. 1, 1873, to Sept. 30, 1874* (W. W. Screws, 1874); . . . *March 4, 1875* (W. W. Screws, 1875); . . . *for the Year Ending Sept. 30, 1877* (Barrett & Brown, 1878); . . . *from Sept. 30, 1878, to Sept. 30, 1880* (Barrett & Brown, 1880); . . . *from Sept. 30, 1880, to Sept. 30, 1882* (Allred & Beers, 1882).

6. *Montgomery Herald,* July 23, 1887.

by economically weak southern states with no money to spend on prisons. To be sure, these authors acknowledge that convict labor grew out of the legacy of slavery, but they also insist that it fed upon capitalist markets. Convict labor and later the chain gang pulled in state revenue and dovetailed nicely with New South ideologies of progress, thrift, and white supremacy.[7]

Studies of the legal prosecution of blacks in the late nineteenth century also stress the racial repression and control endemic to the New South. In one study of Birmingham, Carl Harris emphasizes the relationship between arbitrary arrests of black citizens, official corruption, and white racism. Other analysts show how racist antebellum legal procedures and laws designed to control slaves continued to hound black southerners after emancipation. Albert Smith argues that arson in the Georgia Black Belt was really a form of black protest against the repression of white landowners. And, in a recent exploration of law, race, and sexuality, Mary Berry argues that Old South prejudices regarding proper sexual conduct and legal relations between the races were reimposed by New South judges.[8] Thus, acts designated as criminal in the New South can be understood variously as protest on the part of individuals, as a means of racial repression and control, as a veneer for money making, and as part of broader attempts by those in power to buttress and preserve the status quo.

New South interpretations of leasing and of crime, however,

7. See, for example, Ayers, *Vengeance and Justice;* Ward and Rogers, *Convicts, Coal, and the Banner Mine Tragedy;* and Robert E. Ireland, "Prison Reform, Road Building, and Southern Progressivism: Joseph Hyde Pratt and the Campaign for 'Good Roads and Good Men,'" *North Carolina Historical Review* 68 (April 1991): 125–57.

8. Carl Harris, "Reforms of Government Control of Negroes in Birmingham, Alabama, 1890–1920," *Journal of Southern History* 38 (1972): 567–600. See especially his discussion of the "fee system," in which sheriffs and other law enforcement officers received fees in proportion to the number of arrests or legal notices they served (590–600). Richard H. Haunton, "Law and Order in Savannah, 1850–1860," *Georgia Historical Quarterly* 56 (Spring 1972): 1–24; James T. Currie, "From Slavery to Freedom in Mississippi's Legal System," *Journal of Negro History* 65 (Spring 1980): 112–25; Albert C. Smith, "'Southern Violence' Reconsidered: Arson as Protest in Black-Belt Georgia, 1865–1910," *Journal of Southern History* 51 (November 1985): 527–64; Mary Frances Berry, "Judging Morality: Sexual Behavior and Legal Consequences in the Late-Nineteenth-Century South," *Journal of American History* 78 (December 1991): 835–56.

miss the crucial role of Reconstruction struggles in shaping the origins of the leasing system and as a factor in the growth of the state's prison population. Because these interpretations focus on the relationship between leasing and the economic demands of the New South, they miss the system's origins during Reconstruction. Furthermore, because they see crime as primarily a postbellum version of long-standing racial control, political conflicts peculiar to Reconstruction become obscured from view.

During the 1870s freedmen and freedwomen struggled to capitalize on new freedoms and powers. Large black voting majorities in Black Belt counties in Alabama, coupled with the potential economic power of the freed people, posed many threats to white landowners, merchants, and the Democratic party. Klan activity epitomized the extralegal means of restricting and circumscribing black freedom after the Civil War, but the legal repression faced by many could be just as arbitrary and just as frightening. Laws designed to thwart black economic advancement, social freedoms, and political participation subjected freed people to legal prosecution and incarceration. Emancipation gave black women a voice in labor relations and political participation, as well as new choices in family life and sexuality, but the exercise of such freedoms also left them vulnerable to arrest and imprisonment.

Women incarcerated during the 1870s, white and black, were working people. Thirty-nine of these women gave "house servant" as their occupation, and approximately fifty were designated "laborers"; other occupations included nurse and cook. Among black women prisoners, approximately forty-eight were convicted for larceny and/or burglary, and approximately thirty for murder, manslaughter, and attempted murder. Other convictions included forgery, perjury, bigamy, arson and "not stated."[9] But, without context, the labels alone reveal little.

There is no systematic evidence, such as trial records or testimony, of the circumstances behind these black women's imprisonment, but certainly labor struggles lay at the heart of larceny

9. An occupational breakdown of crimes does not indicate that women in certain occupations were more likely to be convicted of one crime than another. Of the 41 domestic servants in prison, 23 were convicted of larceny and burglary, and 16 were serving time for murder or manslaughter or both. Of the 59 women designated as "laborers," 28 were convicted of larceny or burglary and 22 were in for murder or manslaughter or both.

charges. Women who continued to work for their former owners after emancipation often argued over their wages and their rights. And the old suspicions raised against women slaves accused of poisoning their white owners continued under the new labor relations of freedom. For example, a woman domestic servant identified only as Isabella was convicted in 1866 of attempting to poison her employer and sentenced to twelve years in prison.[10]

Convictions for crimes such as larceny and burglary reflected the changing economic and political relations between the freed people and white property owners and merchants. Beginning in 1874, merchants and planters restricted and undermined black economic activity by regulating the hours during which commerce could occur (sunup to sundown) and designating those to whom cotton could be legally sold.[11] These laws targeted black renters and sharecroppers who sought to sell their cotton shares to white merchants. But perhaps more important, these laws also sought to halt the independent markets that had become a thriving form of commerce among freedmen and freedwomen.

Evidence suggests that freed people engaged in extensive buying, selling, and bartering, a trade that included cotton, cottonseed, dry goods, and luxury items. Moreover, they excluded whites from their trading circles. In 1875 "Farmer" from Forkland in Greene County wrote to the *Eutaw Whig and Observer* that "Negro drummers are constantly seen on the roads and equestrians me[e]t on all sides . . . we suppose of course engaging a few more pounds [of cotton], to be bought with a trifling number of yards of rotten calico, molasses, sugar—peradventure a set of CHEAP JEWELRY. Let a white man attempt a trade! ah! market dull!!! Figures hold out better with the INTELLIGENT negro." Anger over his exclusion led "Farmer" to vow that he would "strenuously endeavor to put a stop" to independent black trading. Clearly, with few markets available to

10. Jacqueline Jones, *Labor of Love, Labor of Sorrow: Black Women, Work, and the Family, from Slavery to the Present* (New York: Basic Books, 1985), 55–57; *Annual Report of the Inspectors of the Alabama Penitentiary, from Oct. 1, 1869, to Oct. 1, 1870,* 8–9.

11. Michael Perman superbly outlines the history of this restrictive legislation in *The Road to Redemption: Southern Politics, 1869–1879* (Chapel Hill: University of North Carolina Press, 1984), 244–50; Eric Foner, *Reconstruction: America's Unfinished Revolution, 1863–1877* (New York: Harper & Row, 1988), 593.

cash-poor southerners, black and white, he wanted a piece of the action. In his outrage, "Farmer" gives a glimpse of the subeconomy of trading and commerce among the freed people. Roger L. Ransom and Richard Sutch specifically point to the fact that the paucity of alternative markets and merchants available to most farmers plunged both the black and white farmers in the South into debt peonage. They do not, however, discuss the existence of independent markets among the freedmen and freedwomen that apparently used cotton and cottonseed as currency and cash. Obtaining goods and cotton this way allowed the freed people to circumvent white merchants.[12]

The list of paying occupations of women prisoners, such as nurse, cook, and servant, as well as the goods that were for sale, suggests that black women participated in these markets. Freedwomen, like freedmen, desired goods, especially calico for clothes, foodstuffs to supplement the family's diet, and jewelry for pleasure. Domestic workers with access to cash, and women agricultural laborers with access to cotton and seed, certainly had either money or barter to trade. As independent markets came under attack in the mid-1870s, all buyers and sellers became vulnerable to legal action. A careful look at one list of convicted prisoners shows that on the same day in 1877 Nancy Rowe and Moza Ann Connolly, both African American cooks, were each sentenced to three years in 1877 for "receiving stolen goods." Along with them Caroline Cheatam, a white cook from the same county, was also sentenced for "grand larceny."[13] For African American women and men, larceny was by far the most common crime.

White Democrats also used the threat of imprisonment against black women who, despite remaining disfranchised, took an active role in the politics of the postbellum black community.[14] For exam-

---

12. *Eutaw Whig and Observer,* October 28, 1875, p. 3; Roger L. Ransom and Richard Sutch, *One Kind of Freedom: The Economic Consequences of Emancipation* (Cambridge: Cambridge University Press, 1977), chap. 7.

13. *Annual Report of the Inspectors of the Alabama Penitentiary for the Year Ending September 30, 1877.*

14. Eric Foner, "Rights and the Constitution in Black Life during the Civil War and Reconstruction," *Journal of American History* 74 (December 1987): 875. Foner acknowledges that the entire community participated in politics; however, the general lack of investigation into the origins of local black leadership and the names of community leaders has led to a "top-down" view

ple, when Alex Webb, a freedman who had worked as a registrar in the town of Greensboro, was murdered in 1867, one black woman publicly threatened to burn the town. The local newspaper remarked that "we shall not be astonished if the first Grand Jury organized in Hale County should give her case their special attention. We heard of several others, of the same gender, whose deportment and language proved that they were ripe for arson, murder, or any other diabolical crime." The *Marengo News-Journal* recalled the activism of black women during the 1874 elections: "Two years ago a lot of negro women collected on the public square here and made all sorts of threats against Democratic 'niggers.'" The editor reminded black women that "[t]he law against intimidation of voters applies to women as well as men." If they continued to harass black Democrats, the paper threatened, they would "find themselves in trouble." Ann Pollard, a black merchant who ran her own stall in Montgomery's downtown market, publicly denounced the Democrats and worked spiritedly on behalf of the Republicans and of black women's rights over a period of many years. In exasperation the *Montgomery Advertiser* exclaimed that "if there is no law to reach her case, one should be devised. . . . We consider her a fit subject for the handcuffs and chains now so plentiful in this happy land."15

Even children in the black community were liable to incarceration by whites seeking to inculcate subservient behavior in former slaves. Ten-year-old Griffin Huckabee of Perry County fought with some white boys in the 1870s and took a dime from one of them. He received two years for "grand larceny." Twenty of the female state prisoners were age eighteen or younger, and, of those, twelve were younger than sixteen. Mary Savage, age fifteen, was sen-

---

of black Reconstruction politics. But black women had leadership roles in the slave community, and clearly that standing carried over into postemancipation politics. See Deborah Gray White, *Ar'n't I a Woman?: Female Slaves in the Plantation South* (New York: W. W. Norton & Co., 1985), especially chap. 4, on the leadership exercised by slave women. Elsa Barkley Brown has written extensively on the topic of black women, community, and politics during Reconstruction. See "To Catch the Vision of Freedom: Reconstructing Southern Black Women's Political History, 1865–1885" (unpublished paper, January 1990, in author's possession).

15. *Alabama Beacon,* June 22, 1867; *Marengo News-Journal,* August 24, 1876; *Montgomery Advertiser,* October 23, 1874, and October 9, 1874.

tenced to two years for "larceny of horse." Lavinia Thomas was twelve years old when she was sentenced for burglary in 1869, and Laura Thompson, another twelve year old, received three and a half years in the penitentiary for burglary in 1877. The end of apprenticeship acts and black codes did not end the power of white law over black children. Black parents knew their children could be taken away for the slightest provocation.[16]

The most serious charge levied against black women was murder, but descriptions contained in pardon appeals show how complicated and varied the circumstances behind a murder charge could be. For example, Martha Aarons was convicted of murdering her child in 1873 and sentenced to the state penitentiary for seventy-five years. A pardon petition, however, revealed that "her step father beat her child to death in her presence." Louisa Stewart, a former slave, was convicted of murder in 1893 for telling a young girl how to induce a miscarriage; according to the petition for her pardon, "She probably thought she was doing a favor in helping that Girl to save her character."[17] Debates and divisions within the black community over sexuality, unwanted children, and the "character" of young girls all contributed to women's incarceration.

For African American women in this period, the "human world" was a political world. Emancipation had enabled many women to act on their economic, political, and sexual visions of freedom, but they did so against power held by white landowners, employers, sheriffs, and Democrats. Struggles against white authority prior to incarceration provide a context for the behavior of black women in prison. Women convicts resisted white authority in prison by complaining, being insolent, defying orders, and escaping. But in order to survive prison, black women carved out valued relationships with male prisoners, children, and each other. This "human world" reflects the importance of family and community to their endurance and survival.

16. *Annual Report of the Inspectors of the Alabama Penitentiary, from March 4, 1875,* 14–15; . . . *from March 1 to Sept. 30, 1873,* 14–15; . . . *for the Year Ending Sept. 30, 1877,* 48–49.

17. It appears that Aarons was held responsible for the death of the child. Petition for the Pardon of Charley Jemison and Petition for the Pardon of Louisa Stewart, both in Pardon and Parole Records, Hale County, 1898 and 1906, respectively, Alabama Department of Archives and History, Montgomery, hereinafter cited as ADAH.

Between 1869 and 1888, women prisoners lived in isolation from each other, often living and working as the sole female in a prison camp. For example, Nellie Boyd was a sixteen-year-old house servant when she was convicted of second-degree murder in 1878. She was the only woman in a prison mining camp of eighty-six men. And Annie Gilmore, a twenty-year-old "House Girl," was the only woman among forty-six men at the prison mine at Newcastle.[18] Their situation was typical. At these camps women performed the so-called domestic work of cooking, cleaning, and being servants to the white superintendents. Women also worked with men at the state's prison farm in Wetumpka, at Thomas Williams's farm nearby, the mining camp at the Pratt mines outside of Birmingham, J. F. B. Jackson's rock quarry and farm, and other prison sites located throughout the state.

To be a woman in a prison camp of men was often a nightmare of hard work, bad treatment, and isolation. No rules governing treatment or punishment existed to protect women. In the 1870s and 1880s all of the county and state prison camps, and the county camps in particular, were notorious for their cruelty, filth, disease, and brutal handling of prisoners.

Whipping was integral to prison discipline and daily life. Several women prisoners testified before a state senate investigating committee in 1888 about their past and present treatment. Every woman who testified had been whipped during her prison life and had seen other women whipped frequently and repeatedly. At one farm a woman was tied to a chair and whipped "till whelps were raised on her back." Women were whipped for quarreling, fighting, "sassing," and being impertinent to the officers. A woman prisoner who had never picked cotton was whipped because she could not pick 125 pounds of it in a day. Flora Adams was whipped "for dancing while the preacher was here on a Sunday."[19] Prison authorities sought to do more than force women to work; they also sought to exercise control over their spirits, their personal behavior, and their sexual activity.

Two events in 1888 changed the environment for women pris-

18. *Biennial Report of the Inspectors of the Alabama Penitentiary, from September 30, 1878, to September 30, 1880,* pp. 34–37, 42–45.

19. Alabama General Assembly, *Testimony before the Joint Committee of the General Assembly, Appointed to Examine into the Convict System of Alabama, Session of 1888–89* (Montgomery: Brown Printing Co. 1889), 125.

oners. First, the Alabama attorney general prohibited the leasing out of state women prisoners to private farms and mining camps and ordered that they be sent to the state penitentiary at Wetumpka, known as the "Walls." Second, the state made the counties switch from a per capita system of leasing prisoners, in which a flat rate was charged for each prisoner, regardless of sex, age, or ability, to a tasking system, which classed prisoners according to their work capacities. Counties were now unable to ask the same price for men and women prisoners, and so they began to send women and indigent prisoners to the state. As a result, the number of women and indigent prisoners living and working at the Walls gradually increased after 1889. After 1888 all state women prisoners moved to the Walls and worked on the state farm under the direct control of an inspector.

Women prisoners had always presented a problem to the state inspectors. R. H. Dawson, the chief inspector of the Department of Corrections, did not want to take on the responsibility of working the women prisoners, whom he found "hard to manage, insolent, and frequently quarreling and fighting." These were not idle observations. On March 15, 1889, Dawson ordered Lizzie Sterrett confined in a dark cell for five days on bread and water for stabbing another woman prisoner with a knife and drawing an axe on the prison yardmaster. But women worked hard, nonetheless. When approximately forty-five to fifty women and fifteen children at the Walls were put to work at a state farm during the growing season of 1889, thirty-five women cultivated 100 bales of cotton, 1,000 bushels of corn, 60,000 pounds of hay, 200 bushels of peas, and 500 bushels of sweet potatoes.[20] The labor of these prisoners provided services vital to the profitable continuation of the leasing system. Their agricultural work provided food, as well as cotton, a cash crop. Moreover, they washed, sewed, and mended prison clothing. Women made up only a small percentage of prisoners, but their labor provided food and clothing to all prisoners.

When women prisoners testified before a state legislative committee in 1888, they suggested that the consolidation of all women prisoners at one site caused them to lose some personal freedoms

20. R. H. Dawson to Gov. Thomas Seay, March 4, 1889, Letter Book, September 11, 1888–May 17, 1889, p. 193, Department of Corrections, ADAH. Also see March 15, 1889, Minutes of the Board of Inspectors, 1883–1913, Department of Corrections, ADAH. Dawson to Seay, Report for the Quarter Ending October 1, 1889, Administrative Files, Papers of Governor Seay, ADAH.

and privileges. Annie Tucker, convicted in 1883, had spent several years working in the Pratt prison mines and preferred that to life at the Walls. She told the state in 1888 that she "was not locked up at mines, cooked, washed, and ironed at mines. . . . Was trusty at mines." What she did not say, however, was that in 1883 P. J. Rogers, the superintendent at the mines, was censured by the Board of Inspectors for "cruel and excessive whipping." R. H. Dawson wrote about Annie Tucker's case in his personal diary. "These are the facts," he stated. "She ran away from Mr. McCurdy's house—was caught and carried to the prison. Col. Bankhead whipped her himself—not severely—After he left by order of Mr. McCurdy, P. J. Rogers stripped her, had her held down, and inflicted 56 lashes upon her with a heavy strap."[21] But despite suffering such brutalities, Annie Tucker said she was better treated at the mines than at any other prison.

Her testimony suggests that although women prisoners were clearly vulnerable to rape, cruel punishment, and exploitation, they also valued freedom of movement and the relationships they established with male prisoners and free men during their time in prison. At the mines, Annie Tucker raised her children and carried on a relationship with their father. "Had two babies at mines— oldest going on five years. State furnishes baby with clothes. Father of children got at mine was a convict." After the mines, she was leased out to work on a prison farm where she said she was poorly treated and "locked up at night." Yet her situation did not prevent her from having a relationship with a freedman, Jack Bozeman. "We got together night and day time." She became pregnant and gave birth to her third child at the Walls. Many of the women prisoners brought to the Walls in 1888 had children with them. One woman testified that there were "sixteen babies here. Some born here and some brought here; seven babies born in the walls this year. Two women will soon have babies; both came lately and were pregnant when they came. The oldest child here is four years old—Annie Tucker's baby."[22]

21. Board of Inspectors to Warden Bankhead, August 25, 1883, Minutes of the Board of Inspectors, 1883–1913, Department of Corrections, ADAH; entry of July 11, 1883, Diary of Reginald Heber Dawson, 1883–1906, fol. 1, ADAH. Col. Bankhead went on to become a U.S. congressmen.

22. Alabama General Assembly, *Testimony before the Joint Committee of*

Not all women wanted children or had their children with them. Thomas Williams testified in 1888 that a woman prisoner died on his farm during an abortion attempt. Several of the women who testified in 1888 said that they had no children. And many women prisoners were forced to leave their children behind with court-appointed guardians. Francis Woods, a woman prisoner, mailed her own money to the probate judge of her county so that her children could come and visit her at the Pratt mines. In order to get them, however, the judge had to serve papers on those who had custody of them.[23]

Like Annie Tucker, most women prisoners did not think that their separate quarters at the Walls represented an improvement. There they were locked up in dark, cramped cells. They endured arduous physical labor, close personal supervision, brutal punishments such as whipping, and the burdens and added pressure of raising children and babies in a prison setting. According to Annie Tucker, at the Walls they were allowed to bathe twice a week. Living together, working together, and raising children in dirty, cramped quarters heightened tensions among women prisoners, and they often quarreled and fought.[24] The only emotional release permitted the women seems to have been preaching and religious services twice a month. The establishment of a separate facility for state women was viewed by some as a triumph in reform, but clearly the new women's prison was designed to control women's behavior, particularly their sexual and personal behavior, more closely. It was concern over their sexual relationships with the male prisoners, and not concern over the hardship of their daily lives, that led the state to establish a separate prison facility for women. Recommending a separate state prison for women, the inspectors wrote to the governor that "where they [men and women] are at the same place, no matter how much care is taken to prevent it, they will sometimes get together; and they are on the look out for

---

the General Assembly, Appointed to Examine into the Convict System of Alabama, Session of 1888–89, p. 125.

23. Francis Woods to Col. Snodgrass, May 10, 1886, and John B. Tally, judge of probate in Scottsboro, to R. H. Dawson, July 7, 1886, Reports of Inspectors and Other Officials, Department of Corrections, ADAH.

24. For example, Lizzie Sterrett was often punished for fighting with other women prisoners. March 15, 1889, and July 22, 1889, Minutes of the Board of Inspectors, 1883–1913.

opportunities of the sort all the time, which makes it difficult to preserve discipline."[25]

In contrast to the women at the Walls, women prisoners at county camps continued to live alongside male prisoners, and their assertions of sexuality continued to undermine prison discipline. This was especially true at the Coalburg prison mine, run by the Sloss Coal and Coke Company, which had a very high rate of death and illness for male prisoners and a notorious reputation for excessive punishments and whippings. Coalburg leased and worked exclusively county convicts—men and women imprisoned for misdemeanors. But a short sentence to Coalburg was often a death sentence. According to the convict inspectors' biennial report of 1890, 101 out of approximately 330 prisoners at Coalburg had died during the preceding two years.[26]

Women prisoners at Coalburg had histories and work demands that differed from those of men. Because of the extra time they had to serve to pay off court costs, the majority of the male prisoners at Coalburg had sentences of over two years. Yet the dozen or so women leased to Coalburg were sentenced for less than one year, including prison costs. And instead of working in or near the prison mines, "several of them were hired out to different persons about Coalburg as cooks and house servants."[27] Their relatively short sentences, and the fact that they were leased to work outside of the prison, appear to have emboldened them. Although incarcerated, the women prisoners at Coalburg refused to wear the badge of prisoner.

For example, after a day of working outside the prison, they refused to wear prison clothing or return to the prison when their work was completed. A. T. Henley, one of the prison inspectors, wrote that "these women are not required to stay at the house where they are hired & it is no uncommon thing on Sundays to see them dressed up in their finest clothes & walking about the village." Civilian clothes gave one the freedom to act as a free person. He continued, "My information is that those who do not sleep in

25. *First Biennial Report of the Inspectors of Convicts to the Governor, from October 1, 1884, to October 1, 1886,* 17.

26. *Third Biennial Report of the Inspectors of Convicts, from Oct. 1, 1888, to Sept. 30, 1890,* 96–97.

27. A. T. Henley to R. H. Dawson, September 1, 1891, Reports of Inspectors and Other Officials.

the prison are allowed to roam at large at night and can be seen almost every night in the company store and about Coalburg wherever they choose to go." Apparently all women prisoners had an aversion to prison dress, and those who stayed inside the prison refused to wear it as well. "I found several of these women [inside the stockade] yesterday, and in one or two instances they were dressed very elaborately."[28]

The rejection of prison dress became a point of contention, because the women's refusal had repercussions throughout the entire prison. "They should be required to wear a uniform at all times," Henley fumed. "There is no reason why the discipline of the prison should not apply to the female convicts as well as the male and any other course is demoralizing." One month later the situation had not improved. "The female convicts at this prison are a very unruly set and give a good deal of trouble. We have had them put in uniform, and try to keep them under control but it is a hard matter."[29] Such outright defiance invited punishment and undermined prison discipline, but it also enabled women to live more humane lives in prison.

As at the Walls, women flirting with male prisoners caused jealousy and high emotions that undermined Coalburg's discipline. Inspector Henley could think of only one solution. "[T]he present plan is to build another prison for them on the mountain above the house of the warden where they can be kept apart from the men. . . . These female prisoners are certainly the most unruly and disorderly convicts that I have ever had to manage and it will be necessary to enforce discipline at the cost of a good deal of punishment I am afraid."[30] The new women prisoners at Coalburg were determined to resist prison life by not acting like prisoners or recognizing the symbols of control such as clothing and sleeping in locked cells—behavior that "made" them prisoners.

Resistance also included appeals to authority, as well as defiance of it. Julia Pearson, a Jefferson County convict, had just arrived at the county road camp outside of Birmingham when she

28. Ibid.
29. A. T. Henley to R. H. Dawson, August 31, 1891, and Henley to Dawson, November 1, 1891, Reports of Inspectors and Other Officials.
30. *Third Biennial Report of the Inspectors of Convicts, from Oct. 1, 1888, to Sept. 30, 1890,* 260; A. T. Henley to R. H. Dawson, October 1, 1891, Reports of Inspectors and Other Officials.

had to fight off the sexual attacks of a guard named Mooney. According to the inspector's report of the incident, Mooney had entered the women's cell on Saturday night and offered Julia Pearson a dollar to go outside with him. When she declined, "he then presented his pistol and told her he would kill her, but immediately said he was joking." After leaving to get some whiskey, he returned, went to Julia Pearson's bed and fell asleep. "Julia says that she asked him repeatedly to go out of their cell and let them alone and finally told him that she intended reporting his conduct to Warden Pittman." Mooney finally left. When he returned at 4 A.M. to gather the women to cook breakfast, "Julia Pearson started towards the gate and said she was going to see Mr. Pittman." He cursed at her. She cursed him back. And then he shot at her twice. The second bullet broke her collarbone.[31] Guards like Mooney posed a real threat to incarcerated women. Another prisoner, Nellie Anderson, was shot and killed at Coalburg by a guard one year later.

Julia Pearson's brave act is significant. Consider the fact that she had been in the prison camp only a few days before the incident. She had been convicted on July 26, 1890, of assault and battery with a knife, and Mooney attacked her the weekend before August 4, 1890. Being new to prison life, Julia Pearson had every reason to think that she, not Mooney, would be disciplined. Her acts of self-defense and her appeal to prison authorities demonstrated how black women drew on their own preexisting sense of rights and self-esteem in their struggles against rape and sexual assault. Such resistance and personal defiance showed that black women entered prison with strong feelings about the limits of the power of authority, their rights under that authority, and freedom.[32]

Women prisoners facing long sentences persevered in their hopes for freedom. Martha Aarons faced a seventy-five-year term in the Alabama State Penitentiary, but after sixteen years she sought help from an attorney in securing a pardon, "as I am so hopeful once more to be free." Aarons had been convicted of murder after witnessing her stepfather beat her child to death. Since 1873 she

31. A. T. Henley to R. H. Dawson, August 5, 1890, Reports of Inspectors and Other Officials, contains a lengthy account of the entire incident.

32. *Third Biennial Report of the Inspectors of Convicts, from Oct. 1, 1888, to Sept. 30, 1890.*

had picked cotton, grown food, scoured uniforms, and performed other arduous work on various Alabama prison farms. Years of exchanging letters with lawyers (and paying fees) had given her hope but had borne little fruit, and by 1889 Aarons was beginning to doubt her incarceration would ever end. "[O]f late I am very dispondent," she wrote, "and when I think that I have for sixteen years been a faithful Slave for the State of Ala, the time has come when she might be generous and forgiving to me."[33] As someone who had known actual slavery, Aarons retained her moral indignation at working hard for nothing and her belief that freedom was a right derived from hard work. Eventually Martha Aarons prevailed, and in 1890 she was pardoned.

After her pardon she visited the penitentiary regularly, for during her time in prison she had fallen "in love with a convick man" by the name of Charley Jemison. Through various methods she tried numerous times to have Jemison pardoned and had even asked her employer, J. W. McLigill, to intercede. In 1898 he wrote to the governor about Martha Aarons and Charley Jemison:

> She is my cook. She has been very true to her prisoner and every thing she makes she give it to Lawers to get Charly out. She paid one lawer 35 dollars in money and 1 bale of cotton weighing over 500 lbs. . . . She will show you the receipt and she paid one lawer 40 dollars in money and they have done nothing. . . . she says she loves him and will marry him if she can get him out. She goes to see him evry month. She has ben true to him.[34]

Using letters, lawyers, money, ingenuity, and persistent appeals to the governor, she hoped to secure Charley Jemison's freedom the same way she had procured her own. Such herculean attempts to free herself and Jemison echo similar antebellum efforts of free blacks to secure the freedom of enslaved family members.

Furthermore, Martha Aarons's devotion to Charley Jemison over many years shows that women formed significant relationships in prison which they then maintained after their release. Indeed, the relationship between Martha Aarons and Charley Jemison illustrates the human world of support and devotion that motivated

33. Martha Aarons to Mr. Stallworth, February 5, 1889, Reports of Inspectors and Other Officials.

34. J. W. McLigill to Governor Johnston, September 26, 1898, Pardon and Parole Records, Hale County, ADAH.

struggle. Aarons's monthly visits to Charley Jemison, her appeals to governors and lawyers on his behalf, and her labor in the cotton fields to earn extra money represent her efforts to create personal independence on her own terms. Her actions caused confusion. Her employer, for one, thought she was being taken for her money. And her persistent efforts to get Charley Jemison released certainly annoyed Thomas Williams, for whom she had worked as a prisoner, and caused him to remark that Martha Aarons was "a much better convict than a free woman."[35] But for Aarons, freedom from prison meant the freedom to struggle for those she loved. Through her relationship with Charley Jemison and her efforts to have him released, Martha Aarons defined herself as a free woman.

Martha Aarons's monthly visits to Charley Jemison illustrate the widespread personal interaction between prisoners and their loved ones that prison authorities resented but could not halt. Indeed, the right to have family visits became a focus of struggle and resistance between male prisoners and authorities. At the very least, prisoners expected their spouses, girlfriends, and other relatives to visit and to write. When men were sent to the prison mines in Birmingham, family members would often follow. And when men were deprived of these visits, they complained. One prisoner, Ezekiel Archey, tried to explain the value he placed on these visits by writing that "our families coming is the next favor to liberty."[36] Inside and outside of prison, women were central to the community support that mitigated the harshness of prison life.

For example, not all women in Alabama prisons were prisoners. Efforts to sustain family ties and the lack of economic options led to women following their husbands into prison, and often, in the county hard labor system, entire families remained with the convicted man at the farm of the leaser. In 1876 the secretary of the state Democratic Executive Committee in Marion, Alabama, wrote to the chairman to complain about the supposedly lax treatment of black prisoners. "It is *no* punishment to a negro to put him at what is *called* hard labor (i.e., to hire him out to the same planter with whom he was living at the time of his sentence and allow him to

35. Letter from Thomas Williams to Governor Johnston, n.d., Pardon and Parole Records, Hale County, ADAH.
36. Ezekiel Archey to R. H. Dawson, May 26, 1884, Reports of Inspectors and Other Officials.

live with his friends and family as before the conviction.)" An article in the *Eutaw Whig and Observer* noted that "it is too often the case, however, that the planter, who thus hires the convicts, can get the control, not only of the convict's services, but that of his entire family for the term for which he is convicted."[37] Emancipation did not mean the end of forced separation for black families. The struggles of these women to keep their families intact demonstrate the importance of family life to the survival of African Americans throughout the South.

The new control black people exercised over their family lives and nonworking time was a social fact of enduring significance. Historians have tended to view emancipation primarily in terms of changing labor relations, analyzing the differences, small and large, between slavery and the experiences of the newly freed black laborers. Indeed, the history of the New South shows that post-emancipation labor relations—ranging from convict labor, to peonage, to sharecropping, to nonunionized wage labor—signaled a continuity of labor coercion, particularly for African Americans. The end of slavery, however, did end the control whites exercised over black family life and the nonworking time of black people. Freedom meant that black citizens now lived open, public, and legitimate family and community lives. But what did this mean for men and women prisoners?

Prisoners forced white authorities to honor these familial ties that connected them to the outside world of family, loved ones, and community, a major change that followed emancipation. Contact with families sustained prisoners, often enabling them to survive and providing hope for the future. Women in prison could go back to their children or look forward to future family lives; men, such as Ezekiel Archey, could anticipate regular visits from female family members and a home life upon release. The high value prisoners and the families of prisoners placed upon family ties highlights the importance of independent personal, family, and community lives in the struggle to survive white oppression both inside and outside prison.

Postemancipation efforts to assert their visions of freedom within

---

37. B. M. Huey to Col. M. D. Graham, August 19, 1876, pardon request for Wm. H. Redding, Pardon and Parole Records, Perry County, ADAH; *Eutaw Whig and Observer*, November 22, 1877.

their communities and against white society shaped the resistance and behavior of black women in prison. These women valued freedom of movement, sexual freedom, wearing their own clothing, and verbally expressing their feelings and dissatisfactions. They valued the appearances associated with freedom as well as the benefits of acting freely. The struggles of black women prisoners revealed their intelligence, courage, personal independence, spirituality, loyalty, and humor. They could also be violent and defend themselves when necessary. Through daily acts of self-assertion that reclaimed personal and social space, women resisted the dehumanizing effects of prison life. The examples of Martha Aarons, Julia Pearson, Annie Tucker, and the women at Coalburg and the Walls show the variety and complexity of that struggle.

"A Far Greater Menace"

Feebleminded Females in the South, 1900–1940

STEVEN NOLL

In March 1918, Superintendent C. Banks McNairy of North Carolina's Caswell Training School for the Feeble-Minded reported that "our greatest problem is the high grade girls' building. . . . [T]hey will curse, fight, destroy clothing, steal, put their clothing, drinking cups, towels, or anything in the sewer pipes, break down doors and knock out windows and run away." McNairy's concerns proved well founded when in December 1918 and January 1919, three high-level female patients burned down two dormitories at Caswell, killing three residents. McNairy explained to his board of directors that "a group of girls formed a pact. . . . The plan was guarded as only a defective mind can guard." In analyzing this tragedy, McNairy revealed the dual purposes of institutions such as Caswell. These girls were "poor, unfortunate, fiendish, yet irresponsible enemies of themselves, society, and the State," he wrote. "Humanitarianism demands their protection, care, and training. Society and good citizenship demand their segregation and asexualization."[1]

McNairy's gender-based notions of the problems caused by fee-blemindedness symbolized wider national concerns about the "dependent, defective, and delinquent classes" and the place of women in a rapidly changing social and economic order. With the advent

I would like to thank Ruth Alexander, Elizabeth Fox-Genovese, Anne Jones, Michael Radelet, and Nicole Rafter for their comments and suggestions.

1. C. Banks McNairy to Board of Directors of Caswell Training School, March 23, 1918; and Superintendent's Report, January 10, 1919, both in Minutes of the Executive Committee of the Board of Directors of Caswell Training School, Caswell Center Archives, Kinston, N.C.

of large-scale industrialization and urbanization in the last quarter of the nineteenth century, the social moorings that had held America together began to unravel. Americans, both men and women, searched for solutions to the problems of a society in flux. In ambiguous and contradictory ways, they often conflated and transposed the causes and effects of the changes underway in a maturing capitalist economy. Concerns about gender and class relations dominated the discussions of social criticism in the first two decades of the twentieth century.[2]

Although the South came later to these problems than the North, its accelerated development following the Civil War made them especially visible and troubling by 1900, when they began to emerge. In these concerns, as in many contemporaneous efforts at reform, southerners frequently turned northward for solutions to pressing social concerns, in the process modifying those answers to fit peculiarly southern situations.

As middle- and upper-class reformers, both men and women, investigated the problems of their rapidly changing society, they increasingly focused on the desperately poor individuals who inhabited America's burgeoning urban areas. With the increasing popularity of evolutionary theories and the concomitant beliefs in the heritability of intelligence, many viewed the lower classes as the cause, not the result, of America's social malaise.[3] Theories about eugenics, or improving the genetic makeup of the human race by preventing the propagation of those deemed unfit, narrowed the concern even further. Since poor and feebleminded women bore poor and feebleminded children, it seemed only logical that, in the words of a 1914 Virginia report, "the assumption by

2. For my explanation of conceptions of gender and their relationship to social change in this time period, I rely on Carroll Smith-Rosenberg, *Disorderly Conduct: Visions of Gender in Victorian America* (New York: Oxford University Press, 1985), especially 167–81; and Noralee Frankel and Nancy Dye, eds., *Gender, Class, Race, and Reform in the Progressive Era* (Lexington: University Press of Kentucky, 1991), especially Dye's Introduction, 1–9.

3. The literature on this subject is voluminous. For two of the more recent and wide-ranging discussions of this paradigmatic shift, see Carl Degler, *In Search of Human Nature: The Decline and Revival of Darwinism in American Social Thought* (New York: Oxford University Press, 1991), 1–55; and Daniel Kevles, *In the Name of Eugenics: Genetics and the Uses of Human Heredity* (Berkeley and Los Angeles: University of California Press, 1985), 3–112.

the State of absolute custody and control of afflicted persons of these classes and of their proper care . . . is the only safe and sure remedy to which we can look." The conflation of gender, class, and assumed mental deficiency constituted, according to sociologist Nicole Rafter, an "attempt to criminalize not an action, but the body itself (i.e., the condition of being both female and a carrier of bad heredity)."[4]

In a time of sweeping social and economic change, reformers looked to science to verify, not challenge, existing beliefs about the order of society. The male-dominated arena of science promulgated a theoretical framework of the inferiority of women. Historian Cynthia Russett concluded that "the overwhelming consensus of this work was that women were inherently different from men in their anatomy, physiology, temperament, and intellect."[5] Scientists preached that women remained childlike all their lives, thus needing protection from the evils of the world. They also asserted that women, again like children, could be highly emotional and difficult to control. From their observations, these male scientists then concluded that these qualities were caused by women's different bodily functions, particularly their cycles of menstruation—functions that frequently underlay the onset of that peculiar late-nineteenth-century malady, female hysteria. A "disease" most often manifest in middle- and upper-class families, hysteria represented the dark and erotic underside of women's childlike nature. Many victims of the disorder were placed in asylums, where a paternalistic regimen of kindness and moral management was expected to cure them. However, as asylums slowly relinquished even the pretense of cure, they devolved into custodial warehouses with little concern for cures.[6]

4. First Annual Report of the Virginia Colony for the Feeble-Minded, 1914, p. 14, Virginia State Library and Archives, Richmond; Nicole Rafter, "Claims-Making and Socio-Cultural Context in the First U.S. Eugenics Campaign," *Social Problems* 39, no. 1 (1992): 17. For more on the investigation of the body as a part of the study of handicapped individuals, see *Disability Studies Quarterly* 12, no. 2 (1992). The entire issue is devoted to the theme of "the body." Particularly interesting is Caroline Bynum, "Writing Body History: Some Autobiographical and Historiographical Reflections," 14–16.

5. Cynthia Russett, *Sexual Science: The Victorian Construction of Womanhood* (Cambridge: Harvard University Press, 1989), 11.

6. For more on female hysteria and its social and scientific construction, see Elaine Showalter, *The Female Malady: Women, Madness, and English Culture, 1830–1980* (New York: Penguin Books, 1987), and Andrew Scull,

Just as scientists centered on women as a distinct and inferior group, they simultaneously developed a similar construction for the lower classes. The discovery of hereditarian laws and the concomitant discrediting of Lamarckian evolution (which maintained a belief in the heritability of acquired characteristics) gave scientists cause to question the efficacy of social welfare programs. Increasingly, scientists viewed the poor as atavistic brutes, throwbacks to an earlier, more primitive time in which physical confrontations and erotic energy were never far from the surface. As the twentieth century moved into its second decade, the scientific community welcomed the use of the standardized intelligence test to determine individual intellectual functioning. The tests were used, however, not to remedy individual learning deficits, but to verify the connection between poverty, criminality, and low intelligence. Intelligence testing gave scientific imprimatur to the belief of inherited inequality. It also provided an avenue for identifying and categorizing those individuals who proved a burden to society and then institutionalizing them as feebleminded.[7]

Most women labeled as feebleminded in the early twentieth century struggled against class prejudices as well as sexual stereotypes. Categorized as childlike and simple by virtue of their sex, these women were institutionalized for their own protection, placed in asylums in the original sense of the term. Yet as members of the "bestial" lower classes, these same women were viewed by reformers as temptresses, as cauldrons of erotic energy waiting to boil over, and, more alarmingly, as transmitters of feebleminded genes to succeeding generations. Lower-class feebleminded women

Social Order/Mental Disorder: Anglo-American Psychiatry in Historical Perspective (Berkeley and Los Angeles: University of California Press, 1989), 267–79.

7. The literature on intelligence testing is large and often highly politically charged. For a view of intelligence testing in a social context, see Stephen Gelb, "'Not Simply Bad and Incorrigible': Science, Morality, and Intellectual Deficiency," *History of Education Quarterly* 29, no. 3 (1989): 359–79. On attempts at a balanced view of the roots of the testing movement, see Michael Sokal, ed., *Psychological Testing and American Society, 1890–1930* (New Brunswick: Rutgers University Press, 1987). For a more jaundiced view, see Russell Marks, *The Idea of IQ* (Washington, D.C.: University Press of America, 1985); and Leon Kamin, *The Science and Politics of IQ* (New York: Halsted Press, 1974).

therefore had to be institutionalized, not only for their own benefit but also for the benefit of society.

Southern attitudes mirrored, and even heightened, national feelings toward women in general, and lower-class women in particular. The 1914 report of the Virginia Colony for the Feeble-Minded verified the concerns about the simmering eroticism of the lower classes when it concluded that "as a matter of choice most of these women lead evil lives."[8] While some southerners saw the threat of feebleminded women as a consequence of their depraved nature, others viewed it as a result of these women's childlike nature and their inability to ward off the advances of unscrupulous males.

Eudora Welty's short story "Lily Daw and the Three Ladies" reveals the latter attitude well. In the story, three matrons of the small Mississippi town of Victory send Lily Daw, a young lower-class resident of their town, to Ellisville State School for the Feeble-Minded, telling her, "It's a lovely place . . . they will let you make all sorts of baskets." Their rationale for removing Lily from the town reflected their desire for protection of and from Lily. "Lily lets people walk over her so," reported one of the women. Another concluded that "Lily has gotten so she is very mature for her age. . . . And that's how come we are sending her to Ellisville." The upper-class matrons of Victory looked after Lily while she was growing up and, according to one of them, "gave Lily all her food and kindling and every stitch she had on." They decided that Lily could no longer remain at large in the community when evidence of her inability to deal with men became apparent.[9] This combination of class-based misplaced benevolence and abject fear forced southern women labeled as feebleminded to struggle under a double burden, from which escape was difficult.

In the 1910s and 1920s, southern states joined the national trend toward institutional provision for those persons categorized as mentally retarded. Between 1914 and 1923, nine states in the South opened public facilities designed specifically to house feebleminded persons (see Table 1).[10] Connected to broader themes of social

8. First Annual Report of the Virginia Colony for the Feeble-Minded, 1914, p. 16.

9. Eudora Welty, "Lily Daw and the Three Ladies," in *A Curtain of Green* (Garden City, N.Y.: Doubleday, Doran and Company, 1943), 8, 11, 4–5, 7.

10. For more on the establishment and organization of southern institu-

TABLE 1
Institutions for the Feebleminded in the South

STATE	INSTITUTION	YEAR FIRST PATIENTS WERE ADMITTED
Alabama	Partlow State School for Mental Defectives, Tuscaloosa	1919
Florida	Florida Farm Colony for Epileptic and Feeble-Minded, Gainesville	1921
Georgia	Georgia Training School for Mental Defectives, Gracewood	1921
Kentucky	State Institutions for the Feeble-Minded, Frankfort	1860
Louisiana	State Colony and Training School, Alexandria	1922
Mississippi	Ellisville State School, Ellisville	1923
North Carolina	Caswell Training School, Kinston	1914
South Carolina	State Training School, Clinton	1920
Tennessee	State Home and Training School for Feeble-Minded Persons, Donelson	1923
Virginia	Virginia [Lynchburg] Colony,	1908, 1914[a]
	Petersburg State Colony, Petersburg	1939[b]

[a]Colony opened in 1908 as an institution for epileptic persons. Feeble-minded individuals were admitted in 1914.
[b]Petersburg State Colony was the South's only institution for black patients.

---

tions, see Steven Noll, "'From Far More Different Angles'": Institutions for the Mentally Retarded in the South, 1900–1940 (Ph.D. diss., University of Florida, 1991). For more on national trends in the institutionalization of retarded persons, see Peter Tyor and Leland Bell, *Caring for the Retarded in America: A History* (Westport, Conn.: Greenwood Press, 1984), 71–122, and R. C. Scheerenberger, *A History of Mental Retardation* (Baltimore: Paul H. Brookes, 1983), 137–78.

welfare and social control, which characterized the Progressive Era, the institutionalization movement represented an attempt to protect society from the perceived threat of the feebleminded, never clearly defined as a class (See Table 2).[11] Southern progressives portrayed the feebleminded as "parasites," "human wreckage," and members of the "anti-social class."[12] Conversely, these leaders viewed feebleminded persons as "helpless and innocents" and "unfortunates." These two seemingly contradictory visions allowed southern institutional leaders to place feebleminded individuals in institutions for their own protection "but also as a matter of protection to the community."[13]

While feeblemindedness itself presented major societal problems, the assumed hereditary nature of the disorder made it even more dangerous. Charles Darwin's theories of evolution, the adaptation of them to the field of eugenics by his cousin Francis Galton, and the rediscovery of Mendelian genetics in 1900 led many in the field of research into feeblemindedness to embrace the view that mental deficiency was carried genetically from generation to generation. In 1916, Edward Johnstone, superintendent of New Jersey's influential Vineland Training School, concluded that "feeble-mindedness is strongly inheritable." Since feebleminded females would bear the children that would carry this hereditary taint, it seemed

11. Important literature on the Progressive Era in the South includes Dewey Grantham's *Southern Progressivism: The Reconciliation of Progress and Tradition* (Knoxville: University of Tennessee Press, 1983) and William Link's *The Paradox of Southern Progressivism, 1880–1930* (Chapel Hill: University of North Carolina Press, 1992), which point out unique parameters of progressivism in a region quite different from the rest of American society.

12. Thomas Haines, "Abstract of the Mississippi Mental Deficiency Survey," *Mental Hygiene* 4 (1920): 682; V. V. Anderson, "Mental Defect in a Southern State: Report of the Georgia Commission on Feeblemindedness and the Survey of the National Committee for Mental Hygiene," *Mental Hygiene* 3 (1919): 529; *Mental Defectives in Virginia: A Special Report of the State Board of Charities and Corrections to the General Assembly* (Richmond, Va.: Superintendent of Public Printing, 1915), 3.

13. Hastings Hart and Clarence Stonaker, "A Social Welfare Plan for Florida," Microfilm 102 CH35, in *The Russell Sage Foundation: Social Research and Social Action in America, 1907–1947: An Historical Bibliography*, ed. David Hammack (Frederick, Md.: University Press of America Academic Editions, 1988), 31; Second Annual Report of the South Carolina State Board of Charities and Corrections, 1916, pp. 7, 31, Department of Mental Health Records, South Carolina State Archives, Columbia.

TABLE 2
Comparison of Descriptive Terminology

GENERAL	1930	1993
	FEEBLEMINDED	MENTALLY HANDICAPPED
	MENTALLY DEFECTIVE	MENTALLY RETARDED
	MENTALLY DEFICIENT	

SUBCATEGORIES		
Mild	Moron	Educable
(IQ 55–70)		(EMH, EMR)
Moderate and	Imbecile	Trainable
Severe		(TMH, TMR)
(IQ 25–55)		
Profound	Idiot	Profound
(IQ <25)		(PMH, PMR)

only logical to institutional leaders that these women would be considered more dangerous than their male counterparts. J. H. Bell, superintendent of Virginia Colony at Lynchburg, summarized this attitude in 1931 in a paper read before the Virginia Medical Society. "The female defective is, generally speaking, more dangerous eugenically than the male . . . and it is therefore evident that if all mentally defective women were sterilized, there would be but little reproduction of feeble-minded persons from these sources."[14]

This scientifically based belief in the genetic transmission of feeblemindedness led to differential admission, retention, discharge, and sterilization rates in southern institutions for males and females. Ironically, even when scientific paradigms shifted, as in the case of eugenics, this discrepancy in the treatment of males and females remained constant. Institutional leaders used ostensibly objective scientific rationales for maintaining two different sets of criteria for male and female patients and, as new scientific paradigms developed, simply shaped them to verify their beliefs about

14. Edward Johnstone, "Stimulating Public Interest in the Feeble-Minded," *Proceedings of the National Conference on Charities and Corrections, 1916* (Chicago: Hildmann Printing Co., 1916), 205; J. H. Bell, "Eugenic Sterilization and Its Relationship to the Science of Life and Reproduction—A Paper Read before the Meeting of the Virginia Medical Society, Roanoke, Virginia, October 7, 1931," pp. 6–7, Pamphlet Collection, Virginia State Library and Archives.

female feeblemindedness. Thus even in the 1930s, when scientific research seemed to destroy the notion that feeblemindedness was strictly heritable, southern superintendents did not reexamine their programs of institutionalization and sterilization. Instead, they simply changed their rationale for these programs.[15] A 1936 North Carolina state survey of mental health services reported that sterilization programs "should be continued . . . on a larger scale." In spite of the debunking of the eugenic reasons for these procedures, the report concluded that "turning to an environmental viewpoint, we often find more reasons than appear from the standpoint of eugenics. . . . Mentally handicapped parents are a liability."[16]

Institutions in the South, like similar facilities nationwide, did not come to grips with the sexual dimension of feeblemindedness. Caught between a belief in the overt sexuality of feebleminded females and a paternalistic desire to protect these women from the advances of predatory males, institutional leaders opted for different treatment patterns based upon gender. In the closed world of the institution, these practices exaggerated, rather than simply reflected, a male-dominated society's ambivalence toward females and the roles they played. Daily institutional life reflected these exaggerations.

The elastic nature of the term *feebleminded* itself, and the arbitrary fashion in which officials used it, led to wide disparities in the admission procedures of southern institutions. Certain categories of feebleminded individuals, those labeled as morons or imbeciles, were often admitted for the protection of society. These persons functioned at the margins of society, and their admission often resulted from their exhibition of deviant behavior. A 1919 Georgia state report concluded that "the depravations growing out of their criminal behavior furnish one of the most satisfactory arguments

15. See especially the influential report of a committee of the American Neurological Association, which reported that "there is at present no sound scientific basis for sterilization . . . [and] we do not believe that society needs to hurry into a program based on fear and propaganda." Abraham Myerson et al., *Eugenical Sterilization: A Reorientation of the Problem* (New York: Macmillan, 1936), 177, 183.

16. *A Study of Mental Health in North Carolina: A Report to the North Carolina Legislature of the Governor's Commission Appointed to Study the Care of the Insane and Mental Defectives* (Ann Arbor, Mich.: Edwards Brothers, 1937), 364, 301.

for a state-wide policy of protection against the menace of feeble-mindedness." Conversely, other feebleminded persons, those labeled idiots, usually were institutionalized for their own protection and to provide relief for families burdened with the care of physically demanding and medically fragile persons. In 1939, Caswell Training School received a letter requesting admission for a six-year-old idiot boy. The child needed institutionalization, the letter read, "not only for his welfare but because of the effect of the strain and worry of having him in the home." The differing demographic variables of the patient population housed in southern institutions greatly affected the functioning of these facilities. Forced to care for and control, in the words of a Louisiana assistant superintendent, "all classes of feeblemindedness," institutions rarely provided more than basic care. "We have white and colored; children and adults; epileptics and non-epilepics; delinquent and non-delinquent," he continued, "educable and custodial cases. The placing of these various classes in one institution makes the problem of their care and training a very difficult one."[17] States organized separate institutions to provide specialized care for individuals categorized as feebleminded and mentally defective. The wide varieties of individuals placed in southern institutions exacerbated an already difficult situation of low funding and little state support. These facilities, therefore, did little to solve the problems of feeble-mindedness in the South.

While the level of mental deficiency remained a paramount consideration in the treatment of institutionalized patients, gender played a major role as well, primarily because of concern about the fecundity of the feebleminded. The 1919 annual report of the South Carolina State Board of Charities and Corrections questioned whether the state would make provisions to prevent the feebleminded from "propagating their kind to add to the ever increasing burden of successive generations." To many leaders in the fight against mental deficiency, this prevention meant taking extra precautions for feebleminded women. In 1931, South Carolina State Training School superintendent Benjamin Whitten reported on the effects of the

17. Anderson, "Mental Defect in a Southern State," 538; Letter in Patient Record No. 2, Medical Records Office, Caswell Center Archives; R. C. Tompkins, "Teaching and Care of Feebleminded in State Institution [sic]," *New Orleans Medical and Surgical Journal* 82 (1929): 161.

Depression on his institution. "You can readily realize what a deplorable situation this is," he concluded, "particularly in the case of girls, who are being held solely to protect them from the depravity of mankind."[18] In response to the presumed special needs of female patients, several eastern and midwestern states opened institutions designed specifically to house feebleminded women. In 1932, the male superintendent of Pennsylvania's Laurelton State School, one of these facilities, defined his institution's purpose as "caring for mentally defective women of the child-bearing age and the segregation of these girls and women in order to prevent their conceiving and reproducing their mental defects in coming generations."[19]

Although southern states did not organize separate facilities for mentally retarded women, they remained cognizant of the gender-based notions of feeblemindedness. The 1915 Virginia survey of mental defectives analyzed the records of 120 Richmond prostitutes and found 86 to be feebleminded. The report suggested that "society should segregate them where they will be protected from licentious men and lewd, avaricious women."[20] Acting upon the recommendations of the survey, Virginia legislators authorized the

18. Fifth Annual Report of the South Carolina State Board of Charities and Corrections, 1919, p. 32, and Fourteenth Annual Report of the South Carolina State Training School, 1928, pp. 7–8, both in Department of Mental Health Records, South Carolina State Archives. Much recent work has been done on the relationship of gender to deviancy in a historical context. See Peter Tyor, "'Denied the Power to Choose the Good': Sexuality and Mental Defect in American Medical Practice," *Journal of Social History* 10, no. 4 (1977): 472–89; Nicole Hahn Rafter, "Too Dumb to Know Better: Cacogenic Family Studies and the Criminology of Women," *Criminology* 18, no. 1 (1980): 3–25; and Stephen Schlossman and Stephanie Wallach, "The Crime of Precocious Sexuality: Female Juvenile Delinquency in the Progressive Era," *Harvard Educational Review* 48, no. 1 (1978): 65–94.

19. LeRoy Maeder, "The Problems of Mental Deficiency in Pennsylvania," *Journal of Psycho-Asthenics* 37 (1931–1932): 35. See also Harry Hardt, "The State Care of Feeble-Minded Women," *Institution Quarterly* 3, no. 1 (1912): 179–86; and Olga Bridgman, "Juvenile Delinquency and Feeble-Mindedness," *Institution Quarterly* 5, no. 2 (1914): 164–67.

20. *Mental Defectives in Virginia,* 66. Other investigations of the same time period showed that the relationship between feeblemindedness and prostitution was not as direct as some assumed. Mabel Ruth Fernald, Mary Hayes, Almena Dawley, *A Study of Women Delinquents in New York State* (New York: Century Company, 1920), 528.

establishment of an institution for the feebleminded on the grounds of an existing facility for epileptics in Lynchburg, giving priority to female patients. The sex of the individuals admitted to the new institution verified the prevailing concerns about the dangers of female feeblemindedness. By 1916, the Virginia Colony for the Feeble-Minded had admitted 138 patients, all of them female.[21]

A 1914 public notice issued by the administration of North Carolina's Caswell Training School confirmed the concerns of the Virginia report. "It is known to students of Social Evil and students of Psychology," the notice read, "that girls of a subnormal mentality are a helpless prey to the men of vicious habits, and a very large percentage of these girls, sooner or later, go wrong. One of the objects of this institution is to segregate and thereby protect these girls." This desire was codified into statute five years later when the North Carolina legislature set provisions for the admission of feebleminded children of both sexes as well as "feeble-minded women between the ages of twenty-one and thirty."[22]

This concern over female feeblemindedness led many reformers to posit the existence of a direct relationship between mental retardation and prostitution. A 1920 survey of 122 Georgia prostitutes found 43.5 percent of them to be feebleminded.[23] By assuming this causal link, leaders in the reform movement viewed prostitutes as victims, as mentally deficient women unable to make correct moral decisions and easily led astray by evil men. Historian Mark Connelly has written that the "feeble-mindedness theory [of prostitution] was

21. Third Annual Report of the Virginia Colony for the Feeble-Minded, 1916, pp. 2, 32, Virginia State Library and Archives. As late as 1938, after males were admitted, females made up 562 of a total institutional population of 1,024. *Twenty-Ninth Annual Report of the State Colony for Epileptics and Feeble-Minded, 1937–1938*, 15, Virginia State Library and Archives.

22. Notice to the Public, n.d., uncatalogued records, Caswell Center Archives; *1919 Laws of North Carolina, Chapter 22, Section 2*, North Carolina Department of History and Archives, Raleigh.

23. Edward Devine, "The Feeble-Minded in Georgia," *Survey* 43, no. 13 (1920): 467. See also Paul Mertz, "Mental Deficiency of Prostitutes: A Study of Delinquent Women at an Army Port of Embarkation," *Journal of the American Medical Association* 72, no. 22 (1919): 1597–99. Mertz tested sixty-nine prostitutes in Newport News, Virginia, and found 53 percent had mental ages ten years or lower. To the author, "these figures add evidence to the already well-established belief that virtually one-half of the country's prostitutes are mentally deficient or feeble-minded" (1599).

as much the product of class and cultural biases as of actual value-free intelligence testing. . . . As in many cases of social labeling, the feeble-mindedness theory reveals as much about those who endorsed it as about the women it purportedly described."[24]

It would, nonetheless, be wrong to assume that only humanitarian concern for the protection of feebleminded females from the dangers of sexual exploitation motivated Progressive Era reformers. More important, according to an 1898 article in the *Journal of the American Medical Association,* authorities placed a mentally defective woman in an institution to "end her danger as a multiplier of her own weakness and the present rapid increase in our dependent population." The 1915 Georgia Survey of Mental Defectiveness verified reformers' concerns for both wayward women and the society at large. "An institution for defective delinquent girls will be a charter of liberty for this most helpless, unfortunate, and potentially dangerous class," it reported, "taking them from the streets and highways, where they have been the defenceless [*sic*] prey of lust and greed. . . . Finally, not the least important of all these benefits is the protection such an institution will afford society."[25]

This need to protect society from potentially defective offspring led superintendents and other officials to institutionalize females for longer periods than males. For the thirteen-year period 1925–1938, females constituted 48.3 percent of the total national institutionalized population, but only 43.1 percent of those were discharged back into the community. These figures showed that the turnover rate for males in institutions also remained higher than for females.[26] These measures signified a desire for social control of

24. Mark Connelly, *The Response to Prostitution in the Progressive Era* (Chapel Hill: University of North Carolina Press, 1982), 42–43. See also Ruth Rosen, *The Lost Sisterhood: Prostitution in America, 1900–1918* (Baltimore: Johns Hopkins University Press, 1982), 1–37.

25. Alfred Wilmarth, "The Rights of the Public in Dealing with the Defective Classes," *Journal of the American Medical Association* 31, no. 22 (1898): 1278; Anderson, "Mental Defect in a Southern State," 546.

26. *Feeble-Minded and Epileptics in Institutions, 1926, Feeble-Minded . . . 1927,* and *Feeble-Minded . . . 1928* (Washington, D.C.: Government Printing Office, 1928, 1929, 1931); *Mental Defectives and Epileptics in Institutions, 1929–1932, Mental Defectives . . . 1933, Mental Defectives . . . 1934,* and *Mental Defectives . . . 1935* (Washington D.C.: Government Printing Office, 1934, 1935, 1937, 1938). See Tyor's "Denied the Power to Choose the Good," 477, wherein the author takes data from midwestern institutions and con-

feebleminded females, reflecting the gender concerns of society. The control of a deviant population remained paramount in the eyes of institutional leaders charged with protecting society from the perceived threat of mentally deficient offspring.[27]

This control manifested itself in longer terms of institutionalization for female residents at southern institutions, mirroring national trends. From 1914 to 1939 at Caswell Training School, for example, 52.1 percent of the males admitted were discharged within three years of admittance. That compared to only 31 percent of the females (see Table 3). Figures from Florida verify the North Carolina data. While males constituted almost 60 percent of Florida Farm Colony's 1,165 admissions from 1922 to 1937, they made up over 65 percent of those discharged during the same time period. Whereas males tended to remain in institutions for shorter periods of time, they also were admitted at earlier ages. Florida Farm Colony admission figures from Alachua County from 1921 to 1949 revealed a mean average male admission age of 10.6, which contrasted with a mean female admission age of 12.42. This two-year differential, similar to the one discovered by Tyor, placed female admission to Florida Farm Colony at approximately the onset of puberty.[28] Both the longer retention rates and later admission ages for female patients demonstrated an official concern that non-institutionalized "girls and women of the child-bearing age" constituted a threat to the social order.[29]

---

cludes that "both mean admission ages and periods of retention were higher for women than men."

27. This notion had broad international currency. See Harvey Simmons, "Explaining Social Policy: The English Mental Deficiency Act of 1913," *Journal of Social History* 11 (1978): 399.

28. *Second Biennial Report of the Superintendent of Florida Farm Colony, 1921–22, Third Biennial Report . . . 1923–25, Fourth Biennial Report . . . 1925–27, Fifth Biennial Report . . . 1927–29, Sixth Biennial Report . . . 1929– 31, Seventh Biennial Report . . . 1932–33, Eighth Biennial Report . . . 1933– 34,* and *Ninth Biennial Report . . . 1935–37* (n.p., n.d.), all in Vault files, Gainesville Sunland Center, Gainesville, Fla. (later reports did not contain this detailed patient movement information); Alachua County Commitment Records, 1921–1940, Alachua County Courthouse, Gainesville, Fla.; Tyor, "Denied the Power to Choose the Good," 481. Males, particularly high-level morons, tended to be admitted earlier than females since their deviance seemed more demonstrable (fighting or stealing) than female deviance at a similar age.

29. See *Laws of Florida, Chapter 7887* 1: 235, Florida State Archives, Tal-

TABLE 3

Average Length of Residence, by Sex, Caswell Training School,
1914–1939

	MALE			FEMALE		
	<3YRS	3–8YRS	>8YRS	<3YRS	3–8YRS	>8YRS
1914–1919[a]	52.1% n=73	9.3% n=13	38.3% n=54	31% n=49	11.4% n=18	57.6% n=91
1920–1924	31.5% n=35	23.4% n=26	45.1% n=50	34.7% n=49	20.6% n=29	44.7% n=63
1925–1929	42.4% n=104	18.8% n=46	38.8% n=95	29.5% n=59	14.0% n=28	56.5% n=113
1930–1934	42.9% n=51	10.1% n=12	47.0% n=56	31.0% n=45	12.4% n=18	56.6% n=82
1935–1939	14.8% n=24	24.7% n=40	60.5% n=98	14.2% n=15	20.7% n=22	65.1% n=69

Source: Patient Admission Book, Medical Records Office, Caswell Center,
Kinston, N.C.
Note: The length of residence was calculated from the date of admission
to the date of dismissal, transfer, escape, or death. The book listed 1,553
admissions to the institution from 1914 to 1939, of which 26 are not calculated in the table, as the year of dismissal, death, transfer, or escape was
listed as unknown in the book. As of September 1988, when this data was
collected, 18 persons (12 male and 6 female) admitted before 1940 were
still living at Caswell Center. They are calculated in the appropriate
column.
[a]Year represents year of admission.

Concerns about hereditary transmission of mental deficiency
and the conflation of promiscuous sexual activity with feeblemindedness distorted the admission procedures of southern institutions. Females, of course, constituted the majority of those committed for such sexual "problems." Compilers of southern state
surveys often cataloged cases of feebleminded prostitutes and bra-

---

lahassee, which recommended preference in admission to those of this category. See also Report of Superintendent C. Banks McNairy to Board of Control
of North Carolina School for the Feeble-Minded, December 16–17, 1914, Minutes of the Executive Committee of the Board of Directors, Caswell Center
Archives.

zenly immoral women. In 1919, the Florida Commission for the
Study of Epilepsy and Feeblemindedness (instrumental in the au-
thorization of the Florida Farm Colony two years later) reported a
case study of a female classified as feebleminded. The "girl . . . has
been openly immoral for years," the survey taker observed. "In the
War Department records, she is classified as a feebleminded moral
degenerate." No records exist as to whether the young woman ever
entered Florida Farm Colony. A Virginia case, however, reveals a
direct relationship between alleged sexual misconduct and institutionalization. In 1928, a Strasburg, Virginia, couple wrote Virginia
governor Harry Byrd, requesting his help "to get our daughter
from the State Colony near Lynchburg. . . . She is feeble-minded.
She was not feeble-minded when she went there. . . . She was sent
there by the Red Cross because she was coaxed away from her
people by outsiders [and gave birth to an illegitimate child]." The
parents, acting as parents for their grandchild, affirmed "the baby
is a well, healthy, and able-bodied child." Of course, this ran con-
trary to the accepted scientific belief in the inherited nature of
feeblemindedness. Not wishing to get involved in the daily problems of the institution, Byrd replied curtly that "there is nothing I
can do about her discharge."[30]

Other southern state institutions also struggled with the problems caused by female sexuality. In Florida, Judge Albert Wiese of
the Tampa Juvenile Court requested admission to Florida Farm
Colony in 1929 for an eighteen-year-old white woman because
"she will live the life of a common prostitute unless she is given
institutional care." Colony staff replied that "it is probable that we
shall be able to take her in the near future," but no further record
indicates whether she was actually admitted. This kind of sexual
admission criterion appeared in North Carolina as well. In 1914, the
superintendent of the Childrens' Home Society of North Carolina
wrote to Caswell Training School superintendent McNairy regarding a female patient admitted as one of the first residents of the

30. Case Study reported in "Florida's Feeble-Minded," *Survey* 42 (August 9,
1919): 705. See a similar case study, voluminously detailed, in Madeline
Bragar, "The Feeble-Minded Female: An Historical Analysis of Mental Retardation as a Social Definition, 1890–1920" (Ph.D. diss., Syracuse University,
1977), 111–29. Mr. and Mrs. Burner to Governor Harry F. Byrd, February 20,
1928; Byrd to the Burners, February 24, 1928, Papers of Governor Harry Byrd,
RG 3, box 29, State Colony fol., Virginia State Archives, Richmond.

new state institution. "I would not know how to categorize Edna's special form of feeblemindedness," he wrote, " . . . though a report from a recent home she was in indicated that the sexual instinct was very strong. . . . Her future safety" and presumably the safety of society from her feebleminded offspring, "depends on her being segregated and receiving institutional care."[31]

The working papers of the South Carolina Report on the Feeble-Minded of 1916–1917, which investigated high-level mentally defective individuals in the community, verified the prevailing perception that female mental deficiency and sexual immorality went hand in hand. Of the twenty-three Columbia, South Carolina, females identified in the report as feebleminded, eighteen were categorized as immoral or sexually active in one form or another. One young woman married without her mother's consent and "went out in automobiles with men." Another young female was classified as feebleminded in spite of her "claim to be a junior at Lander College." The report categorized her as feebleminded because of her illegitimate pregnancy, which left her "family very much disgraced at her conduct."[32]

Although institutions admitted many moron women because of sexual "problems" and promiscuity, it should not be assumed that superintendents considered this procedure as mere punishment for misdeeds. In a form of paternalism similar to that practiced by slave owners in the antebellum era as well as by males in the Victorian time period, the social welfare bureaucracy placed females in institutions for their own protection as well as for the protection of society. Relying on their belief in the lascivious nature of male behavior, superintendents felt their facilities truly acted as asylums for impressionable and vulnerable women, offering protection and refuge from males intent on taking advantage of women unable to protect themselves from untoward sexual advances. A 1934 North Carolina state publication reported that "it is especially important to safeguard the feeble-minded girl . . . from exploita-

31. Application form of August 30, 1929, and Superintendent Colson's reply of September 2, 1929, both in Superintendents' Correspondence, Vault Files, Gainesville Sunland Center, Gainesville, Fla.; William Streeter to C. Banks McNairy, May 11, 1914; and patient information in patient file 4, Medical Records Office, Caswell Center Archives.

32. Cases 76 and 55, Working Papers of the South Carolina Report on the Feeble-Minded, South Carolina State Archives.

tion from unscrupulous persons. [She] is otherwise led to become a sex delinquent, spreading disease, and giving birth to illegitimate offspring who themselves become charges of the State."[33]

Running institutions for the feebleminded seems to have been exclusively a male profession, and male officials did not always sympathize with the plight of sexually exploited young women. The 1914 annual report of the Virginia Colony concluded that "immoral women in this institution . . . are adept in the use of the vilest language and practices, common among women of their class, and their effect on the children patients is demoralizing in the extreme."[34] Whether the motivation was protection or control, however, did not seem to matter. With societal concern about inherited feeblemindedness at a peak, young, poor, promiscuous women ran the risk of being labeled as feebleminded and placed in an institution for the retarded.

Eugenic sterilization, removal of the reproductive capacity for genetic and not punitive reasons, offered officials an alternative to the long-term institutionalization of their patients. The 1934 superintendent's report of Florida Farm Colony concluded that "a step towards checking this on-rushing horde now devouring civilization would be the surgical sterilization of every feeble-minded person."[35] The surgical removal of reproductive organs seemed quick, relatively inexpensive, permanent, and at the cutting edge of the latest scientific research. It also solved a major social problem by preventing the propagation of feebleminded offspring.

Institutional leaders nationwide were more likely to initiate sterilization procedures on female patients than on males. Females represented 64.1 percent (15,996) of the 24,957 mentally retarded individuals sterilized in the United States from 1907 to 1949. In Virginia and North Carolina, the two southern states that sterilized the most patients, the figures are 60 percent and 80 percent females sterilized, respectively.[36] Could the disparities between the

33. *A Brief History of the Care of the Underprivileged Child in North Carolina,* Special Bulletin 13, issued by the North Carolina State Board of Charities and Public Welfare, 1934, p. 24.

34. First Annual Report of the Virginia Colony for the Feeble-Minded, 1914, pp. 11–12.

35. *Eighth Biennial Report of the Superintendent of Florida Farm Colony, 1932–1934,* 7.

36. Moya Woodside, *Sterilization in North Carolina: A Sociological and*

numbers of men and women sterilized simply have occurred because, in the words of the director of the North Carolina Eugenics Board, "men are less willing to believe that the only effect of
sterilization is the prevention of parenthood"?[37]

Superintendents recognized this sex differential as more than
either a statistical aberration or the result of men not believing in
the efficacy of the procedure. In 1925, Virginia Colony superintendent Dr. A. S. Priddy responded to a question concerning who at
his institution would benefit from sterilization. "I should think from
75 to 100 women," he replied. "The men have other anti-social
tendencies just as glaring as child-bearing, and we would have to
keep them there [in the institution]—they rank below the tramps
and hoboes."[38]

Superintendents saw several causes for the preponderance of
females sterilized. Concerned that people might wonder that women
were being singled out for the procedure at the Virginia Colony (of
the first 447 persons sterilized there, 328 were female), colony
superintendent J. H. Bell addressed the issue in 1931 as he spoke
before the Virginia Medical Society. "There has been no disposition on our part to create this difference," he assured his fellow
doctors. Males "of a suitable type for sterilization and release"
simply "are able to evade serious contact with welfare agencies
and local officials" and "therefore [are] not in a position to be
sterilized." Females should be sterilized for their own protection,
he argued, since they "fall an easy prey to the sexual aggressions
of males of superior intellect as well as to those of her [*sic*] own
mental level." Conversely, "the feeble-minded male cannot enter
into serious competition with the normal male for the affections of
the feeble-minded female." Bell concluded by announcing that

Psychological Study (Chapel Hill: University of North Carolina Press, 1950),
194. In North Carolina, women comprised 680 of the 858 persons sterilized;
in Virginia, 2,011 of the total 3,453. Statistical data from Eleanor Welborn,
*Eugenical Sterilization in the United States, with Particular Attention to a
Follow-up Study of Non-Institutional Cases in North Carolina, April 5, 1933 to
January 1, 1939* (master's thesis, University of North Carolina, 1940), app. A.

37. Clarence Gamble, "Eugenic Sterilization in North Carolina," *North
Carolina Medical Journal* 12, no. 11 (1951): 550.

38. Testimony of A. S. Priddy in *Buck v. Bell*, in Harry Laughlin, *The Legal
Status of Eugenical Sterilization* (Chicago: Free Publication of the Municipal
Court of Chicago, 1930).

"the female defective is, generally speaking, more dangerous eugenically than the male . . . and it is, therefore, evident that if all
mentally defective women were sterilized, there would be but little
reproduction of feeble-minded persons from these sources."[39]

Bell's predecessor, Dr. Priddy, also believed that the sterilization
of women provided the key to a successful state eugenics program. Again, his rationale combined concern about the sexual
immorality of those he labeled "the high-grade women of the anti-
social class" and the protection of "unsterilized, physically attractive young women," since, upon release, "it is not infrequent for
them to be returned to the institution pregnant."[40] The gender and
class stereotypes of institutional officials, combined with their belief in concerted, scientifically based state action, led to the dispro-
portionate sterilization of lower-class women.

North Carolina's 1933 sterilization statute allowed for the sterilization of noninstitutional cases upon the recommendation of county
welfare agencies. This made North Carolina unique in the South,
where all other sterilization laws pertained only to institutionalized
persons, usually as a prerequisite for discharge. The sexual dis-
parity appeared even more pronounced in North Carolina's non-
institutional cases, with women constituting nearly 90 percent of
the 229 persons sterilized between 1933 and 1939.[41] In examining
the implications of noninstitutional sterilization in Orange County,
North Carolina, researcher J. McLean Benson concluded that "we
tolerate the actions of men where we do not tolerate similar actions in women." Benson's study of the nineteen cases in that
county verify his conclusions. Of the nineteen operations performed in Orange County between 1934 and 1936, only two were
on males. Sex delinquency was the major rationale for the female
sterilizations. One young woman, sterilized for that problem, was
"very obviously a case for Caswell Training School, but authorities
were unable to get her into the School." Another young woman,
listed as poverty stricken and afflicted with venereal disease, was
sterilized for being "boy-crazy." The operation did little for her

39. Bell, "Eugenic Sterilization and Its Relationship to the Science of Life
and Reproduction," 6–7.
40. A. S. Priddy, quoted in Cynthia Pegram, "Dr. Priddy Backed Law,"
Lynchburg News, March 27, 1980, C4.
41. Welborn, *Eugenical Sterilization in the United States*, 95. There were
206 women out of the total 229 persons sterilized.

malady, "for she is as boy-crazy as she ever was. However," the report concluded, "she will not propagate her kind."[42]

The treatment of feebleminded women in the South was inextricably bound up with the class and gender stereotypes in the minds of institutional officials. These leaders associated feeblemindedness with pauperism and dependency. They also considered female mental deficiency as synonymous with sexual immorality and promiscuity. Drawing upon these presuppositions as well as a scientific mind-set that assumed feeblemindedness was genetically transmitted, male superintendents established institutional policies that viewed female feebleminded individuals as more dangerous than their male counterparts. The desire for a stable social order, one not upset by "those who are the greatest menace to the community," became the primary rationale for the institutionalization and sterilization of women labeled as feebleminded.[43]

42. J. McLean Benson, *Sterilization with Special Reference to Orange County, North Carolina* (master's thesis, University of North Carolina, 1936), quote: 59, case studies: 31. Of the 206 women sterilized statewide in North Carolina outside institutions, 109 were categorized as sexually promiscuous. Welborn, *Eugenical Sterilization in the United States*, 101.

43. Hastings Hart, "The Extinction of the Defective Delinquent—A Working Program," Microfilm 102 CH10, in David Hammack, ed., *The Russell Sage Foundation*, 2.

"Better Babies"

Birth Control in Arkansas during the 1930s

MARIANNE LEUNG

In 1930 when the first birth control association in Arkansas was organized, Rabbi Ira Sanders recalled, "It was suggested that because the movement [birth control] might evoke criticism on the part of a rather orthodox and staid community, that we call it the Arkansas Eugenics Association on the grounds that nobody would object to being well born." Sanders, one of the founders of the Little Rock Birth Control Clinic, claimed that the above line of reasoning sufficed at a time when the Little Rock community faced severe economic difficulties. According to the constitution of the newly formed Arkansas Eugenics Association, the purpose of the association was to promote "the eugenic development of the human race under favorable physical, economic, and social conditions."[1] But the Little Rock clinic directed its efforts toward poor women only.

An examination of the ideas and the work of this and other local

Work on this essay was supported in part by a research award from the History of Medicine Associates, University of Arkansas for Medical Sciences Library, Little Rock, and the Medical Education for Arkansas of the Arkansas Medical Society.

1. Rabbi Ira E. Sanders, interview by Charlotte Gadberry, Little Rock, Ark., January 18, 1978, Ira E. Sanders Papers, box 9, file 37.2, Special Collections, University of Arkansas, Little Rock Library, University of Arkansas at Little Rock; the Constitution of the Arkansas Eugenics Association, art. 2. The files from the Little Rock Birth Control Clinic and the Arkansas Eugenics Association are housed in Special Collections Archives, University of Arkansas for Medical Sciences Library, Little Rock, under the collection name History of Public Health in Arkansas—Birth Control, hereinafter referred to as the UAMS Collection.

birth control clinics across America reveals a complex picture of what occurred at the grassroots level of the birth control movement. Among other things, local community groups embraced various ideas of different national movements and, depending on the local situation, adopted only what would work to their advantage at the time. Judging from both the name adopted for the Arkansas birth control movement, the Arkansas Eugenics Association, and much of the public rhetoric it employed, this local birth control movement adhered to the ideas of the American Eugenics Society.[2] When one probes deeper, however, it becomes clear that the Arkansas birth control advocates were actors and reactors within a complex web of changing ideas; but they looked mainly to the national birth control movement for guidance and support. They knew that to obtain their goals, community support was crucial, and therefore they shrewdly selected the appropriate context in which to introduce safe and effective birth control into their community.

Hilda Kahlert Cornish, a respected member of the Little Rock community in Arkansas, initiated and directed the Arkansas birth control movement. She was the connecting link between the Birth Control Clinical Research Bureau, directed by Margaret Sanger in New York, and the Little Rock Birth Control Clinic. Hilda Cornish, the widow of banker Edward Cornish, had a reputation of working for the betterment of the poor and destitute citizens of Little Rock. She also belonged to the library board and had important connections with influential individuals in the local community.[3]

Cornish came in contact with families in poverty through her active participation in volunteer work. Her interest in the issue of birth control for poor families arose at the time when her son, Ed Junior, and Margaret Sanger's son, Stuart, roomed together at Yale University. She studied the work of the New York clinic in June 1930 and learned much from lengthy conversations with Margaret Sanger. That summer, Cornish also visited a clinic in Denver, Colo-

2. See, for further discussion, Carl J. Bajema, ed., *Eugenics Then and Now* (Stroudsburg, Pa.: Dowden, Hutchinson and Ross, 1976), 239, 265, 268; Ellsworth Huntington, *Tomorrow's Children: The Goals of Eugenics* (New York: John Wiley and Sons, 1935), 46–51.

3. Hilda Coates (daughter), interview by Marianne Leung, Little Rock, Ark., July 12, 1989, 2, Oral History Research Office, Memphis State University, Memphis, Tenn.

rado, and learned valuable information from its leader, Ruth Vincent Cunningham.[4]

Cornish quickly shared what she had learned, and by November the same year, an organized group was meeting regularly in Little Rock. The group met in the rooms of the future clinic in the basement of Baptist Hospital on January 28, 1931, and agreed to call itself the Arkansas Eugenics Association. Its goal was to make safe and effective contraceptives available to poor white women in the community at a time when Arkansas was experiencing severe economic hardships. An executive committee, including two physicians, led the work of the new association. The clinic opened its doors on February 1, 1931, and operated for the duration of the decade.[5]

Declaring that the purpose of the clinic was to serve married indigent women, the Arkansas Eugenics Association swiftly disseminated information in the community.[6] Following the lead of Margaret Sanger's Birth Control Clinical Research Bureau, the local birth control advocates kept careful records on women who approached the clinic for contraceptive information. Among other things, information about each woman included reproductive history (number of previous pregnancies), present economic situation, age, marital status, previous contraceptive method used, and reasons for requesting contraceptive information. The clinic summarized and printed some of this information in reports disseminated to interested community members. The reports informed the public about the goals of the Arkansas Eugenics Association in order to establish the legitimacy of the clinic and to solicit community support.

Like many other local birth control clinics at the time, the Little Rock center offered weekly clinics at which a physician was available to give gynecological examinations and fit women with contraceptive devices such as the diaphragm and spermicidal jelly. In

4. Ibid.; [Sylvia Cornish?], memo-report, [ca. 1937], describes the early beginnings of the Little Rock Birth Control Clinic and the motivations of Hilda Cornish, box 6, file 4, UAMS Collection; Hilda Cornish to Margaret Sanger, July 24, 1930, Margaret Sanger Papers, container 129, reel 84, Manuscript Division, Library of Congress.

5. Report of the Little Rock Clinic of the Arkansas Eugenics Association for February 1, 1931–January 31, 1932, box 6, file 4, UAMS Collection.

6. Ibid.

accordance with the national movement, women in Arkansas learned about the clinic from different professionals with whom they came into contact. These included social agencies, doctors, nurses, and health agencies. Former clients and clinic publicity sufficed as additional sources of referrals. The clinic also offered literature that clearly described contraceptive methods. Both medical professionals and interested community members in general sought out these informational sources.[7]

One of the major events in the history of the Arkansas state birth control movement was the 1935 resolution adopted by the Arkansas Medical Society at Fort Smith. It urged the American Medical Association to initiate a comprehensive program concerning contraceptives, to undertake scientific study of contraceptives, and to work for legislative changes to remove restrictions affecting physicians. A year later, *United States v. One Package* removed long-standing restrictions against disseminating contraceptive advice and information to the public. Then, in 1937, the American Medical Association decided to study contraceptive practices. In effect, the AMA approved of birth control as having a definite place in medical practice.[8] The Arkansas birth control advocates reached their immediate goal when the Arkansas State Health Department, in January 1940, took on the responsibility to make contraceptive advice and devices available to low-income families.[9] The name, Arkansas Eugenics Association, changed to the Planned Parenthood Association of Arkansas in 1942.

The Little Rock clinic is of interest to women's history for many

7. Reports about work at individual birth control clinics were published in the *Birth Control Review* between the years 1928 and 1932. Hilda Cornish responded to letters requesting contraceptive information by recommending that the letter writer borrow books from the library at the clinic. Books and pamphlets available at the clinic were listed in a letter dated January 21, 1938, from Mrs. Ed Cornish to an unknown man in El Dorado, Ark., box 6, file 3, UAMS Collection.

8. Resolution adopted at the 1935 annual meeting of the Arkansas Medical Society, box 5, UAMS Collection, and reel 84, Margaret Sanger Papers; *New York Times,* June 9, 1937, p. 1, col. 2. Hilda Cornish and Enid Aubrey Branner (Arkansas Legislative representative to the National Committee on Federal Legislation for Birth Control) participated in the 1935 annual meeting of the AMS.

9. Robbie Moreland, "Humanitarian's Goal: Safe Birth Control," *Arkansas Magazine,* September 14, 1986, 5.

reasons. At first glance, the Arkansas Eugenics Association seemed to advocate a eugenic population program focused on the poor. According to the national eugenics organization, the American Eugenics Society, to disseminate contraceptive information to poor women benefited future generations. In the view of eugenicists, local birth control clinics helped prevent the "undesirable" elements of society from contributing to the future gene pool.[10]

Eugenics had two manifestations, as a social science and as a reform movement. Eugenics as a science sought to determine the direction and rate of genetic change in human populations brought about by natural selection and to study the impact of genetic changes on society. For example, some eugenicists argued that wars alter natural selection and that the deaths of great numbers of individuals, with genes deemed beneficial to humanity, have negatively affected the quality of future generations.

As a reform movement, eugenics tried to modify the way in which natural selection operated on human populations. The American Eugenics Society saw as its purpose social reform and hoped to improve the quality of future generations through selective breeding of human beings. The American Eugenics Society peaked during the mid-1930s. It supported both the idea that people with undesirable characteristics should limit the number of children they reproduced and the idea that people with desirable characteristics should be strongly encouraged to have many children. Advocates in the movement argued that if nature proceeded undisturbed, the result would unnecessarily delay social betterment and cause human suffering. Intervention, they argued, was more humane than natural reproduction.[11]

Eugenics literature emphasized "negative eugenics," which discouraged less "fit" people from reproducing. The literature, however, failed to specify who was undesirable. Some eugenicists care-

10. See, for further discussion, Linda Gordon, *Woman's Body, Woman's Right: A Social History of Birth Control in America* (New York: Grossman, 1976), 274–90.

11. For further discussion see Bajema, ed., *Eugenics Then and Now;* Kenneth M. Ludmerer, *Genetics and American Society: A Historical Appraisal* (Baltimore: John Hopkins University Press, 1972); Daniel J. Kevles, *In the Name of Eugenics: Genetics and the Uses of Human Heredity* (Berkeley and Los Angeles: University of California Press, 1985), 174; and Huntington, *Tomorrow's Children.*

fully avoided defining what kinds of people should not have children. They more often mentioned desirable traits. For example, in 1935, Ellsworth Huntington, the president of the American Eugenics Society, outlined some desirable characteristics: "These include emotional stability, strong character, considerateness for other people, the tendency to uphold or improve moral standards, intelligence, adaptability, and originality. Even more important, perhaps, is the quality which makes people feel a personal responsibility for the public welfare." In the same publication, the society also discussed the need for a test to separate desirable from undesirable families and suggested the following: "It is the general reputation of a family among persons of all types who know it well. Honesty, sobriety, industry, freedom from quarrels, and especially the altruistic spirit which expresses itself in neighborliness, community service, and honest zeal for public welfare are among the important elements of this test."[12] If people failed to pull their own weight in society and became burdens to others, they were "undesirable."

Reports for the Arkansas Eugenics Association distributed throughout the 1930s included statements suggesting that the people directing the work of the clinic indeed listened to the ideas of the American Eugenics Society. In the early part of the 1930s these statements emphasized birth control and economic issues. They suggested that more poor people would result in an additional economic burden to the already strained economic situation. The annual report for 1931–1932, for example, included the following statement: "Many long time charity cases may not have been a charge on our community had mothers, in their early married lives, been given contraceptive aid. The welfare agencies are now providing care for the third generation of some of these families."[13] The association urged Little Rock community members to consider that money spent on supporting birth control would save taxpayers from paying for the support of future indigent people whose births could have been prevented. This information should be understood in its proper historical context.

Arkansas had been hit hard by both the Great Depression and the

12. Huntington, *Tomorrow's Children,* 35, 37.
13. Report of the Little Rock Birth Control Clinic of the Arkansas Eugenics Association, February 1, 1931–January 31, 1932, box 6, file 4, UAMS Collection.

drought of the early 1930s. The Hoover administration declared the
state a disaster area in 1930 but hesitated to give direct aid in the
form of food to hungry Arkansans. The Great Depression caused
economic difficulties in the nation as a whole. Workers in the
South, however, traditionally earned less than workers in other
parts of the country.[14] Closely related to issues of economics was
that of safe and effective birth control. The Great Depression gave
doctors and lay people a special interest in the practice of birth
control, as parents had grown fearful of their ability to support
additional children and appealed for assistance in limiting family
size.[15] The members of the Little Rock community therefore appreciated the work of the Little Rock birth control advocates.

Later reports showed more evidence of an agreement with the
American Eugenics Society on the view of social eugenics as a
method of reform. In the report for 1931–1933, Rabbi Sanders, then
a member of the Arkansas Eugenics Association's executive committee, stated: "Birth control offers the only sane and logical solution to a world over-populated and as a result economically mal-
adjusted. Fewer and better children would go far to stabilize the
economic security of the future, and thus place the ages to come in
a more happy and receptive mind to receive those blessings that
civilization will have in store for them."[16]

The Little Rock clinic highly recommended the booklet *The
Truth about Birth Control* by Norman Himes, a historian of birth
control technology. The reports for 1931–1934 and 1931–1935 included the following excerpt from this booklet: "Birth control, if
wisely directed, is one of the greatest forces of social, economic
and racial regeneration that man has succeeded in wresting from
nature. It is the sober judgement of those most competent to speak,
that birth control is an effective instrument for reducing (but not

14. Roger Lambert, "Hoover and the Red Cross in the Arkansas Drought of
1930," *Arkansas Historical Quarterly* 29 (Spring 1970): 3–9; Douglas L. Smith,
The New Deal in the Urban South (Baton Rouge: Louisiana State University
Press, 1988), 104.

15. The decade of the 1930s saw an overall decline of the birthrate, with
an all-time low in 1933. See Louis I. Doublin, "The Trend of the Birth Rate
Yesterday, Today, and Tomorrow," *Bulletin of the New York Academy of Medicine* 19 (August 1943): 564.

16. Reports of the Arkansas Eugenics Association for 1931–1933, box 6,
file 4, UAMS Collection.

eliminating) infant and maternal mortality, poverty, population pressure, abortion, marital discord caused by sexual maladjustment, mental disease and deficiency."[17]

In response to the statements published to promote the work of the clinic, members of the community let the Arkansas Eugenics Association know how they had understood its message. Because the association expressed concern with both the welfare of the individual married woman and the economic burden that larger poor families posed to taxpayers, it received a variety of responses from the community. In one letter, typed on official Young Men's Christian Association (YMCA) stationery, the general secretary of the local YMCA, J. B. Withee, clearly stated his motives for supporting the clinic:

> This is a wonderful work you are doing, and I sincerely wish I had plenty of means so that I could back this program in a big way. To me this is our only hope for ever breeding a stock of people that will be able to develop. In fact, the Anglo-Saxon Race will be exterminated in no time unless we educate along this line. People who should have children are not having them, and people who should not have children are having them. Enclosed find $2.00 which will help a little.[18]

On paper, the Arkansas Eugenics Association was affiliated with the American Eugenics Society, but the Arkansans seemed largely oblivious to the ideas promulgated by the parent organization and the criticism engendered by eugenics in the academic world of biological, sociological, and anthropological scholars.[19] They simply found the language of the eugenics movement useful. The methods used to direct the clinic and to communicate with the local community came mainly from the national birth control movement, especially the American Birth Control League and the Birth Control Clinical Research Bureau, and not from the American Eugenics Society. Little evidence exists that the Little Rock birth con-

17. Norman Himes, *Medical History of Contraception* (1936; reprint, New York: Gamut Press, 1963); reports of the Little Rock Clinic of the Arkansas Eugenics Association for 1931–1935, box 6, file 4, UAMS Collection.

18. J. B. Withee to Mrs. Ed Cornish, March 15, 1934, box 6, file 3, UAMS Collection.

19. For example, Franz Boas, "Eugenics," *Scientific Monthly,* November 1916, 473; Ludmerer, *Genetics and American Society,* 121, 126; and Kevles, *In the Name of Eugenics,* 129–47.

trollers corresponded regularly with the American Eugenics Society, but members of the Little Rock group frequently wrote Margaret Sanger and the Birth Control Clinical Research Bureau in New York.[20] In other words, while adopting the rhetoric of the national eugenics movement, the group closely followed the methods of the American Birth Control League led by Margaret Sanger.

To people in Little Rock, Margaret Sanger and the American Birth Control League represented radical feminism. By the late twenties and early thirties, however, Margaret Sanger no longer adhered to radical methods. While she spoke for women's rights early in the history of the movement, by the 1920s, Sanger had aligned with the more conservative members of society.[21] Even though she agreed with the basic premises of eugenics methods, she disagreed with the movement's tendency to restrict its ideas of sex to a purely procreative function.[22] The ideas promoted by the Little Rock birth control advocates seemed to follow the national lead, in that they both changed to become more reflective of eugenics ideas as time passed.

The importance of the opinion of the medical community to both the national and the local Arkansas birth control movements is quite clear. The Arkansas Eugenics Association made a special effort to inform the public that the medical scientific community approved of contraceptive information and devices. Physicians who aligned with the Arkansas movement did not regard safe and effec-

20. Among the few documents related to the eugenics social movement filed by the Arkansas Eugenics Association were the following: "Summary of State Laws on Birth Control and Sterilization," a reprint from *Birth Control Review* (November 1932); *U.S. Maps Showing the States Having Sterilization Laws in 1910–1920–1930–1940,* published by Birthright, Inc., Box 441, Princeton, N.J.; and *Eugenic Sterilizations Performed in State Institutions under State Laws up to January 1, 1953,* published by the Human Betterment Foundation in Pasadena, Calif., box 5, UAMS Collection.

21. For further discussion, see Gordon, *Woman's Body, Woman's Right,* 249–300; Joan M. Jensen, "The Evolution of Margaret Sanger's 'Family Limitation' Pamphlet, 1914–1921," *Signs* 6 (Spring 1981): 548–67.

22. James Reed suggests that Sanger hoped that "women in control of themselves would become a revolutionary force by choosing to rear children only under the best possible conditions, thereby eliminating not only poverty but mediocrity as well." *From Private Vice to Public Virtue: The Birth Control Movement and American Society since 1830* (New York: Basic Books, 1978), 68.

tive birth control for women as their main concern during the 1930s. To them, the issue of socialized medicine topped the agenda. Physicians in Arkansas, however, gave enough support to keep the Little Rock clinic open while other clinics across the nation closed because of lack of community support.[23]

Many physicians who did not actually volunteer at the clinic helped in other ways in disseminating contraceptive information to low-income families. Hilda Cornish surveyed doctors both in Arkansas and neighboring states in order to learn who would possibly treat patients referred by the Little Rock clinic. She then compiled a list of doctors who had responded favorably and organized it according to county. Individuals interested in contraceptive information but unable to visit the clinic in Little Rock received the list. This procedure gave more individuals an opportunity to obtain contraceptive advice and devices.[24]

Even though most physicians accepted the use of contraceptives, not all were supportive. Dr. L. E. Biles, secretary of the organized medical community in Woodruff County, Arkansas, declared his opposition to the use of contraceptives by upper-class women when responding to elicitation of support by the Arkansas Eugenics Association. He replied that "[I] don't think it's right [the use of contraceptives] and that it's practiced by those who should bear children to [sic] much. Hell will be crowded with such people."[25]

Even among those physicians who approved of contraceptives in general, some had reservations concerning who should use them. One such reservation, based on eugenics beliefs, came from Dr. W. C. Langston. He delivered a talk to the Arkansas Medical Society's meeting in March 1939 in which he conveyed the following:

> Recent reports indicate that the unemployed population of certain areas of the country are reproducing at a rate 60 per cent greater than that of the employed of the same social strata. I am not saying that an unemployed person is by nature unfit to be a parent but, by virtue of his being unemployed, is adding to the economic burden of society by increasing at too great a rate. And this is not because

23. Sheila Rothman, *Woman's Proper Place: A History of Changing Ideals and Practices, 1870 to the Present* (New York: Basic Books, 1978), 203–6.

24. Correspondence and summarized reports compiled by Hilda Cornish, box 6, file 8, UAMS Collection.

25. Dr. L. E. Biles in response to a survey conducted by the Arkansas Eugenics Association in 1934, box 6, file 8, UAMS Collection.

he wants it that way. If the ever-decreasing number of productive individuals earn less and less to care for the ever-increasing number of non-productives, we shall eventually have a dramatization of the well known irresistible force meeting the equally well known immovable body.

Not only are we allowing the less desirable elements of our American society to furnish population replacements but we are taking definite steps to kill the already decreasing minority of our intelligent, educated, and skilled citizens.[26]

The above individuals were not directly involved in the daily work at the clinic, but others were. What motivated those men and women who did give their skills and time to the clinic? Evidence shows that these individuals believed in the betterment of their community through activism and volunteer work. Their work at the clinic did not occupy all their talents or energy. Rather, it figured only as part of their busy lives as community volunteers for many causes.

In order to keep the clinic open to poor women, all workers at the clinic had to serve on a volunteer basis. During the clinic's first year of operation, nine women volunteered as "assistants."[27] The Arkansas Eugenics Association raised money only to cover the costs of supplies and public relations. For economic reasons and in order to evoke community support, physicians also donated their skills to the clinic. That Little Rock had enough committed physicians seems apparent in light of the fact that the clinic kept its doors open for such a long time.

The physicians were the only medically trained individuals at the clinic. They examined the women and fitted them with contraceptive devices. There is no evidence to suggest that any nurses or midwives volunteered at the clinic. The power struggle of the previous decade between physicians and public health personnel, represented by both administrators and medically trained persons such as nurses and midwives, partly explains this absence of involvement. The Little Rock community had previously reached out to help women in economic distress. The Sheppard-Towner Act of

26. Dr. William C. Langston, "Medical Research in the Contraceptive Phase of Preventive Medicine" (speech delivered to the Arkansas Medical Society, March 27, 1939), UAMS Collection.

27. First Annual Report . . . for the Period February 1, 1931–January 31, 1932, box 6, file 4, UAMS Collection.

1921 established a maternity and infant health care program that nurses and midwives strongly supported. Physicians felt threatened and worried about socialized medicine. As a result, the power struggle between physicians and nurses for control over health care split the medical community.[28] As Margaret Sanger did on the national level, Hilda Cornish chose to align herself with the physicians rather than with the poor women's traditional caregivers, midwives and public health nurses. Thus the curious absence of nurses and midwives in the establishment and work of the Little Rock Birth Control Clinic. This might be one explanation why African American women were not invited to the clinic from its start in 1931. The health care systems for white and African American women were separate and different. Mrs. Cornish and the Little Rock birth control advocates did not align with the members of the African American health care community and saw little reason for doing so at the time.

Hilda Cornish Coates, the oldest daughter of Mrs. Cornish, volunteered at the clinic from its start in 1931. She accompanied each woman into the "fitting" room at the time of a physical examination and fitting of a diaphragm. In an interview in 1989, Mrs. Coates remembered that "having a woman there in the doctor's office, that was medical ethics. You had to have the nurse there with the doctor. We would hand things to him. We never did fit a diaphragm." She saw herself as being the assistant to the physician and made a point to stress the medical legitimacy of the clinic by referring to herself as the "nurse." There was at the time some confusion concerning the legality of what they were doing, and Mrs. Coates remembered that her group was "tiptoeing around" in order not to attract the attention of the law enforcers.[29]

Hilda Cornish Coates did not participate in the local birth con-

---

28. Elissa Miller, "From Private Duty to Public Health: A History of Arkansas Nursing, 1895–1954" (Ph.D. diss., Memphis State University, 1989), 112–28. See discussions published in *Journal of the Arkansas Medical Society* during the years 1930 to 1940, for example, Leonce J. Kosminsky, "Annual Address," 31 (June 1934): 1.

29. Coates, interview, 8, 3–4. According to "Summary of State Laws on Birth Control and Sterilization," Arkansas had no statutes restricting physicians from disseminating contraceptive information to their patients. Because many states did have restrictive laws, physicians were confused as to what the law actually allowed.

trol movement in order to aid in the liberation of women from their traditional roles as mothers. She had no plans for her own life to diverge from the callings of wife and motherhood. She saw her role at the clinic to be instrumental in assisting women who, for medical or economic reasons, sought to limit the size of their families.

Another volunteer with key responsibilities at the clinic was Raida Pfeifer. She acted as the clinic's receptionist from 1931 and as a member of the Board of Governors of the Arkansas Eugenics Association from 1933. As an economics major at Vassar College in the late 1920s, young Raida found a special interest in the issues of population control. Returning to Little Rock in the early thirties, she learned about the clinic through Rabbi Sanders. Its work coincided with her view that "an increased population would be a runaway problem for the whole world in time unless pregnancies were controlled."[30]

In general, the contemporary Little Rock community did not label these women as radicals. Some people objected to their work and felt that the birth control movement turned women away from their primary duty—motherhood—and instead encouraged women to "entertain at parties, wear fine clothes and drive fine cars."[31] But the women running the clinic did not advocate new roles for women. This is evident in the restriction of services to married women only; unmarried women were publicly discouraged from using contraceptives. Contraceptives should only be used within marriage and then only when women faced economic difficulties or had medical problems. People often asked Hilda Cornish why she advocated birth control when she herself had six children. She replied that she had enough money to take care of them. "We love a big family. When you cannot take care of a big family, I try to help you."[32]

The Little Rock community faced severe economic hardships in the early 1930s, and it is not difficult to understand why the work of

30. Report of the Little Rock Birth Control Clinic of the Arkansas Eugenics Association, February 1, 1931, to January 31, 1934, box 6, file 4, UAMS Collection; Raida Pfeifer, interview by Marianne Leung, Little Rock, Ark., March 16, 1990, p. 2., interview in the possession of the author.

31. Anonymous letter addressed to the Arkansas Eugenics Association and attached to a picture of Margaret Sanger, Hilda Cornish, and Mrs. Fitzhugh. The letter was originally received March 31, 1937, box 6, file 3, UAMS Collection.

32. Coates, interview, 20.

the clinic gained community support. The first report of the Arkansas Eugenics Association stated that the Little Rock clinic registered 161 white women during its first eleven months of service. Of these women, 115 had sought advice because of economic reasons whereas others approached the clinic because of medical reasons or a combination of the two.[33] By 1940, the clinic had served 1,500 white and 150 African American women.[34] While the information promoting the clinic in the early years invited any married woman whose family income did not exceed seventy-five dollars per month, until 1937 only white women actually had the opportunity to receive services.[35]

Before 1931, only physicians in private practice prescribed contraceptives for Arkansas women. That is, women could gain access to safe and effective contraceptives, but all women did not have the same options. The physician wanted fees both for his services and for the birth control devices. In effect, until the Little Rock Birth Control Clinic opened in 1931, only women who could spare the money had access to safe and effective birth control. Then after the clinic opened, only white women had access to affordable contraceptive advice. African American women, despite their substantial numbers, had to wait until October 1937, when the clinic finally opened its doors to them.[36] Then, in accordance with social customs at the time, the clinic held separate hours for white and African American women.

There is no evidence suggesting that African American women visited the clinic before 1937. The Arkansas Eugenics Association did not have a truly eugenics-oriented agenda because, in the South especially, the danger during the 1930s was that eugenics would be directed against African American people. While some

33. Twenty-one women sought advice because of economic and health reasons, and only five gave health as their primary reason for contacting the clinic. Report . . . for the Period February 1, 1931–January 31, 1932, box 6, file 4, UAMS Collection.

34. Ten-Year Report of the Arkansas Eugenics Association, p. 2, box 6, file 4, UAMS Collection.

35. If earning more than seventy-five dollars per month, the family was referred to a private physician. The clinic created a sliding scale of fees ranging from fifty cents to five dollars.

36. *Your Community and Birth Control,* pamphlet distributed by the Arkansas Eugenics Association in 1937, box 6, file 4, UAMS Collection.

historians argue that eugenicists in the South targeted African Americans, others suggest southerners feared a decline in the African American population and therefore discouraged any attempts to reduce it. This was especially true in the rural communities that depended on an agricultural economy.[37] If the Little Rock group had adhered closely to the arguments of the American Eugenics Society, which was not subscribing to the fear of a declining African American population but to a race suicide theory, the African American women would have been targeted at an earlier time. There is no evidence to suggest that the Little Rock birth controllers sought out African American midwives or nurses in order to convey birth control information to the African American community. The fate of the African American women was not a central concern to the leaders of the Arkansas Eugenics Association during the early 1930s.

In other parts of the nation at the same time, African American women received contraceptive advice at clinics associated with the American Birth Control League.[38] Most of these clinics were segregated. In the South, the Baltimore Birth Control Clinic had seen African American women since 1928. It reported in 1929 that of 168 patients advised, 29, or 17.3 percent, were "colored."[39] Obviously it is difficult to draw parallels between Arkansas and Baltimore, because the southern rural values and race relations in Arkansas differed from the metropolitan race relations found in Baltimore.

37. See, for further discussion, Gunnar Myrdal, *An American Dilemma: The Negro Problem and Modern Democracy* (New York: Harper and Row, 1944), 179–81; Gordon, *Woman's Body, Woman's Right,* 330; and Simone Marie Caron, "Race, Class, and Reproduction: The Evolution of Reproductive Policy in the United States, 1800–1989" (Ph.D. diss., Clark University, 1989), chap. 4, p. 24; Pete Daniel, *The Shadow of Slavery: Peonage in the South, 1901–1969* (Urbana: University of Illinois Press, 1972).

38. For example, the Detroit Birth Control Clinic, six clinics in Illinois directed by the Illinois Birth Control League, the Cincinnati Clinic on Maternal Health, and the Mothers' Health Clinic of Alameda County, California. Reports were published in the *Birth Control Review* between 1929 and 1933 indicating that African American women represented a significant number of the clients at these clinics.

39. Jessie M. Rodrique, "The Black Community and the Birth Control Movement," in *Women and Power in American History: A Reader,* vol. 2, ed. Kathryn Kish Sklar and Thomas Dublin (Englewood Cliffs, N.J.: Prentice Hall, 1991), 160–74; "The Baltimore Clinic," *Birth Control Review* (May 1929): 137.

The point is that birth control clinics affiliated with the organized national birth control movement had a history of reaching out to African American women long before the Arkansas advocates actually did.

The pertinent question for Arkansas is why the Little Rock clinic opened its doors to African American women in 1937. Simone Caron, in her examination of reproduction policy in the United States between 1800 and 1989, argued that with the case of *United States v. One Package* in December 1936 the public debate heightened and many more birth control clinics opened. The confusing state concerning the legality of disseminating contraceptives by physicians ended, and public health facilities took on the responsibility of directing birth control clinics. This heightened public debate and acceptance of birth control might have been what prompted a donation by a community member in Little Rock in 1936. An unknown person, interested in "furthering the movement" by inviting African American women to receive affordable contraceptive advice, made the donation. As a result, the Arkansas Eugenics Association had by September of 1937 inaugurated a clinic for African American women.[40]

What Jessie M. Rodrique found to be true at the Baltimore Birth Control Clinic rings true for Arkansas: no matter what physicians, community leaders, or politicians thought to be an appropriate context for introducing a birth control clinic into the community, women had their own agendas. Letters to the Arkansas Eugenics Association from men and women in Arkansas suggest that they desperately needed safe and effective contraceptives and would accept help from whomever offered it. A woman in Mt. Olive, Arkansas, wrote the following letter in 1941. It speaks for the situation of many women in the South during most of the 1930s.

> We are terribly poor. We have four children, oldest 8 ½ years, baby 13 mths. I live in terror that I will become pregnant again. I honestly do believe I will die if I give birth again. We do not have

40. Caron, "Race, Class, and Reproduction," chap. 4, pp. 22–23. [Sylvia Cornish?], memo-report, [ca. 1937], box 6, file 4, UAMS Collection. Also, the report of the Little Rock Birth Control Clinic of the Arkansas Eugenics Association for 1931–1934 reported that "if sufficient funds are available the Association will establish a charity clinic for the negro women and also arrange for services in the rural section, where the needs are the greatest," box 6, file 4, UAMS Collection.

enough to eat, never have milk. Life is just a dull, drab ache of fear. My husband is now a W.P.A. worker and has had no work for a year and half. He has only drawn one W.P.A. check. Will you please tell me where, if possible I can buy whatever contraceptives that are safe and how much they cost. My doctor says he does not know.[41]

The total number of white and African American women registered at the clinic between 1931 and 1940—1,650—certainly attests to the demand for safe, effective, and affordable contraceptives in Arkansas.

Studies of other local efforts to disseminate birth control information could provide a fresh perspective on birth control nationwide. The February 1932 issue of *Birth Control Review* (pp. 59–61) reported on 104 "centers for contraceptive advice" as of January 1932. Most birth control clinics listed in the *Birth Control Review*, published by the American Birth Control League, had names connected with a local birth control league, a hospital, or a "mothers' health clinic" or "mothers' health association." Only one other clinic besides the Arkansas Eugenics Association identified itself by name with eugenics: the Canon Kip Eugenics Clinic in San Francisco.

Local birth control movements sometimes closely followed the lead of Margaret Sanger and the American Birth Control League, and at other times they had their own agendas. Some local clinics survived only for a short time. Other clinics, such as the one in Little Rock, gained community support and became a permanent component of community life. It will be difficult to speak of a "national" birth control movement until a large number of local birth control movements have been examined. What explains their successes and failures will be a crucial part of the story of a national birth control movement. In re-creating this complex story, students of women's history should be careful drawing conclusions about the benefits of the birth control movement to women based on information created either for fund-raising efforts or in an attempt to solicit community support. Successful community activists shrewdly promoted ideas and programs publicly that were acceptable to their specific communities at the time. However, women in these communities took advantage of the situation without much consideration for motives of the birth control promoters.

41. Jessie M. Rodrique, "The Black Community and the Birth Control Movement," 160–74; letter to Dear Sirs or Madam from a woman in Mount Olive, April 1941, box 6, file 3, UAMS Collection.

GENDER ROLES AND GOVERNMENT

They Called It "Motherhood"

Dallas Women and Public Life, 1895–1918

ELIZABETH YORK ENSTAM

In 1895 a small group of mothers in Dallas asked the Board of Education to spread gravel on the playground of the McKinney Avenue Public School. When the board denied their request, the women called their friends together and met, now numbering an even dozen, in their leader's living room. The easiest thing to do, they decided, was to chip in five dollars apiece and themselves buy the gravel. Upon hearing of their project, however, a neighbor donated the gravel from a creek bed on his property, so the mothers used their money to pave the school's walkways and plant shrubs on the grounds. They then purchased reproductions of famous paintings and hung them in the classrooms and halls. The name they gave their organization, the Public School Art League, indicated their intentions for the future. And indeed, during the next eight years, these women sponsored lectures in Dallas by well-known artists and arranged exhibitions of the Traveling Gallery belonging to the Texas Federation of Women's Clubs. In 1903 they joined the art committee of the public library to form the Dallas Art Association, which founded the art museum that exists in the city today.[1]

In addition to their work with art, the league's members soon found reasons to resume functioning as the McKinney Avenue

1. Photocopy, unidentified booklet, a history of the Dallas City Council of PTAs [1970s] (hereinafter cited as PTA History), 1–2, Dallas City Council of PTAs Archives; *Dallas Morning News,* November 9, 1901, January 12, 1902; Geraldine Propper Cristol, "The History of the Dallas Museum of Art" (master's thesis, Southern Methodist University, 1970), 10–12.

Mothers' Club, and in the latter capacity they approached the Board of Education again. When the women reported that the school needed a new furnace, the men complied at once. But in 1898, when the mothers asked that indoor toilets be installed, the school trustees denied their petition. The mothers tried to appeal to the mayor, who refused even to see them. With an apparently instinctive understanding of pressure-group politics, the women then appointed a committee to visit the mayor's office every day until he agreed to discuss their concerns. Within the year, the McKinney Avenue Public School had modern plumbing, and the same tactics extended a city sewer line to the school.[2]

These mundane requests for a neighborhood school were among white Dallas women's earliest—and may well have been their first—direct encounters with government. Relatively wealthy and socially prominent, married to successful professionals and businessmen, the twelve McKinney Avenue mothers were educated and privileged housewives. They were questioning male judgment about the public schools at a time when numerous Dallas women had begun to explore new possibilities. In 1893 and 1894 the earliest conventions of the Council of Women of Texas met during the state fair in Dallas for presentations on a wide variety of topics that interested women. The Dallas Equal Rights Club was organized less than a year before the request for the playground gravel, and three years later, in 1898, five organizations formed the Dallas Federation of Women's Clubs and affiliated with the state federation.[3]

Intent on improving the place where their children spent much of each day, the McKinney Avenue mothers most likely had no inkling of the political implications of their actions. Yet their experiences forecast the way Dallas women would become involved in politics—inadvertently, and for the sake of the children. Between 1895 and 1918, about twenty articulate, capable officers of four women's organizations plunged into public life and politics. In the process, these leaders of the Council of Mothers, the Dallas Federa-

2. PTA History, 2. "Dallas Mothers Council Comes of Age" [memories of Olivia Allen Dealey], *Dallas Morning News,* June 22, 1930.
3. The Dallas Equal Rights Club (1893–1897) was not the same organization as the Dallas Equal Suffrage Association (1913–1920), although in numerous cases, the membership of the second included women who had joined the first.

tion of Women's Clubs, the Woman's Forum, and the Equal Suffrage Association developed a political agenda and style as directly related to gender expectations as their purposes and goals were.[4] Motherhood, with its actual responsibilities and its sentimental connotations, provided an almost unassailable rationale for entering affairs customarily managed by men.

As Dallas women extended their projects and activities ever further into the functions and concerns of government, they insisted, at least until 1909, that what they did was not political. But *political,* as we now understand the term, can refer not only to officeholding and law and elections but also to making the decisions, setting the policies, defining the regulations by which people live and conduct their activities. At its most primeval, *political* refers to power—who decides how people will live and behave and order their affairs. Politics, then, goes much beyond government and, some would say, reaches into personal relationships and all human institutions and organizations.[5]

Because the McKinney Avenue children attended a tax-supported institution, mothering collided with government. The women's attempts to improve a single school led to confrontations with elected officials. Simply by demanding that the school board spend some public money, the McKinney Avenue mothers sought to influence, very modestly to be sure, matters of public policy. They did so again later and on a larger scale when they joined two other mothers' clubs and persuaded the Board of Education to retain the district's

4. On club projects that required dealing with the male power structure: Elizabeth York Enstam, "The Forgotten Frontier: Dallas Women and Social Caring, 1895–1920," *Legacies* 1 (Spring 1989): 20–28; Jackie McElhaney, "'The Only Clean, Bright Spot They Know,'" *Heritage News* 11 (Fall 1986): 19–22; Michael V. Hazel, "The Dallas Public Library: Opening the Doors to the World of Books," *Heritage News*, 15–19; Hazel "Dallas Women's Clubs: Vehicles for Change," *Heritage News* 11 (Spring 1986): 18–21.

5. For a discussion of politics as more than elections and of women's political culture, see Paula Baker, "The Domestication of Politics: Women and American Political Society, 1780–1920," *American Historical Review* 89 (June 1984): 621–22, 624–25; Maureen A. Flanagan, "Gender and Urban Political Reform: The City Club and the Woman's City Club of Chicago in the Progressive Era," *American Historical Review* 95 (October 1990): 1033–34, 1046, 1048, 1050; and Nancy F. Cott, "What's in a Name? The Limits of 'Social Feminism'; or, Expanding the Vocabulary of Women's History," *Journal of American History* 76 (December 1989): 820–23.

only music teacher, to hire a school sanitary inspector, and to upgrade the regulations for heating and ventilating school buildings. In 1906, having learned the value of alliance, six mothers' clubs formed an association, the Council of Mothers, which affiliated with the Texas Congress of Mothers when it organized in Dallas three years later.[6] Their experience with male authority was to recur numerous times for other leaders and officers of Dallas women's clubs and associations.

Despite repeated claims that they intended nothing political, in time the clubwomen accepted the full implications of their actions. By 1917 several hundred of them, including most of the major club leaders, belonged to the Dallas Equal Suffrage Association. Between 1895 and 1917 the women had learned that to a large extent health and safety in the home depended on factors that were public by definition, including services, laws, ordinances, organizations, and agencies whose effects were community wide. As a result, in the name of their socially sanctioned "sphere," the privacy of the home, white Dallas women claimed a number of public matters as rightfully theirs and developed their own strategies to work for change. The resulting campaigns and projects created new functions in public life for women even as the women continued to accept traditional definitions of their "place."

Dallas women's interest in public affairs may well have been encouraged by an event that attracted nationwide publicity. In 1893 at the World's Columbian Exposition in Chicago, Texas clubwomen attended sessions of the World's Congress of Representative Women. They heard speakers and panels discuss the relation of women to issues ranging through such fields as religious philanthropy, social injustice, law, and politics. A few months later, during the state fair in October, Dallas women who were officers of the Texas Woman's Press Association hosted the first meeting of the Texas Woman's Congress. The organizers intended, one told a *Dallas Morning News* reporter, to "wake up the women of Texas to an understanding of . . . what they can do."[7]

The delegates from fourteen cities and towns represented reli-

6. PTA History, 3.
7. *Dallas Morning News,* October 27, 1893; Judith N. McArthur, "Motherhood and Reform in the New South: Texas Women during the Progressive Era" (Ph.D. diss., University of Texas at Austin, 1992), 2–5.

gious and secular groups, missionary as well as literary societies, temperance as well as study organizations. The daily sessions in 1893 reflected this wide range of concerns. An audience of perhaps a dozen on the first day and over three hundred by the third heard papers with titles such as "Woman in the Church," "Temperance Instruction in the Public Schools," "The Evolution of American Literature," and "Women as Educators." Scheduled with these presentations were others that forecast change in women's lives and interests. The president of the Dallas Equal Rights Club gave an address entitled "Equality, Not Supremacy," and the president of the Texas Equal Rights Association, "The Coming Woman in Politics." "The Vocations Open to Women," "Professional Women from a Physician's Standpoint," "Women's Opportunities in Journalism and Literature," "Women in the Labor Organizations," and even "Bee Culture and Poultry Raising . . . Industr[ies] for Women"— these speeches focused their listeners' attention beyond domestic interests.[8]

Similar papers did so again at the annual meetings of the next two years, also during the fair in Dallas. Spokeswomen in 1894 hoped the congress would "bring together women for all lines of work" and "make better known to the general public the magnitude and variety of woman's work for humanity." Announcing that they would not work for woman suffrage "or any other specific reform," they urged, among other things, equal educational and professional opportunities for women and girls. With one comment in favor of "an equal standard of purity for men and women," they tacitly denounced prostitution and expressed hostility toward male privilege.[9] And they wanted women's traditional work in the home to receive the recognition due its real importance to American society.

Appearances mattered, too, and at this second meeting the congress renamed itself the Council of Women of Texas. The word *congress,* the members feared, carried political connotations.[10] Re-

8. *Dallas Morning News,* October 22, 23, 25, 26, 28, 1893.
9. For statements of the organization's purposes: *Dallas Morning News,* October 6, 1895.
10. Stella L. Christian, ed. and comp., *The History of the Texas Federation of Women's Clubs* (Houston: Texas Federation of Women's Clubs, 1919), 6, hereinafter cited as *TFWC History.* Christian is correct that the Texas Woman's Congress changed its name in 1894, but errs in saying it first met that year.

flecting Texas clubwomen's lack of experience with public life, this attitude contributed to the early demise of the state's first suffrage organization, which lasted only from 1893 to 1896. Strong and very able leaders adopted a nonpartisan stance, but the suffragists could not deny the overtly political nature of their cause. Neither could they overcome the belief of many club leaders and employed women alike that in addition to being inappropriate for women and dangerous to the home the vote had little to do with their lives.[11]

Within this domestically oriented, traditional climate of opinion, the organization of the Council of Women of Texas suggested that Texas women had, at least in urbanized areas, created a "women's culture." With its grounding in widely accepted theories that women were innately gentle, nurturant, spiritual, life giving, the women's culture first produced intensely close friendships and a special empathy among women, then belief in their special mission to society, and finally the courage to enter the male realm of public life.[12] In addition to their work in charity and benevolence, during the late 1880s and early 1890s clubwomen in Dallas founded several organizations and institutions devoted to concerns that women believed they understood specifically because they were women. The Woman's Home and Day Nursery (1886), the Woman's Exchange (1887), and Girls' Co-Operative Home (1891), the Methodist rescue home Sheltering Arms (1893)—all these met needs experienced only by women.

At the base of the women's culture lay factors attributable, for the most part, to urbanization. In Dallas the women's literary and music study clubs, all organized during the 1880s, included as members the daughters of the city's original families. By contrast, the club founders, officers, and leaders came, almost to a woman,

11. On the first suffrage association in Texas, see A. Elizabeth Taylor, "The Woman Suffrage Movement in Texas," in *Citizens at Last: The Woman Suffrage Movement in Texas,* ed. Ruthe Winegarten and Judith N. McArthur (Austin: Ellen C. Temple, 1987), 13–25, first published in *Journal of Southern History* 27 (May 1951): 194–215. For antisuffrage comments by a clubwoman and a female clerical worker, see *Dallas Morning News,* April 22, 1894, and April 29, 1895, respectively.

12. For discussion of the concept of a "women's culture," see Linda K. Kerber, "Separate Spheres, Female Worlds, Woman's Place: The Rhetoric of Women's History," *Journal of American History* 75 (June 1988): 14–18.

from the newcomers who nearly quadrupled the population from 10,358 in 1880 to 38,067 by 1890. Most clubwomen in this second wave of pioneers were upper- or middle-class native southerners who had been reared on plantations or in small market towns. In Dallas these women established nuclear households, which they ran with the help of servants, whether a full staff or only a laundress and a cook who doubled as a maid. The urban environment separated their daily lives and work from those of their husbands, while distance from their ancestral homes freed them, if not from the tentacles of propriety, at least from the most crippling social pressures of extended family, evangelical church, and traditional community.[13] Diversified by a number of midwesterners and by southerners educated in northeastern colleges, the Dallas club leaders had by the early 1890s created their own culture alongside the city's burgeoning commercial development and rampant boosterism.

With the institutions they founded for women, Dallas women were creating public spaces for their particular uses and, at the same time, moving into areas usually assumed to "belong" to males. Their literary and music clubs met in private homes, and the missionary societies met either in private homes or in the churches. But the Dallas Equal Rights Club rented an office in the business district on Main Street. To be sure, downtown department stores, certain theaters, and a few restaurants welcomed women as customers and patrons. But upper- and middle-class Dallas women had begun to define their own needs and work to meet those of less-privileged white women.[14]

13. Elizabeth Hayes Turner, "Women Progressives and the Origins of Local Suffrage Societies in Texas" (paper presented to the Houston Area Southern Historians, October 1991). In *The Enclosed Garden: Women and Community in the Evangelical South, 1830–1900* (Chapel Hill: University of North Carolina Press, 1985), Jean E. Friedman attributes the slowness of southern women to create a separate women's culture to the persistent strength of the patriarchal family, the evangelical church, and the local ties of community. Suellen M. Hoy identified the "municipal housekeepers" as housewives, not professional or employed women, in "'Municipal Housekeeping': The Role of Women in Improving Urban Sanitation Practices, 1880–1917" in Martin V. Melosi, ed., *Pollution and Reform in American Cities, 1870–1920* (Austin: University of Texas Press, 1980).

14. Kerber, "Separate Spheres," 36; Sarah Deutsch, "Learning to Talk More Like a Man: Boston Women's Class-Bridging Organizations, 1870–1940," *American Historical Review* 97 (April 1992): 389–90.

Other urban Texas women shared these experiences, and by 1897 they, too, were ready to do more than present papers and lead discussions about social problems. In 1896, attendance declined significantly at the annual Council of Women of Texas sessions, and a year later interest seemed so low that officers postponed the meeting "until a more propitious time," which never came. Attention was shifting toward the Texas Federation of Women's Clubs, founded in Waco earlier that year, 1897. Soon afterward, the state federation affiliated with the General Federation of Women's Clubs and accepted the national organization's goals to widen women's influence in American life by recommending reforms to legislative bodies.[15]

Nonetheless, Texas Federation officers stated that they had no desire "to meddle" in politics. With Dallas women prominent among the charter members, the federation's leaders decided to pursue their concerns only through private influence and indirect means. Because they allied with no party and, by implication, avoided deals and bargains, they saw their methods and purposes as non-partisan and therefore nonpolitical, unselfish, and altruistic, inspired only by their concern for children and for other women unable to speak in their own behalf.

Instead of appointing a legislative committee, the Texas Federation president sent out periodic circular letters to identify her administration's policies and goals. Local clubs could fund and operate free kindergartens and traveling libraries, plant trees and shrubbery around public buildings, and resolve not to buy hats decorated with the plumage of Texas birds. But founding the women's College of Industrial Arts in Denton (now Texas Woman's University); repealing the annual tax on library associations; building a women's dormitory at the University of Texas; passing child labor and compulsory education laws; and amending the poll tax to add money to the state's public school budget—these and similar measures required contact with the legislature. For several years federation presidents urged members to take advantage of parties, dinners, and other social occasions to pressure, with great tact and discretion, their husbands, brothers, and male friends among the state's

15. *Dallas Morning News*, October 10, 1897. For a contemporary account of the early women's organizations in Texas, see *Dallas Morning News*, November 22, 1903, and *TFWC History*, 9–15, 44.

political and business leaders. These tactics brought success with the least controversial matters but left issues like child labor and compulsory education unresolved.[16]

Within about four years the clubwomen sought to pursue their purposes in more direct, if no less modest ways, and their methods may be seen at work in Dallas. In 1898 delegates from five literary and culture clubs, among them the women who had helped to organize the state federation, founded the Dallas Federation of Women's Clubs. Including the city's most prominent society leaders within their ranks, the officers sought as the years passed to reach beyond their particular circles. By 1910 the federation's roster included the Council of Jewish Women, and by 1917, the Graduate Nurses' Association and the Women's Auxiliary of the Typographical Union, whose members were the wives of printers, typesetters, and machinists. With about one thousand members in thirty-two clubs by 1917, the Dallas Federation grew to include roughly twice as many women in fifty-three clubs by 1920. On the occasion of its original organization in 1898, the federation set as its first goal the building of a public library.[17] With the library's opening three years later, its foremost concern became the welfare of children.

In 1903 a column on the "woman's page" of the *Dallas Morning News* galvanized city federation leaders into a major statewide reform effort. Two children, a girl and a boy, were arrested in an unnamed Texas town for stealing a few spools of silk thread. For this theft of goods worth about thirty dollars, they were arrested, jailed with adults, and subjected to the regular courts for trial, which, in the opinion of reformers, was outrageous treatment for youngsters not yet ten years old.[18]

16. *TFWC History,* 44–47, 50, 55, 56, 68, 86–88, 90–91. In 1903 the Texas legislature passed a child labor law, but the law was not enforced until after 1909, when the state Bureau of Labor Statistics opened. Ruth A. Allen, *East Texas Lumber Workers: An Economic and Social Picture, 1870–1950* (Austin: University of Texas Press, 1961), 44, 51–65. A compulsory education law passed in 1915.

17. Dallas Federation of Women's Clubs Minutes and Roster, January–August 1917 and February–December 1920, Texas/Dallas Collection, Dallas Public Library; National League for Women's Services, Minutes, May 24, [1917], File A43115/Msb-10, Dallas Historical Society; *History of the Dallas Federation of Women's Clubs* (Dallas: Dallas Federation of Women's Clubs, 1936), 16, hereinafter cited as *History DFWC.*

18. *Dallas Morning News,* February 2, 1903. And see Jackie McElhaney,

The president of the Texas Federation of Women's Clubs, a Dallas resident, made creation of a separate court system for children a central issue for her administration, but unlike her predecessors in the office, she accepted the necessity of dealing with politics and government. Taking care, nonetheless, to observe social expectations, she joined leaders of the Dallas women's clubs in tactics that were direct, though still essentially private in appearance. Visits to state representatives and senators to lobby for the juvenile court were attempts to exert direct influence on lawmakers, yet they were actually not very different from pressuring a (legislator) friend at a dinner party. Inviting officeholders to a meeting to hear an authority on the subject was similar to a private social event, especially when a reception for the speaker followed his address.

A project so clearly related to government as creation of a new arm of the state justice system could hardly avoid genuine political participation, however behind the scenes it remained. The campaign for the juvenile court bill was characterized by close cooperation among its women and men advocates. Impressed by the women's knowledge of the problem and agreeing with their solution, the Texas Association of County Judges and Commissioners asked them to work with a legal committee to draft a bill to present to the legislature. The women also wrote letters to politicians in Austin and to the delegates attending the state Democratic convention in 1906. Prejudice lingered against women speaking before mixed or male audiences, but the clubwomen made short "personal talks" before businessmen's clubs and small groups of legislators.[19]

In 1907 the Texas legislature passed two laws, one for dependent and neglected children and the other for delinquents. Requir-

---

"Pauline Periwinkle: Crusading Columnist," *Heritage News* 10 (Summer 1985): 15–18.

19. *Dallas Morning News,* October 30, 1938; *History DFWC,* 33; Dallas Woman's Forum, *Yearbook, 1907–1908,* 31, Dallas Woman's Forum Archives, Dallas Woman's Forum Clubhouse, hereinafter cited as DWF; Martha Livinia Hunter, *A Quarter of a Century History of the Dallas Woman's Forum* (Dallas: Dallas Woman's Forum, 1932), 13; *TFWC History,* 134, 143, 187–88, 208–10, 219–20. For a contemporary critique of women's "passive" methods, as well as analysis of the clubwomen's work in Texas and other states, see Martha E. D. White, "The Work of the Woman's Club," *Atlantic Monthly* 90 (May 1904): 619, 621.

ing separate legal procedures for minors, the statutes granted to the county and district courts the jurisdiction to sit as the juvenile court when hearing cases involving children.[20] Responsibility for implementation lay with each county, so Dallas women conducted additional campaigns during the next six years for county funding to pay the salary of a probation officer and to open a detention center. They also worked with the Texas Federation to acquire funds for the state industrial homes and training schools for youngsters convicted in the juvenile courts.[21]

As might be expected, the campaign for the juvenile justice system attracted severe criticism, especially from men who objected as a matter of course to women's organizations. In a letter to the *Morning News* in January 1906, the Dallas Federation's new president defended the clubwomen and justified their civic involvement as work that indeed encompassed motherhood. Women had gone "out beyond the home circle," she reminded readers, specifically "for love of home and children." Men simply did not have time to do all "the work of the world, . . . yet it is vitally important that it should be done."[22] Women's duties, in other words, lay within the domestic realm, but the valid interests and concerns of the home extended beyond the four walls of any individual house.

Despite continuing criticism, as the years passed, the clubwomen found male allies in addition to the county judges, attorneys, and legislators. Among the men of their own class were many who, as members of the Texas Democratic Party's progressive wing, sympathized with the women's causes.[23] In 1906 a group of such men, professionals and businessmen who were members of Dallas's commercial elite, translated their economic dominance

---

20. *General Laws of the State of Texas Passed at the Regular Session of the Thirtieth Legislature . . . January 8, 1907 . . . [to] April 12, 1907* (Austin: n.p., 1907), 135–41. Janet Schmelzer, "Thomas M. Campbell: Progressive Governor of Texas," *Red River Valley Historical Review* 3 (Fall 1978): 52–63.

21. "The State Industrial Training School for Juveniles, Report of the Committee Chairman," in *Club Woman Argosy* 6 (December 1909): 13, single issue in Mrs. Percy V. Pennybacker Papers, Eugene C. Barker History Center, University of Texas at Austin; *TFWC History,* 208–10, 219–20, 243, 311; *History DFWC,* 11, 52–53.

22. *Dallas Morning News,* January 15, 1906; *History DFWC,* 30–35.

23. Deutsch, "Learning to Talk More Like a Man," 391.

into direct political influence. With an economy based on supplying farm equipment and consumer goods, Dallas was the regional distribution center for northern and western Texas, Arkansas, and Oklahoma. To a large extent, the wholesale and retail firms owned by these men *were* the city's economy. Advocating the Dallas city commission plan pioneered in Galveston, nearly one hundred leading merchants and bankers urged reorganization of Dallas government.[24]

"Imagine," they said to voters, "a city without graft and almost without politics." Within an electorate already heavily employed in white-collar jobs and with African Americans virtually disfranchised, the businessmen won acceptance of the new city commission charter by a margin of almost two to one. In April 1906 their slate of candidates was elected to municipal offices. Later named the Citizens' Association, this organization would lead Dallas government for the next decade and remain a significant factor in local politics throughout the 1920s.[25]

Before World War I, the Citizens' Association leaders were usually willing at least to listen to the women's goals. In a letter written to the Texas Federation president in April 1911, one Dallas Federation officer bragged that Dallas clubwomen had "the hearty co-operation, advice and financial aid of our City and County officials, and our progressive business men."[26] On a number of occasions, success for the women's programs meant working to influence these influential men, who, once convinced, would take the issue to the voters.

24. Bradley Robert Rice, *Progressive Cities: The Commission Government Movement in America, 1901–1920* (Austin: University of Texas Press, 1977), 25–28, 30, 32, 63–66, 72–76, 92, 95–96; Lewis L. Gould, *Progressives and Prohibitionists: Texas Democrats in the Wilson Era* (Austin: University of Texas Press, 1973), 25–26, 36–40, 285–86.

25. Quotation: Sam Acheson, *Dallas Yesterday,* ed. Lee Milazzo (Dallas: Southern Methodist University Press, 1977), 165; U.S. Bureau of the Census, Special Reports, *Occupations at the Twelfth Census* (Washington, D.C.: Government Printing Office, 1904), 437, 439; U.S. Bureau of the Census, *Thirteenth Census of the United States . . . 1910,* vol. 4, *Population 1910: Occupation Statistics* (Washington, D.C.: Government Printing Office, 1914), 221, 223, 225. On the Citizens' Association: Acheson, *Dallas Yesterday,* 165–68, 170–77, 188–90.

26. Ella (Mrs. P. P.) Tucker to the President of the Texas Federation of Women's Clubs, April 3–5, 1911, Dallas Federation of Women's Clubs Records, Texas/Dallas Collection; Deutsch, "Learning to Talk More Like a Man," 391.

Before launching their first major local campaign, the Dallas Federation officers widened their base among Dallas's female population. In the summer of 1906 they founded a new organization, the Woman's Forum. A department club patterned after the Athenean Club of Kansas City, the forum offered study in nine areas— art, Bible and sacred history, music, philosophy and science, literature, household economics and pure food, civics and philanthropy, and current events. These topics were intended to attract women then on waiting lists to join the existing clubs, all of which limited their size. Stressing the importance of club membership for women's self-development, the forum's first president urged an activist approach to city problems. She encouraged the women to seek "practical results," and in her inaugural address promised that the forum would consider any matter concerning life in Dallas in order to "study and correct wrongs and abuses wherever woman's influence is needed." The forum immediately joined the Dallas Federation, and with almost three hundred members by the end of its first year, provided additional leadership and expanded resources for numerous civic programs that the federation officers would soon launch.[27]

Any subject related to family belonged within the purview of mothers, and few matters reached as directly into home life as a woman's purchases of milk, foods, and medicines. The Woman's Forum thus had little difficulty justifying its first major project, the passage of a pure food and drug ordinance for Dallas. In August 1906, barely six weeks after President Theodore Roosevelt signed the Meat Inspection and Pure Food and Drug Acts, delegates from the forum began discussions with the newly elected city commissioners about a pure food law and the appointment of a city chemist. With this campaign the women were not only pitting their judgment against male authority, they were also affecting the livelihoods of hundreds of small-business owners.

The forum's committee was composed of mothers who defined for the city standards of cleanliness equal to those in their own kitchens. The women wanted inspection of all places selling food

27. Dallas Woman's Forum, *Yearbook, 1907–1908,* 30–31, 34; Edna Frances Wesson, "Through the First Twenty-One Years with the Dallas Woman's Forum," typescript; Dallas Woman's Forum, *Yearbook, 1910–1911,* 14–15 (second quotation), and *Yearbook, 1911–1912,* 16–19—all in DWF; Hunter, *Quarter of a Century,* 5–6 (first quotation).

and drink, prohibition of the sale of "unwholesome, adulterated" products, and specific penalties for violations. They wrote an ordinance that prescribed exact methods for cleaning and sterilizing implements, receptacles, and storage areas for milk processing, demanded truthful labeling, and set fines for health department employees who connived or assisted in violations of the law. Appalled by the proposed law's stringency, dairymen, farmers, grocers, and druggists resisted the ordinance, then asked for delay in implementation. The women were a more effective interest group than their opponents, and the forum committee's pressure on city government never wavered. On March 1, 1907, Dallas's new pure food and drug ordinance went into effect.[28]

The pure food and drug laws illustrated the crux of gendered politics. After the Dallas ordinance passed, the "woman's page" columnist for the *Morning News* noted the differences in the positions of women and of men on several issues, particularly with regard to the safety of commercially processed food. Each year in the United States, she wrote, an estimated half a million children under the age of two died from "preservatives in milk and adulterated foods." While "the Congress of men" had stalled for seventeen years before passing a pure food law, within only a year of receiving farmers' complaints, they appropriated thousands of dollars for studies of the boll weevil. Plentiful cotton crops, to be sure, fed and clothed the children of farmers. But among lawmakers, commercial interests took precedence over the interests of mere human beings.[29]

The pure food and drug campaign initiated a long series of women's projects that fell within the category of "municipal house-

28. *Dallas Morning News,* January 1, February 2, February 3, and February 7, 1907; *History DFWC,* 4, 37–38, includes names of the federation committee appointed at the city's request to help with enforcement; Dallas Woman's Forum, *Yearbook, 1907–1908,* 31, DWF; Hunter, *Quarter of a Century,* 4, 44; City of Dallas Minutes, vol. 32: November 7, 1906, p. 315; November 13, 1906, pp. 331–32; December 11, 1906, p. 371; August 14, 1906, p. 214; September 25, 1906, p. 261; October 4, 1906, p. 275; October 9, 1906, p. 298; January 22, 1907, p. 419; and *Ordinance Records of the City of Dallas,* vol. 13, p. 459; vol. 19, pp. 177–81, 231, 609—both in the Office of the Secretary, City of Dallas; "Report of the City Chemist," *Annual Reports of the City of Dallas, 1906–1907* (Dallas: n.p., 1907), 131–40, in Texas/Dallas Collection.

29. *Dallas Morning News,* February 11, 1907; Flanagan, "Gender and Urban Political Reform," 1032–33.

keeping." All had economic aspects, for they required tax money or special public bond issues. Of equal significance was the fact that all had political implications, for either openly or tacitly, they revealed a rejection of the way men were running city departments. With such challenges to male dominance of public affairs, the clubwomen may be designated "cultural feminists." As such, they did not necessarily seek the vote. Believing, however, that they understood certain social problems and needs better than men, they rarely hesitated to make their wishes known.[30]

With regard to their results, in Dallas the measures described as municipal housekeeping served not so much to clean up behind dirty industry or careless manufacturers as to supply city residents with basic services that had never been established. During the early years of the twentieth century, Dallas more than tripled in size as the population increased from about 43,000 in 1900 to almost 159,000 by 1920. The crush of newcomers seriously aggravated old problems that city leaders had long neglected—waste disposal, for example, and water, which had rarely been adequate and never really clean.[31]

Although the Citizens' Association included husbands, brothers, and family friends of Dallas Federation and Woman's Forum members, the men were not always sympathetic to the women's plans. Dallas business leaders held more or less progressive views with regard to some social issues, but they also retained a tendency to harbor essentially rural assumptions, for example, that each family could adequately make its own arrangements for water, fuel, and waste disposal. Whereas they understood how plentiful, readily available water benefited economic growth, they accepted very limited responsibility for public well-being. Matters of health, in

30. Cott, "Limits of 'Social Feminism,'" 815, 826; Josephine Donovan, *Feminist Theory: The Intellectual Traditions of American Feminism* (New York: Frederick Unger, 1985), 31–60; Karen Blair, *The Clubwoman as Feminist: True Womanhood Redefined, 1868–1914* (New York: Holmes & Meier, 1980), 5. Blair uses the term "domestic feminism" rather than "cultural feminism."

31. M. E. Bolding and Erie H. Bolding, *Origins and Growth of the Dallas Water Utilities* (Temple, Tex.: privately published, 1981), 11–12, 18–20, 21, 44, 48, 56–59, 65–68, 71–72, 73–74, 92; Stuart Galishoff, "Triumph and Failure: The American Response to the Urban Water Supply Problems, 1860–1923," and Joel A. Tarr et al., "The Development and Impact of Urban Wastewater Technology: Changing Concepts of Water Quality Control, 1850–1930," both in Melosi, ed., *Pollution and Reform*, 35–57, 59–82.

other words, lay within the private sphere, with each separate household.[32] Hence, when they decided to expand the city water system, they planned to avoid the cost of a purification plant. Water from relatively clean streams would mix with that from sources long known to be polluted, but the city chemist, they figured, could just "doctor" the water whenever "the need became evident"—that is, when the causes of a major epidemic could be traced directly to the reservoirs.

Despite the area's history of typhoid fever and frequent vague, unspecified illnesses, the clubwomen had to campaign for five years for the bond issue to build a filtration plant. With research, reports on sanitation and water systems in other cities, lectures by visiting experts, speeches to men's clubs, and numerous letters to the editors of local newspapers, the women sought to educate and inform the city leaders and the taxpayers. By lobbying city commissioners and other public officials, the women again functioned as a pressure group—unenfranchised but influential by reason of their status as mothers. Men initially unmoved by health matters were at last persuaded that a safe, as well as plentiful, water supply could attract new businesses and the residents who would provide a labor force. The filtration plant opened in May 1913. After this struggle, which they later remembered as "long and sometimes bitter," the clubwomen considered the city's clean water to be their foremost achievement.[33]

For smaller projects a more direct method worked quite well. When they failed initially to convince Dallas leaders to accept a program, the clubwomen launched it themselves. A Dallas Federation committee, for example, introduced the concept of the play park with an activity program run by trained directors, whose salaries the women paid from the federation budget. The federation also hired the county's first probation officer, the city's first police matron and truant officer, and visiting nurses for the schools. Members of the mothers' clubs began the practice of providing lunches in the public schools. For all these programs the club-

32. Baker, "Domestication," 641; Deutsch, "Learning to Talk More Like a Man," 390.

33. *History DFWC*, 1–2, 6–7, 56–60, 65; *Dallas Morning News*, December 8, 1909, and October 30, 1938; Bolding and Bolding, *Dallas Water Utilities*, 56–57, 71–75, 92. On the adverse economic effects of poor water, see Galishoff, "Urban Water Problems," 36–38.

women were able to acquire public funding after the need was proven. With the personnel hired, the program in operation, or the institution founded upon secure public support and tax money, the women relinquished control, often retaining contact only through an advisory committee.[34] Despite the long-term results of taking women's work out of women's hands, this approach did vastly expand their effects on city problems.

In 1908, less than two years after their victory with the food and drug ordinance, the activist clubwomen led their organizations into the most direct of political events, an election. Officers of the mothers' club at the William B. Travis (formerly the McKinney Avenue) School circulated petitions for voters' signatures to add the names of two women to the list of candidates for the Board of Education. Although women could not vote at any level in Dallas, the state constitution specified males or qualified electors for only two minor offices, both appointive. Women had, in fact, already served on the school boards in two Texas towns, Denison and Wills Point.[35] Both the female candidates in Dallas had years of experience as club leaders. One was the organizer of several mothers' clubs, and she would earn a statewide reputation for advocacy of fire safety and prevention measures. The other had served as president of both the Texas and Dallas Federations and the Woman's Forum.[36]

With its obvious similarities to traditional female roles, service on the school board was a reasonable extension of motherhood into public life. Yet once again, clubwomen sought to evade that word "politics." They argued, with somewhat precious reasoning, that education could not be a partisan issue because "all good citizens stand for divorcement of school interests from politics" and because even though the board had only five seats, the women were independent candidates and thus not running against anyone.

The race provides a study in how Dallas women gingerly stretched the rules of propriety and cautiously claimed public

34. *Dallas Morning News,* February 26, 1906, February 16, 1914; *History DFWC,* 8–9, 11, 32, 37, 48–52, 57–58; PTA History, 7, 9.

35. *Dallas Morning News,* May 3, 1918.

36. Michael V. Hazel, "A Mother's Touch: The First Two Women Elected to the Dallas School Board," *Heritage News* 12 (Spring 1987): 9–12; Diana Church, "Mrs. E. P. Turner: Clubwoman, Reformer, Community Builder," *Heritage News* 10 (Summer 1985): 9–14.

spaces.[37] The Dallas Federation's election workers canvassed voters and distributed literature in every "proper" ward, avoiding, that is, the areas where known brothels operated and, more than likely, most African American neighborhoods. Seeking to answer complaints that "it did not look right in a Southern woman to take a prominent place," federation leaders reminded the public that in Kentucky, Florida, Louisiana, Mississippi, and Oklahoma women had at least limited rights regarding school matters. With such strict examination of their every move, the candidates could not possibly "electioneer" at the polls, especially after federation members expressed dismay merely at the idea.

The female candidates conducted themselves with resolute graciousness. A rival suggested that their names be placed at the top of the ballot because they were handicapped in the race: they could not campaign in the same ways as the men, nor could they vote. Both women refused to accept any special favors and insisted on drawing for their places like the others.

Apparently, neither woman ever spoke in her own behalf, except possibly at small private gatherings. Other clubwomen made statements in their favor to the newspapers, while men conducted much of the public campaign, speaking for the women at teas and receptions, and even at a meeting of the Council of Mothers. Upon hearing of their candidacy, a member of the outgoing board withdrew his name for reelection in order to work for one of the women. In lengthy letters and short personal statements to the *Morning News,* business leaders supported the women's election largely in the very terms voiced by the women themselves.

Their platform was simply "the welfare of the child," and they argued that because they were women, they, not men, knew what children needed most. Both candidates were mothers, one with four sons and the other with two sons and four daughters. Certainly a crucial factor in the race was support by the Citizens' Association (identified only as "a group of citizens from every section of the city"), which included the women's names among

37. Deutsch, "Learning to Talk More Like a Man," especially 390; Kerber, "Separate Spheres," 36. For the events and rhetoric of the 1908 School Board elections, see *Dallas Morning News* on these dates in 1908: March 23, March 25, March 26, March 28, March 29, March 31, April 4, April 5, April 6, April 8, April 9.

the candidates it favored for city offices. Both women won, one easily and the other with a slim majority.[38]

Despite their great care not to offend traditional sensibilities even as they challenged tradition, the two Dallas school board candidates reflected the changing attitudes of Texas clubwomen toward politics. Protected by—but armed with—the rhetoric of motherhood, by 1908 the state's clubwomen were well organized, sure of their purposes, confident of their ability, and increasingly less apologetic about their visibility in public debate, especially regarding matters related to children. About this time, too, the annual meetings of the Texas Federation began to include reports on the legal status of women and the property rights of married women in Texas. Instead of pronouncements denying a wish "to meddle" in politics, after 1909 the organization's presidents urged "agitation and personal letters to our legislators" with regard to child labor, working conditions for women, and prison reform. In 1910 the federation advocated the appointment of women to all state boards handling matters that affected women and children. This assertiveness in dealing with state government for the sake of children and less fortunate women did not extend to the club-women's own political rights. The Texas Federation refused to endorse woman suffrage until 1915 and then did so only informally.[39]

Because they justified their invasion of the male realm with their responsibilities as mothers, it was perhaps inevitable that the clubwomen would, sooner or later, challenge not merely conditions that particularly affected children but also those firmly embedded in the contemporary mores. In April 1916, when the Dallas Council of Mothers launched a citywide campaign to ban alcoholic beverages from the state fair, it attacked a custom traditionally accepted as a male privilege. The women chose an opportune time to endorse prohibition, for "dry" forces seemed to be gathering strength. In February 1915, for example, the brewers had lost a major antitrust suit brought by the Texas attorney general. With the issue saturating state politics at every level, the mothers announced

38. *Dallas Morning News,* March 25 and 26, April 9, 1908.

39. *TFWC History,* 37, 135, 177, 182, 244, 234, 249, 260; Dallas Woman's Forum Executive Board Minutes, January 31, 1907, 7, DWF; Marguerite Reagan (Mrs. John) Davis to Minnie Fisher Cunningham, October 27 and November 5, 1915, and Dora Hartzell (Mrs. Fred) Fleming to Cunningham, May 5, 1916, all in the Jane Y. McCallum Papers, Austin History Center, Austin Public Library.

that they wished to protect their husbands as well as their sons from temptation.[40]

The women first had to get the issue on the ballot for the upcoming city elections, so they began their campaign by employing the initiative, a tool of direct democracy adopted as part of the 1906 city charter. Previous experience with club projects proved beneficial, for gathering the signatures of registered voters was hardly more bold than standing on street corners each year on Tag Day to ask passersby for donations to the Empty Stocking Fund or the Infant Welfare and Milk Stations. Officers of the Council of Mothers worked with the city attorneys to draft a charter amendment that excluded Fair Park from Dallas's saloon laws. Because they were dealing with the electorate and not just with city officials or state lawmakers, representatives from the mothers' clubs spoke this time not only before small exclusive groups and receptions in private homes but also in meetings open to the general public.[41]

The women found businessmen and local officials firmly allied against them, for this fight involved economic issues as well as those of morality and personal behavior. The city stood to lose money because of its contracts with concessioners who sold food and drinks at the fair; tens of thousands of visitors from other areas of Texas would feel the drying effects of such a regulation; the state fair board would lose much-needed revenue from the sale of beer. Morality took precedence over financial gain, the women responded, and in letters and statements to the *Dallas Morning News* they lectured their opponents as though the men were little boys being called to task by their mothers. The twenty-one mothers' clubs received strong support from the churches, the Anti-Saloon League, and the Dallas Pastors' Association. Sharing the ballot with candidates for the Board of Education and eight additional city charter amendments, the prohibition issue attracted more votes

40. *The Brewers and Texas Politics* (San Antonio: Anti-Saloon League, 1916), Texas/Dallas Collection; PTA History, 10–11; Gould, *Progressives and Prohibitionists,* 167–74. On the temperance movement as an attack on male privilege, see Jack S. Blocker, Jr., "Separate Paths: Suffragists and the Women's Temperance Crusade," *Signs* 10 (Spring 1985): 463–64, 466, 469, 471, and 472.

41. *Dallas Morning News,* January 25, January 26, January 27, January 29, February 8, February 15, 1916.

than any other provision and passed easily.[42] Expedience lay with the "wets," but the voters agreed with the mothers.

By 1917 many of the very clubwomen who had wished to remain nonpolitical in the mid-1890s were members of the Dallas Equal Suffrage Association.[43] Their conversions were often as instructive as the experiences of the McKinney Avenue mothers. In a special *Dallas Times Herald* weekly series entitled "Why I Am a Suffragist," about two dozen women explained their reasons for wanting the ballot. Changing times had made one seventy-year-old club leader "strongly in sympathy with the feminist movement." Another viewed the vote in direct relationship to women's duties, at this time particularly with regard to World War I. Women citizens, she believed, would be "much more efficient had they been trained in city, county, state, and national politics." And the suffragists invoked the metaphors of motherhood. "When I became a Mother, I became a suffragist," a third woman stated. Articles with titles such as "Political Dominance of Men Is an Evil to the Mothers," "There Is Need of the Mother Heart in Legislation," and "Women in Home Should Have Voice in Government" linked women's responsibilities to home and children with the vote.[44]

Suffragists could not deny the overtly political nature of their cause. Nor could they consider remaining nonpartisan when faced with the machinations of such powerful foes as Governor James E. Ferguson and former United States Senator Joseph Weldon Bailey, probably the most influential politicians in Texas. Because their goal was so obviously political, Dallas suffragists had little to gain from the tactics used in the genteel campaigns of the Dallas Federation and the Woman's Forum. Routinely, suffragists worked in conference with attorneys, legal scholars, and party leaders; lobbied state and national representatives and senators; and spoke at meetings open to the public.

42. *Dallas Morning News,* January 21, January 28, January 30, February 1, February 11, April 2, April 4, April 5, 1916. R. E. L. Knight, who donated the gravel for the McKinney Avenue Public School's playground in 1895, was now president of the state fair and a strong opponent of the Dallas Council of Mothers.

43. "Pauline Periwinkle" column, *Dallas Morning News,* February 12, 1912; and *History DFWC,* 56–57.

44. *Dallas Times Herald,* June 10, December 30, September 2, August 26, July 22, June 24, 1917.

Officers of the Dallas Equal Suffrage Association accompanied state suffrage leaders and visiting national organizers on automobile tours to speak in small towns throughout the state. Although they did not hold parades and open-air rallies, which were so successful in Houston and Galveston, they employed other popular or mass political tactics. When they hosted the annual Suffrage Day at the state fair in 1915, for example, they rode in the automobile parade to the park and, like the state suffrage leaders, spoke to crowds of fairgoers from the open cars. October 23 of that year was also Traveling Salesman Day at the fair, so after the speeches, the suffragists spread throughout the fairgrounds and persuaded all the "drummers" to wear the bright yellow "Votes for Women" ribbons on their lapels. Three years later, to gather signatures for petitions and register women to vote in the 1918 primary, the local suffragists went throughout Dallas and Dallas County—to homemakers in residential neighborhoods, to office workers in downtown buildings, to operatives in the factories and mills, to clerks in the department stores, to teachers in the public schools after classes, and to employed women during lunchtime at the YWCA cafeteria.[45]

Activities by the clubwomen such as the campaigns for the 1909 school board race and their 1916 prohibition victory risked alienating the public. For this reason, and because they were working for women as women and not just as mothers, Dallas suffragists devoted a great deal of effort to maintaining the image of an organization whose members participated in regular, "normal" community activities. In the competition for the Style Show Parade of March 1916 they entered a car decorated with yellow and white flowers that spelled "Votes for Women" and "Victory in 1917." While recruiting new members at small teas and receptions, they held their annual conventions in the best hotels. Suffragists joined the Dallas Federation's welcoming committee for the ranchers' wives when the Cattleman's Association met in Dallas; they stood in receiving lines for the annual meetings of the Texas Congress of Mothers. At every opportunity they took great pains to spurn such "radical"

45. *Dallas Morning News*, October 23, 24, 1915; Nonie Boren Mahoney to Minnie Fisher Cunningham, December 6, 1916, and Vernice Reppert to Cunningham, November 9, 1917, McCallum Papers; and *Dallas Morning News*, March 6, 8, 9, and July 2, 3, 10, 1918.

behavior as that of the women who picketed the White House and criticized President Wilson.[46]

Above all, the suffragists participated in war work. They marched in the Patriotic Parade on April 10, 1917, to show their support for American entrance into the European conflict. In the following months they organized their own Red Cross auxiliary, sold war bonds and savings stamps, planted victory gardens, wrote articles on food conservation, and knitted constantly during each of their regular meetings. Their press secretary made sure not only that all such activities got into the newspapers but also that the women were identified specifically as suffragists. These occasions, in addition to enhancing their image, provided further opportunities to seek support for the cause; suffragists carried pamphlets and copies of prosuffrage articles everywhere in the chance that they might meet a potential recruit. "When suffrage is first," a Dallas woman once wrote, "one works without hardly realizing it."[47] The suffragists, in short, turned virtually everything they did into a political statement.

Between 1895 and 1918, through the work of white clubwomen in Dallas, gender invaded politics at the point where public policy touched private life. To many, probably the majority of women, arguments about justice and rights were abstractions. By contrast, safe water and pure food, protection from the evils of alcoholic beverages, good education in school buildings that were "fire-proof," sanitary, adequately lighted and ventilated—all were practical matters of everyday life. The concerns of mothers for home

46. Marguerite Reagan Davis to Minnie Fisher Cunningham, June 19, July 5, 1916; and Katherine (Mrs. Isaac) Jalonick to Cunningham, August 2, 1917, both in the McCallum Papers; *Dallas Morning News,* February 23, 1916; Mamie (Mrs. J. J.) Hardin to Cunningham, September 8, 1917, Minnie Fisher Cunningham Papers, Houston Metropolitan Research Center, Houston Public Library; *Dallas Morning News,* October 4, 1917; Edith League to Texas Erwin Armstrong, October 17, 1917, McCallum Papers; *Dallas Morning News,* October 1, 7, 23, 1915. See Michael McGerr, "Political Style and Women's Power, 1830–1930," *Journal of American History* 77 (December 1990): 870–71, 879, 883.

47. *Dallas Morning News,* April 10 and 11, 1917; Katherine Jalonick to Minnie Fisher Cunningham, December 3, 1917, McCallum Papers; *Dallas Morning News,* May 1 and 3, 1917; November 15 and 20, and March 5, 1918; May 24, 1917; Vernice Reppert to Cunningham, May 7, 1917, Cunningham Papers; Nona Boren Mahoney to Jesse (Mrs. Roger P.) Ames, October 22, 1918, McCallum Papers.

and family and especially children, in other words, defined the issues that women pushed into the political arena. The programs that grew from those issues in turn expanded the responsibilities of government to its citizens.

Gender considerations also determined the evolution of the women's political style. Clubwomen skillfully developed effective strategies and tactics that were also "gender appropriate." By adapting familiar and acceptable social forms to pressure-group methods, they turned receptions into occasions for lobbying and teas into functions for recruiting supporters. The practice of asking for donations on a busy street corner once a year on Tag Day resembled the mass approach necessary for petition drives and for canvassing voters and, only a few years later, for telephone duty on election day.

Unfortunately, white clubwomen extended little of their developing expertise to the well-being of minority children. With a very small number of Hispanic residents in Dallas before 1917, the Dallas Federation of Women's Clubs seemed unaware of their presence until 1918, when a clubwoman proposed building a play park for Mexican children.[48] In 1913, black mothers could buy inspected milk at reduced prices from the Infant Welfare Station by going to the side door, but only if they did not come "in such numbers" as to be "objectionable to white people." The Infants' Welfare Association at last established a clinic for African American children in 1922. With their problems and needs ignored except by a few white individuals, black mothers had the strength and initiative to take care of their own. After 1900, teachers and middle-class housewives organized several reading, Bible study, and culture clubs, which routinely added charitable projects to their regular assignments. They founded other associations solely for charitable purposes, and by 1919 the Texas Federation of Colored Women's Clubs ran a settlement house in south Dallas.[49]

48. *Dallas Morning News*, November 10, 1918; *Hispanic Beginnings of Dallas: Into the Twentieth Century, 1850–1976* (Dallas: Hispanic Beginnings of Dallas Project, 1990), 18, photograph.

49. The Reading Circle, organized in 1891, may have been the first club for black women in Dallas. See *African American Families and Settlements in Dallas: On the Inside Looking Out: Exhibition, Family Memoirs, Personality Profiles and Community Essays*, vol. 2 (Dallas: Black Dallas Remembered, 1990), 25; Elizabeth L. Davis, *Lifting as They Climb: The National Association of Colored Women* (facsimile of 1933 edition; Ann Arbor: University Microfilms,

Whatever their shortcomings, the white clubwomen achieved an enviable record, and their accomplishments appear especially impressive given their relatively small numbers within the Dallas female population. In a city of over 26,000 adult white women by 1910 and nearly 41,000 by 1920, the Dallas Federation's size in 1917 was about 1,000, barely twice that three years later. Even before the clubwomen produced suffragists from their ranks, they functioned as an adept pressure group to extend women's influence beyond the "woman's sphere" to the point of affecting the way their city was run. With motherhood providing purposes, a rationale, and, in a sense, a "cover," the projects of four organizations—the Dallas Federation of Women's Clubs, the Woman's Forum, the Council of Mothers, and the Equal Suffrage Association—took the twin ideologies of maternalism and domesticity into the male realm of politics.

1971), 397–98. Notices of regular meetings and community projects of African American women's clubs appeared in almost every issue of the *Dallas Express* in 1919, in the earliest surviving numbers of this black-owned newspaper.

"Ideals of Government, of Home, and of Women"

The Ideology of Southern White Antisuffragism

ELNA GREEN

In 1894 the *San Antonio Express* took an opinion poll of sorts, asking local men and women what they thought of the issue of woman suffrage. The opinions expressed by those Texans not only demonstrate the fervency with which woman suffrage was discussed in the late-nineteenth-century South, they also conveniently summarize the most widely used arguments against woman suffrage in the region. Those arguments rested upon the fear of the loss of southern chivalry, the belief that men already represented their women, the "Negro question," and the doctrine of separate spheres based on gender and ordained by God.[1]

Twenty years later, Mississippi suffragist Nellie Nugent Somerville cataloged what she considered to be the most commonly heard objections to woman suffrage in the South: the fear of enfranchising black women, biblical injunction, apathy toward the ballot by women themselves, and the fact that Mississippi men repre-

---

1. *San Antonio Express,* July 22, July 29, 1894. The volume of literature on the southern suffrage movement is large and multiplying rapidly. Among the more important recent works not noted elsewhere in this essay are: Evelyn A. Kirkley, "'This Work Is God's Cause': Religion in the Southern Woman Suffrage Movement, 1880–1920," *Church History* 59 (December 1990): 507–22; Anastatia Sims, "'Powers That Pray' and 'Powers That Prey': Tennessee and the Fight for Woman Suffrage," *Tennessee Historical Quarterly* 50 (Winter 1991): 203–25; and Marjorie Spruill Wheeler, "Mary Johnston, Suffragist," *Virginia Magazine of History and Biography* 100 (January 1992): 99–118.

sented their women at the polls.[2] These two examples illustrate a much larger phenomenon: throughout the more than three decades of suffrage agitation in the South, the pool of arguments against the enfranchisement of women remained essentially unchanged.

The ideological consistency of the southern antisuffrage position becomes significant when contrasted to the evolution that took place in the rhetoric of both the prosuffrage movement and the national antisuffrage movement. A description of those changing ideologies, set beside an analysis of the implications of the static southern antisuffrage ideology, can also illuminate some of the forces at work in the suffrage movement. Suffragists and antisuffragists were locked in something resembling a strategic Ping-Pong game, with each side forced to respond to actions by the other, and the two stories are best told together.[3]

As the heirs of the Enlightenment, with its emphasis on natural rights and equality, American suffrage theorists in the mid-nineteenth century insisted that women deserved the vote because they were citizens, and equal citizenship alone was enough to entitle them to the ballot. Elizabeth Cady Stanton, Susan B. Anthony, Lucretia Mott, and other early suffragists grounded their feminism in concepts of equal justice and equal rights. As part of a larger feminist agenda intended to bring women into full and equal partnership with men, nineteenth-century suffragism constituted a radical innovation. Accompanied by demands for other reforms such as a single standard of morality, equality of pay, lenient di-

2. Report of Legislative Work, 1914, Nellie Nugent Somerville Papers, Schlesinger Library, Radcliffe College, Cambridge, Mass.

3. Some notes about terminology: Unless otherwise stated, the terms *suffragist, antisuffragist,* and *southerner* refer to whites only. The phrase *southern suffragist* refers to the majority of southern suffrage supporters, who advocated ratification of the Nineteenth Amendment, not to that minority faction that demanded state constitutional amendments. These so-called states' rights suffragists, led by Kate Gordon, while extremely important in the suffrage contests in the South, cannot be examined in the brief context of this paper. See Kenneth R. Johnson, "Kate Gordon and the Woman-Suffrage Movement in the South," *Journal of Southern History* 38 (August 1972): 365–92; Elna C. Green, "The Rest of the Story: Kate Gordon and the Opposition to the Nineteenth Amendment in the South," *Louisiana History* 33 (Spring 1992): 171–89; and Marjorie Spruill Wheeler, *New Women of the New South: The Leaders of the Woman Suffrage Movement in the Southern States* (New York: Oxford University Press, 1993), chap. 5.

vorce laws, and equal access to education and the professions, suffrage was only one part of a wider vision of equality for women.[4]

Yet a number of powerful forces whittled away at many of the more controversial demands of the nineteenth-century feminists, eventually leaving suffrage as one of the few reforms upon which all the various women's movements could agree. A series of public scandals (like the Victoria Woodhull affair), a general rise in conservatism in American society at the end of the century (in response to the new immigration, social Darwinism, and the acquisition of an overseas empire), and the rise of a new generation of national suffrage leaders (including Carrie Chapman Catt), themselves a product of a more conservative climate, all worked to redefine the "woman's rights movement" as the "woman suffrage movement."[5] Another element influencing suffragism's retreat from radicalism was the emergence of a southern wing of the suffrage movement. The highly symbolic National American Woman Suffrage Association Annual Convention of 1903, held in New Orleans, testified to the change. With southern women featured prominently in the convention, the delegates voted to accept a states' rights structure that would allow southern suffrage organizations to work for state suffrage amendments and permit the exclusion of black women from their associations.[6]

Reflecting both the changing nature of the suffrage movement itself and new currents in contemporary American thought, suffrage ideology near the turn of the century evolved into what Aileen Kraditor has called the "expediency" argument. Suffragists increasingly claimed that women, as women, had special talents and proclivities that should be applied to government and politics. Those areas in which women "excelled," such as education, morality, and homemaking, could be profitably applied to the public

4. Ellen Carol DuBois, "The Radicalism of the Woman Suffrage Movement: Notes toward the Reconstruction of Nineteenth-Century Feminism," *Feminist Studies* 3 (Fall 1975), 63–71.

5. Beverly Beeton, *Women Vote in the West: The Woman Suffrage Movement, 1869–1896* (New York: Garland Publishing, 1986), 150; William O'Neill, *Everyone Was Brave: The Rise and Fall of Feminism in America* (Chicago: Quadrangle, 1969), 21–47; Kathleen Barry, *Susan B. Anthony: A Biography of a Singular Feminist* (New York: New York University Press, 1988), 200–210.

6. B. H. Gilley, "Kate Gordon and Louisiana Woman Suffrage," *Louisiana History* 24 (Summer 1983), 295.

sphere. Women would clean up politics, vote in needed reforms, and help to usher in good government by use of their municipal broom.[7]

Similarly, the national antisuffrage movement felt the impact of changing conditions in the twentieth century and responded with some modifications of its rhetoric. The first antisuffrage organization in the country, formed in Massachusetts in 1882, soon grew into a national association with chapters in more than twenty states.[8] The National Association Opposed to Woman Suffrage (NAOWS) served as an information clearinghouse for antisuffragists through its official journal, the *Woman's Protest*. In addition to its own columns and original articles, each issue contained reprinted articles from across the country, giving its readers access to some of the best antisuffrage rhetoric published.

Kraditor was the first scholar to examine the arguments employed by the antisuffrage movement. She classified the most commonly used arguments against the enfranchisement of women into three categories—theological, biological, and sociological.[9] In 1917, however, that pool of arguments felt the impact of internal conflict within the national antisuffrage organization as the NAOWS under-

7. Aileen S. Kraditor, *Ideas of the Woman Suffrage Movement, 1890–1920* (New York: Columbia University Press, 1965). Although Kraditor's model of natural rights versus expediency has been softened by years of challenges, it remains a common line of interpretation. For recent accounts incorporating this paradigm, see Peter G. Filene, *Him/Her/Self: Sex Roles in Modern America,* 2d ed. (Baltimore: Johns Hopkins University Press, 1986), 37; Glenda Riley, *Inventing the American Woman: A Perspective on Women's History* (Arlington Heights: Harlan Davidson, 1986), 157; and Sara M. Evans, *Born for Liberty: A History of Women in America* (New York: Free Press, 1989), 153–54.

8. On the national antisuffrage movement, see Jeanne Howard, "Our Own Worst Enemies: Women Opposed to Woman Suffrage," *Journal of Sociology and Social Welfare* 9 (September 1982): 463–72; Catherine Cole Mambretti, "The Battle against the Ballot: Illinois Woman Antisuffragists," *Chicago History* 9 (Fall 1980): 168–77; Susan E. Marshall, "In Defense of Separate Spheres: Class and Status Politics in the Antisuffrage Movement," *Social Forces* 65 (December 1986): 327–51; Louise L. Stevenson, "Women Anti-Suffragists in the 1915 Massachusetts Campaign," *New England Quarterly* 52 (March 1979): 80–93; Thomas James Jablonsky, "Duty, Nature, and Stability: The Female Anti-Suffragists in the United States, 1894–1920" (Ph.D. diss., University of Southern California, 1978); and Jane Jerome Camhi, "Women against Women: American Antisuffragism, 1880–1920" (Ph.D. diss., Tufts University, 1973).

9. Kraditor, *Ideas,* chap. 2.

went a complete restructuring. In what one historian has interpreted as a palace coup, the NAOWS suddenly replaced its entire slate of officers, moved its headquarters, and renamed its journal the *Woman Patriot*. Responding to the Bolshevik Revolution and the outbreak of World War I, the new journal took as its motto For Home and National Defense against Woman Suffrage, Feminism, and Socialism. Its rhetoric became stridently antiradical as it attempted to associate suffragism with bolshevism, anarchism, and subversion. Its pages were peppered with stories of socialists who demanded woman suffrage and with character assassinations that grew increasingly shrill. Previously a conservative organization devoted to opposing suffrage and changes in the family, the NAOWS became a reactionary group dedicated to ferreting out radicalism, pointing accusatory fingers in numerous directions.[10]

This evolution in antisuffrage ideology made little headway in the southern states, however, as southern antisuffrage rhetoric remained firmly based in its nineteenth-century origins.[11] Unlike northern antisuffragism, which cities seemed to generate,[12] the southern variety flourished on the plantation, in the Black Belt, and in the country town. Southern antisuffragism was the product of rural conservatism, an expression of the values of plantation-based economic elites. The leaders of the movement spoke for the big agriculture and big textile nexus, the New South's heirs of the Old South's traditions. Southern antisuffragists came from that small inner circle of social and economic elites that had controlled south-

10. For numerous examples of northern antisuffragists' proclivity for red-baiting, see the *Woman Patriot*. For analyses of the red-baiting tendency, see Jablonsky, "Duty, Nature, and Stability," 187–200, and O'Neill, *Everyone Was Brave*, 228. Jablonsky interpreted the change of leadership as a palace coup, but one that ultimately changed the direction of the antisuffrage movement (189).

11. Texas was a notable exception to this generalization. The rhetoric of antiradicalism was used early and often there. See, for example, Mrs. James B. Wells, *Why I Am Opposed to Woman Suffrage* (Austin: n.p., 1915). Its emergence may be explained by the presence in Texas of a relatively large foreign population, particularly Mexican and German, and an unusually large and active Socialist Party in the early twentieth century. See James R. Green, *Grass-Roots Socialism: Radical Movements in the Southwest, 1895–1943* (Baton Rouge: Louisiana State University Press, 1978).

12. Jablonsky, "Duty, Nature, and Stability," 19, 120; Camhi, "Women against Women," 3.

ern politics since before the Civil War.[13] Firmly rooted in the plantation economy, the opponents of woman suffrage frequently traced their family lines back to the Revolution or beyond, and could point to significant landholdings, slaveholdings, and political offices in their genealogies. As the *Montgomery Advertiser* exulted, "The personnel of the Anti-Ratification League of Montgomery is representative of the highest type of Southern womanhood; its members are from Alabama families, which have exemplified the best in Southern life and they grew up and have lived in the atmosphere of the culture and traditions of the South."[14]

Southern antisuffragists saw the world as an integrated whole; class, gender, and race relations were set in a permanent configuration, each mutually reinforcing the others. This ideal world consisted of a traditional patriarchal hierarchy, a sort of triangular structure with elite white males at the top and everyone else in their assigned positions beneath. A blow to any part of the edifice might endanger the integrity of the entire structure. Antisuffrage senator Joseph Weldon Bailey of Texas emphasized, "We have our ideals of government, of home and of women." To which educator Eugene Anderson of Georgia added, "We appreciate the Negro *in his proper relationship*."[15]

Antisuffragists believed that this social structure was in the best interest of all concerned: male, female, black, white, rich, poor. But, in fact, this social system served their own best interests, as it protected the social and economic status quo, a hierarchy at the top of which they and their families were comfortably located. The ideal world created by this class institutionalized inequality. Antisuffragists witnessed with horror the trend toward wider participation in the electoral system and fought the implied social equality that came with political equality. As one southern woman put it, "Negro women would be placed on the same par with white

13. Paul D. Escott, *Many Excellent People: Power and Privilege in North Carolina, 1850–1900* (Chapel Hill: University of North Carolina Press, 1985).

14. Elna C. Green, "Those Opposed: Southern Antisuffragism, 1890–1920" (Ph.D. diss., Tulane University, 1992), chap. 2; editorial, *Montgomery (Ala.) Advertiser,* June 25, 1919.

15. Bailey quoted in Sam Hanna Acheson, *Joe Bailey, the Last Democrat* (New York: Macmillan, 1932), 357; Anderson quoted in *Woman Patriot,* August 9, 1919, 2 [emphasis mine]. For more extensive summary of the southern antisuffrage arguments, see Green, "Those Opposed," 188–207.

women." And Virginia antisuffragists reminded their legislators that "every argument for sexual equality in politics is, and must be, an argument also for racial equality. There is no way around it. If the white woman is entitled to the vote because she bears, has borne, may bear, or might have borne children, the Negro woman is entitled to the same right for the same reason."[16]

The fundamental unit of this world was the family, not the individual, as the antisuffragists made quite clear in their literature. Eugene Anderson saw the suffrage movement as "an attempt at individualism and an attack on the home." He remained unwilling to "set up Individualism in America in place of the family unit," since it was the "purpose of the founders of the government to make the family the unit and to encourage family unity, and not to encourage individualism." A Kentucky editor wrote that woman suffrage "means the breaking up of the family which has been the basal institution of human welfare thus far from the very dawn of history. . . . 'Votes for women' means that the individual and not the family is to be the unit of the State."[17]

Of course, the man was the head of the family. An attorney from St. Louis objected to woman suffrage because "where there is substantially universal manhood suffrage . . . all persons, including women and children, are practically represented by the voters." A southern minister projected that "if a woman is elected governor of a state, she becomes the head of all the men in that common-wealth, and if she is elected president of the United States, she becomes the head of all the men who are citizens of the United States and even head of her husband, and thereby changes God's order completely which has fixed man for the headship of the woman."[18] The family as a unit could have only one head. Anything else endangered the survival of the institution.

Their adherence to this mythic ideal world explains why the

16. Newspaper clipping [January 1918], Era Club Papers, Louisiana Collection, New Orleans Public Library; *Woman Patriot,* August 30, 1919, 2.

17. Eugene Anderson, *Unchaining the Demons of the Lower World; or, A Petition of Ninety-Nine Per Cent against Suffrage* (Macon, Ga.: n.p., [1918]), 2, 5, 11; *Berea (Ky.) Citizen,* April 1, 1920; quoted in *Woman Patriot,* April 24, 1920.

18. George Lockwood, *Why I Oppose Woman Suffrage* (St. Louis: n.p., 1912), 4; Isaac Lockhart Peebles, *Is Woman Suffrage Right? The Question Answered* (Meridian, Miss.: Tell Farmer, 1918), 14.

antisuffragists described a postsuffrage world in such apocalyptic terms. Fernand Mouton, Louisiana's lieutenant governor, claimed that "[t]here is nothing in the form of disaster, yellow fever, cyclones, or earthquakes that could wreak the ruin of the South as effectively as the operation of the Susan B. Anthony amendment." Another Louisiana antisuffragist wrote that woman suffrage "would lead to the end of family life and finally to the end of our civilization."[19] This extreme rhetoric was not raving exaggeration. The antisuffragists understood how precariously balanced their world's structure was, and they knew that they had the most to lose should it collapse.

In one sense, the antisuffragists were right. American society *was* moving from an emphasis on the family unit toward an emphasis on the individual. But no amount of tinkering with the electorate could stop the trend, for it was being produced by economic and demographic forces that the political process was powerless to halt. The enfranchisement of women served as a recognition of economic and demographic changes; it did not produce those changes.

Southern antisuffragists continued to cherish the nineteenth-century ideals of separate spheres and republican motherhood. The *Jackson (Miss.) Clarion-Ledger* warned suffragists that "they had better be at home . . . instructing their sons, future voters, in lessons of good citizenship and in the shaping of them into citizens into whose hands in future years the affairs of State may be safely placed." And Congressman Frank Clark of Florida rhapsodized about the power of the "queen of the home": "As the mother, as the wife, as the sister she exercises a broader and deeper and mightier influence than she can ever exercise or hope to on the stump and in the byways of politics in this land."[20]

These were not just male-imposed values. Female antisuffragists also clung tenaciously to their separate sphere, which they saw as providing a guaranteed area of power and influence. A world without the separate sphere might just be a world where women had no influence at all. Annah Watson of Memphis wrote

19. *New Orleans Item,* June 29, 1919; E. von Meyrenberg to Miss M. W. Coate, January 8, 1912, Grace Chamberlain Papers, Louisiana Historical Center, Louisiana Museum, New Orleans.

20. *Jackson (Miss.) Daily Clarion-Ledger,* January 22, 1914; quoted in Kraditor, *Ideas,* 18.

in 1895 that women's power lay "in their influence with husbands, brothers and sons, . . . in their power to direct the votes of those nearest and dearest for the accomplishment of the uplifting of society. This may seem slow in method and practical results but it is safe." In 1919 the Alabama Anti-Ratification League affirmed, "We are home keepers and the mothers of children, and we seek to discharge our duty to our country and to the cause of civilization and right living, not by voting and holding office, but . . . by instilling into our children love of their country and devotion to high ideals."[21]

Southern antisuffragists believed that suffragism meant a final refutation of the doctrine of the separate sphere. They never forgot the claims and the arguments of the nineteenth-century suffragists, which had struck at the foundations of family structure and gender relations. They remained suspicious of the suffragists' more recent moderation, and taunted them unmercifully with examples of past extremism. In 1918 Isaac Peebles of Mississippi was still using Elizabeth Cady Stanton's *Woman's Bible* as evidence of the "free love" values of suffragists. The *Easley (S.C.) Democrat* suggested that suffragists "bring Mrs. [Mary Elizabeth] Lease and Mrs. Victoria Woodhull and some of the Yankee female viragoes" to speak on behalf of a suffrage bill.[22]

So southern antisuffragists continued to demand separate spheres for the sexes. For the races they demanded separate castes. Their dedication to the ideal of white supremacy was unmatched, and their efforts to protect it unfailing. An antisuffrage pamphleteer opposed woman suffrage because he was "uncompromisingly and unalterably opposed to anything approaching social equality between whites and blacks, and any and everything that may lead to, or further, such equality, or may give political power to the negro." Newspaper editor Hiram Henry boasted, "The best brain of Mississippi was employed to disqualify the Negro men as voters, in the Constitutional Convention of 1890, and the work of . . . that notable

21. Annah Robinson Watson, "Attitudes of Southern Women on the Suffrage Question," *Arena* 63 (February 1895): 367; Petition to the Legislature of Alabama [1919], Alabama Equal Suffrage Association Papers, Suffrage Organization Records, Alabama Department of Archives and History, Montgomery.

22. Peebles, *Is Woman Suffrage Right?*, 15; quoted by A. Elizabeth Taylor, "South Carolina and the Enfranchisement of Women: The Early Years," *South Carolina Historical Magazine* 77 (April 1976), 117.

body will not be set aside at the behest of a few fanatical suffragettes, who do not seem to comprehend that the Susan B. Anthony amendment would make their cooks and washerwomen voters." He was wrong. The suffragists knew full well the implications of their demands. They could not help but know, since the antisuffragists reminded them at every turn. But as one southern suffragist declared, "The time has come to lay, once and for all, this old, old ghost which still stalks, [but] has outlived its time." The progressive North Carolina jurist, Walter Clark, asked, "From what reserve [other than women] can we draw the votes to offset the 25,000 colored soldiers, or other colored men, who *will assuredly vote* in this State at the next Presidential Election [in 1920]?"[23] Suffragists argued that woman suffrage, even if black women voted, would not damage white supremacy, and that was enough.

"White supremacy," however, inadequately describes the antisuffragists' goal. "White monopoly" more nearly indicates their objective.[24] Antisuffragists insisted upon a lily-white electorate, whereas the suffragists were willing to accept a black voting minority. As the always outspoken James K. Vardaman put it: "I am opposed to Negro voting; it matters not what his advertised mental and moral qualifications may be. I am just as much opposed to Booker Washington as a voter . . . as I am to the . . . typical little coon, Andy Dotson, who blacks my shoes every morning. Neither is fit to perform the supreme function of citizenship." A self-styled "Old Line Democrat" questioned "the patriotism of any white person who believes that one single negro ought to be allowed to cast a ballot in Alabama." And a San Antonio woman argued that blacks were "never intended for power of *any kind*."[25]

23. George R. Lockwood, *Woman Suffrage a Menace to the South* (St. Louis: n.p., 1917), 7; Henry quoted in *Woman Patriot,* December 20, 1919, 8; Mrs. Guilford Dudley, *The Negro Vote in the South: A Southern Woman's Viewpoint* (New York: NAWSA, 1918), [unpaginated pamphlet]; Clark quoted in David Morgan, *Suffragists and Democrats: The Politics of Woman Suffrage in America* (East Lansing: Michigan State University Press, 1972), 135 [emphasis mine].

24. Although he did not use the phraseology that I have employed, my interpretation of the distinction between white supremacy and white monopoly has been informed by my reading of Paul E. Fuller, *Laura Clay and the Woman's Rights Movement* (Lexington: University Press of Kentucky, 1975), 62.

25. Vardaman quoted in Paul Lewinson, *Race, Class, and Party: A History of Negro Suffrage and White Politics in the South* (London: Oxford University

While southern suffragists pointed out time and again that white women outnumbered black men and women combined and would in fact increase the relative strength of the white electorate, the antisuffragists remained unswayed. To them, allowing even *some* black voters was dangerous, because "the colored population is not distributed with exact equality, like the sugar in a pudding" and thus could permit the election of blacks to office in some districts. And former Texas governor Oscar B. Colquitt argued, "The point is that when you give the ballot to women, you give it to all women, regardless of color. . . . you abandon your state's right and you make it possible for negro equality such as you suffered in the carpet bag days."[26]

The danger of political equality lay in its tacit admission that blacks had the right to vote simply because they were citizens. Moreover, political equality implied social equality, and as a Louisiana judge remarked, white women "side by side with the Negro women, voting with them, would be outrageous indeed." Texas's deposed governor, James E. Ferguson, agreed: "This talk about equal suffrage also means equal nigger." Antisuffragists acknowledged this implication over and again, as they linked the two together in their literature. An anonymous broadside entitled *Planks from the Suffrage Platform* stated it succinctly: "Suffrage stands for race equality—social and political." Three antisuffrage women warned the citizens of Nashville that the "dangerous principles" that lurked within woman suffrage included "Race equality."[27]

Indeed, to some it seemed that political equality meant not only racial equality but black supremacy. James Callaway, a tireless antisuffrage editorial writer from Georgia, believed that the "Susan B.

Press, 1932), 84; "A Protest against Woman's Suffrage in Alabama," Alabama Equal Suffrage Association Papers, Suffrage Organization Records, Alabama Department of Archives and History, Montgomery; Mrs. Charles Florian, *San Antonio Express,* July 22, 1894 [emphasis mine].

26. Quoted in Loretta Zimmerman, "Alice Paul and the National Woman's Party, 1912–1920" (Ph.D. diss., Tulane University, 1964), 176; Colquitt quoted in Ruthe Winegarten and Judith N. McArthur, eds., *Citizens at Last: The Woman Suffrage Movement in Texas* (Austin: Ellen C. Temple, 1987), 179–80.

27. Judge Gilbert Dupre, Opelousas, La., to Editor, *Jackson (Miss.) Clarion-Ledger,* October 2, 1918; *Ferguson Forum* (Tyler, Tex.), May 22, 1919; anonymous undated broadside, in Lizzie Elliott Papers, Tennessee State Library and Archives, Nashville; Mrs. George Washington, Mrs. James Pinckard, and Mrs. Ruffin Pleasant to Editor, *Nashville Tennessean,* August 6, 1920.

Anthony Amendment" meant black rule. Having seen a photograph of Carrie Chapman Catt marching between two black women in a suffrage parade, Episcopal bishop Thomas Gailor interpreted it to mean that Catt "may have been proclaiming the supremacy of the negro race." A Mississippi legislator contended that "every vote cast for the adoption of the Anthony amendment is a vote cast for Negro supremacy." Nancy MacLean's assessment of the Ku Klux Klan might be equally applied to the antisuffragists; their inability to imagine an egalitarian world led them to interpret struggles for black equality as efforts to establish black supremacy.[28]

In sum, even though southern suffragists and antisuffragists used the language of white supremacy in this discussion, it is clear they were talking about two different things. The pervasive phrase, "white supremacy," seemingly so clearly defined, actually was open to interpretation, and the proponents of woman suffrage defined it differently than their opponents. Distinguishing between white supremacy and white monopoly helps to explain the problem Aileen Kraditor could not solve: why did suffragists fail to convince southern legislators to enfranchise them when both sides claimed to believe in white supremacy?[29]

Implicit in the suffrage position was the acknowledgment that some blacks, both male and female, indeed *would* vote. The Kentucky suffragist, Madeline McDowell Breckinridge openly admitted that some black women would vote, but insisted that southern men must "ask themselves if they were going to deprive intelligent white women forever for that reason." As Anna (Mrs. Guilford) Dudley asked rhetorically, "Do you think [a southern woman] would hesitate [to vote] even if her cook should be in front of her?"[30] Clearly she considered that an acceptable situation.

28. Undated broadside entitled "Elihu Root Warns the South," Elliott Papers; Thomas P. Gailor to Josephine Pearson, September 13, 1920, Josephine A. Pearson Papers, Tennessee State Library and Archives, Nashville; A. J. Whitworth, "Disgrace, Dishonor, and Disaster," *Woman Patriot,* January 10, 1920, 5; Nancy L. MacLean, "Behind the Mask of Chivalry: Gender, Race, and Class in the Making of the Ku Klux Klan of the 1920s in Georgia" (Ph.D. diss., University of Wisconsin-Madison, 1989), 200.

29. Kraditor, "Tactical Problems of the Woman-Suffrage Movement in the South," *Louisiana Studies* 5 (Winter 1966), 304.

30. Melba Dean Porter, "Madeline McDowell Breckinridge: Her Role in the Kentucky Woman Suffrage Movement, 1908–1920," *Register of the Kentucky*

Dudley and others who shared her views saw no reason to fear black voters. Although it is doubtful that many of these southern whites were eager to enfranchise black southerners, they nevertheless were willing to accept black voters as an inevitable and benign by-product of woman suffrage. Indeed, some southern suffragists went even further, exhibiting remarkable racial moderation for their time and place. The Tennessee suffrage association proudly recorded the successful cooperation between black and white women voters in 1920.

> In Nashville they [black women] registered about 2,500 and voted almost their full quota. They organized under the direction of the [white] suffrage association, had their own city and ward chairmen[,] and worked with an intelligence, loyalty and dignity that made new friends for their race and for woman suffrage. There was not a single adverse criticism of them from any ward. They kept faith with the white women even when some of their men sold out the night before the election to a notorious political rounder. They proved that they were trying to keep step with the march of progress and with a little patience, trust and vision the universal tie of motherhood and sisterhood can and will overcome the prejudice against them as voters.[31]

In another unusually overt instance of racial moderation, the Birmingham suffrage league found itself nearly split in two over a resolution condemning segregation, with a minority of its members favoring the resolution, debated in 1913.[32]

By placing suffragism in its context against a background of antisuffrage conservatism, it is possible to argue that southern suffragism was more progressive than often interpreted. Its racial moderation, even more than its critique of contemporary gender roles, placed the southern suffrage movement at the forefront of southern progressive thought. Mainstream southern suffragists were willing to part company with white monopoly, and showed themselves willing to accept black women voters in the electorate. The

---

Historical Society 72 (October 1974), 345; Dudley quoted in A. Elizabeth Taylor, *The Woman Suffrage Movement in Tennessee* (New York: Bookman, 1957), 42.

31. Elizabeth Cady Stanton et al., eds., *History of Woman Suffrage,* 6 vols. (Rochester: Fowler and Wells, 1889–1922), 6:606.

32. Ethel Armes to Alice Stone Blackwell, June 26, 1913, Alabama Suffrage Associations Papers, NAWSA Papers, Manuscripts Division, Library of Congress.

admission of any blacks to the polls implied their fundamental right to be there. Thus southern suffragists directly challenged the post-Reconstruction racial settlement.

By contrast, northern suffragism (in the current state of the historiography) was a conservative, middle-class movement by women who did not challenge the current status quo but who merely wished to be admitted to it. Suffragists took pride in the fact that their movement was in the mainstream, and proudly announced that suffragism was a bourgeois movement. The national movement had shed its nineteenth-century radicalism, with its demands for a feminist restructuring of society, and by the turn of the century merely asked for the vote for women of the middle classes.[33] Southern suffragists, at least those who subscribed to the federal suffrage amendment,[34] tacitly agreed that black women had the same inherent right to vote that white women had, an extremely progressive proposition for their time and place.

Dewey Grantham has emphasized the way in which southern progressivism was proscribed by southern traditions. He argued that southern progressivism rested upon a foundation of broad agreement by whites that blacks, both male and female, must be kept out of southern politics. More recently, William A. Link has challenged the concept of a unified white opinion about race and racial qualifications for voting.[35] The evidence presented here shows that there remained some room for debate within that broad con-

33. Kraditor, *Ideas,* 211; Morgan, *Suffragists and Democrats,* 55; Kraditor, *Ideas,* 26. Not everyone agrees with this interpretation. Ellen Carol DuBois, for example, argues that the northern suffrage movement had a more radical critique of American society and a more broadly based organization than past historians have seen. "Working Women, Class Relations, and Suffrage Militance: Harriet Stanton Blatch and the New York Woman Suffrage Movement, 1894–1909," *Journal of American History* 74 (June 1987): 34–57. While I agree that historians have erred in portraying northern or eastern suffragism as a monolithic middle-class movement, I do not accept Harriet Stanton Blatch as representative of the ideology of the national movement as a whole. Moreover, DuBois's own evidence points to the slim progress that Blatch made in converting her fellow New Yorkers to her more progressive views.

34. I am of course not including in this discussion the so-called states' rights suffragists, led by Kate Gordon.

35. Dewey W. Grantham, *Southern Progressivism: The Reconciliation of Progress and Tradition* (Knoxville: University of Tennessee Press, 1983), xix, 10, 126. William A. Link, *The Paradox of Southern Progressivism, 1880–1930* (Chapel Hill: University of North Carolina Press, 1992), xi and passim.

sensus. Suffragism is one area in which southern women tried to storm the fortress of tradition. Understanding the ideological basis of southern suffragism, and its willingness (albeit with some suffragists being more willing than others) to jettison white monopoly, will place southern suffragism firmly in the vanguard of the southern progressive movement.

Southern antisuffragists wished to protect as long as possible the last remaining vestiges of "the world the slaveholders made." The patriarchy of the past, with its clearly defined race, gender, and class relations, provided a haven of security and stability in a changing and confusing world. The mythic world the antisuffragists desired, where everyone had a place and knew it, constituted a systematic ideology, and Kraditor erred to argue otherwise.[36] While the arguments the antisuffragists devised might indeed be contradictory at times, the theoretical underpinnings of that antisuffrage position were rock solid. Southern antisuffragists saw race, gender, and class relations as inseparably intertwined.

This discussion of antisuffrage ideology cannot be complete without some consideration of the generally ignored phenomenon of southern *black* antisuffragism. It must be treated separately however, since its ideological basis was wholly different from that of the white antisuffragists.

That African Americans in the South disagreed among themselves over the issue of woman suffrage should come as no surprise, although the subject remains uninvestigated to date. Those southern blacks who advocated the enfranchisement of women did so with two major principles in mind: first, women, as citizens, had the right to vote to protect their interests; and, second, black women could use the ballot in order to help their race. A group of black citizens in Atlanta, for example, pledged to "exert our righteous efforts until not only every eligible black man but EVERY ELIGIBLE BLACK WOMAN shall be wielding the ballot proudly in defense of our liberties and our homes." And black women formed suffrage organizations throughout the South, although their existence has often escaped notice by historians, who have generally looked only at sources generated by white suffragists.[37]

36. Kraditor, *Ideas,* 23.
37. Rosalyn Terborg-Penn, "Nineteenth-Century Black Women and Woman Suffrage," *Potomac Review* 7 (Spring–Summer 1977), 20; citizens quoted in

Black southerners, however, approached the question of woman suffrage cautiously, for they knew that open demands for black woman suffrage might unleash white fury on all southern blacks. The fear of reprisals, in an era when lynchings happened daily and the Ku Klux Klan rode nightly, caused many to stop and weigh the potential dangers of suffrage advocacy. In 1913, for example, the *Nashville Tennessean* reported that local blacks were "manifesting interest in a debate . . . between members of their race on the question of woman suffrage." The very fact that such a debate was noted in the white press could only have encouraged more caution in the black community. One black woman leader in Tennessee later insisted that even though woman suffrage was discussed and debated, blacks still undertook no organized suffrage work in the state.[38]

Fear of a white backlash to black suffragism produced not only caution but outright opposition to the suffrage movement from other southern blacks. North Carolina's Annie Blackwell, a black temperance leader, provides one example of opposition to woman suffrage based on concerns for the African American community as a whole. Blackwell reasoned that, should the Nineteenth Amendment be ratified, southern states would pass "grandmother" clauses designed to prevent black women from voting. Woman suffrage would effectively mean white woman suffrage. While such an outcome might be acceptable if white women could be counted on to vote in the interests of and in support of their black sisters, events in the recent past made it doubtful that white women would be the source of sisterly solidarity. White women had participated in lynchings, had encouraged the Wilmington race riot of 1898, and had campaigned for disfranchisement of blacks in 1900.[39]

Harry Gamble, *Federal Suffrage a Racial Question in the South* [privately printed pamphlet, 1918], 26, copy in Antisuffrage Literature, NAWSA Papers. See Terborg-Penn, "Nineteenth-Century Black Women," 19–21, for a discussion of the historical invisibility of black suffragists.

38. Taylor, *Tennessee*, 55–56. One can only speculate if Taylor, a white historian doing an interview in the 1950s, might have gotten a different response than a black interviewer doing an interview in the 1970s or the 1990s.

39. Only recently have historians begun to examine the role of white women in encouraging and supporting racial violence. See Glenda Elizabeth Gilmore, "When Woman Shall Have Entered Every Door of Usefulness: The

There was a second ideological position for southern black opposition to woman suffrage, one that closely reflected the conservative values of white antisuffragists. Some southern black men opposed the reform because of their adherence to the doctrine of separate spheres. "We want supper, our socks darned, buttons sewed on, children dressed, our tired brow and head rubbed. Therefore let us hear, not of sermons she must go and preach, [or] of conventions she must hold."[40] Southern blacks were not immune to the cult of true womanhood and the doctrine of the separate spheres, especially if they judged that their acceptance by the white community depended on their adoption of the values of the white community.

In sum, black opposition to woman suffrage in the South stemmed from concerns about race and gender. As was true for southern whites, southern blacks could not judge woman suffrage merely on its own merits. It could not be treated as a natural right or as simple justice. The potential impact on all African Americans in the South, not just women, had to be utmost in the minds of southern blacks. For many, their position on the suffrage issue was watchful waiting; for others, outright opposition.

It is important to note that these black antisuffragists, male and female, were never included in the organizational efforts to defeat woman suffrage in the southern states. White antisuffragists could not bring themselves to build an interracial movement, even when it would have been one dedicated to the protection of prescribed gender and race relations. Their racial views prevented them from incorporating black antisuffragists into their movement, an act that would have implied an unacceptable degree of social equality between the races.

In conclusion, southern antisuffrage rhetoric tells us much about those who espoused it. Southern white antisuffragists believed that

---

Double-Edged Feminism of Southern Black Women, 1892–1920" (paper presented at the Berkshire Conference on the History of Women, New Brunswick, N.J., June 1990), 13–14; Nancy MacLean, "White Women and Klan Violence in the 1920s: Agency, Complicity, and the Politics of Women's History," *Gender and History* 3 (Autumn 1991), 287–303; Kathleen M. Blee, *Women of the Klan: Racism and Gender in the 1920s* (Berkeley and Los Angeles: University of California Press, 1991).

40. *Star of Zion,* August 11, 1898, 4, quoted in Gilmore, "When Woman Shall Have Entered," 13.

any changes in the status quo would affect them most of all, as they stood at the peak of the social hierarchy created by their grandfathers. Therefore, the ideology they forged served to buttress contemporary class, race, and gender constructs. Having the most, they had the most to lose.

"Both in the Field, Each with a Plow"

Race and Gender in USDA Policy, 1907–1929

KATHLEEN C. HILTON

Progressive Era reformers promoted numerous strategies for melio-rating United States economic, social, and political ills. In the spirit of the times, United States Department of Agriculture administra-tors officially inaugurated, in 1907, one of the most prominent and durable public policy initiatives for revitalizing rural life. The USDA's Extension Service hired state directors and farm and home demon-stration agents and charged them with confronting rural economic and social crises.[1] Administrators in Washington, D.C., defined both the crises and acceptable solutions for this highly centralized program. Administrative structures, job descriptions, directives, and publications for agents and participants promulgated the orga-nizers' unwavering commitment to mutually exclusive male and

I wish to thank the Women's Research Institute of Virginia Polytechnic Insti-tute and State University, Blacksburg, Virginia, for partially funding this research; the archivists of Hampton University, Virginia State University, VPI&SU, and the National Archives for their research assistance; USDA Extension Service retirees and administrators who generously shared their experiences and files; and Mary Neth and Peggy Barlett for helpful comments on earlier drafts of this work.

1. On Extension Service as an initiative within the Progressive reform tradi-tion, see David Danbom, *The Resisted Revolution: Urban America and the Industrialization of Agriculture, 1900–1930* (Ames: Iowa State University Press, 1979); Pete Daniel, *Breaking the Land: The Transformation of Cotton, Tobacco, and Rice Cultures since 1880* (Urbana: University of Illinois Press, 1985); C. W. Warburton, *Interpretation of the Smith-Lever Act,* Circular No. 87, July 1928, 3–4, in Circular Letters, March 1908–June 1944, States Relations Service, Miscella-neous Records, United States Department of Agriculture, Records of the Federal Extension Service, RG 33, National Archives, hereinafter cited as NA. All cita-tions of Extension Service sources at the National Archives are from RG 33.

female economic roles. In spite of this apparent internal consistency, however, the program embodied assumptions about race and gender that subdivided the USDA's constituency. While gender had a deterministic impact on white women's work, it was race, rather than gender, that frequently defined black women's work.

Prescriptively and practically, southern women shared common experiences as female participants in this public policy initiative. Local USDA employees prescribed innovations which reflected the organizers' assumptions that men and women filled separate, unequal economic roles within the rural household. This practice simply reinforced most husbands' perceptions. In addition, Extension Service projects clearly modified rural women's labor patterns. Home demonstration work sometimes added tasks to women's daily routines; more frequently, participants learned new methods for accomplishing familiar duties. The program also created female networks that increased the visibility and status of domestic labors, affecting the context in which women worked.

However, "local agent" and "homemakers' clubs," the distinctive titles for black agents and female clubs, only hinted at ways in which race reconfigured the program for black women. Segregation and discrimination, which perpetuated race hierarchy in the South, made African American women vital assets within a minority community determined to flourish against daunting odds. The resultant program design and implementation reveal what rural women, black and white, shared by virtue of being female in a patriarchal society, as well as the ways that race established disparate boundaries for being female.[2] Both revelations are critical to understanding the history of black women who remained in the rural South and participated in Progressive Era reform initiatives.

Unlike many of their contemporaries, Extension Service administrators paid little attention to age in formulating policies. Seaman A. Knapp, the first director of the Office of Extension Work South, found adult farmers highly resistant to scientific agriculture (his

2. Although most data cited are for Virginia, and some of the conclusions remain appropriately tentative, this is much broader than a case study of one state. All state directors, county agents, and specialists received directives from the USDA offices in Washington, D.C., used identical report forms, and were held accountable for conducting the program according to established guidelines. In addition, several sources report data from all southern states, and none cite Virginia as exceptional.

antidote to the boll weevil) and so turned to their sons in desperation in 1907. Because Knapp and his successors had no reason to presume that farmers' wives would be any more receptive to innovation, the agency initially approached girls. According to the USDA plan, female work began in a girl's one-tenth-acre garden plot, progressed into the kitchen, and ultimately interested the mother. Ella G. Agnew and Marie Cromer, the first home demonstration agents, began conducting girls' work in Virginia and South Carolina in 1910. Black supervising teachers, supported by the Jeanes Fund, had already undertaken comparable work in 1906; but Lizzie A. Jenkins, the first African American woman to organize work with black girls and women in Virginia under USDA auspices, received her appointment in May 1913. Extension Service personnel deliberately organized separate clubs for youths, but demonstrated uncharacteristic respect for black and white adolescents as economic producers who could help solve rural problems.[3] Other reformers guided youth toward age-specific tasks that eliminated interaction with the adult world of work. Instead, these club organizers recognized young people for outstanding yields, regardless

3. "Report of the Secretary," in *Annual Reports of the Department of Agriculture for the Year Ending June 30, 1910* (Washington, D.C.: Government Printing Office, 1911), 82–83; *Annual Reports of the Department of Agriculture for the Year Ending June 30, 1916* (Washington, D.C.: Government Printing Office, 1917), 314–15; Franklin M. Reck, *The 4-H Story* (Chicago: National Committee on Boys and Girls Club Work, 1951); *Annual Report, Farmer's Co-Operative Demonstration Work for 1914* (Blacksburg: Virginia Polytechnic Institute, in Co-Operation with USDA, 1915), 9; Arthur D. Wright, "The Jeanes Fund and the Jeanes Teachers," reprinted from *Annual Report of the John F. Slater Fund,* for the year ended June 30, 1936, 5–6, Extension Department Collection, Hampton Archives, Hampton University, Hampton, Va., hereinafter cited as HA; J. B. Pierce, "Brief History of Home Demonstration Work in Virginia, 1907–1914 Inclusive," April 14, 1938, typescript in personal Extension Service files of Ann Frame, Blacksburg, Va.; Thelma Hewlett, "Lizzie A. Jenkins," and John Baptist Pierce folder, both in box 1, RG 26, University Archives and Special Collections, Newman Library, Virginia Polytechnic Institute and State University, Blacksburg, Va., hereinafter cited as VPI&SU. Most Progressive Era initiatives, including compulsory high school attendance, effectively relegated adolescents to age-segregated settings that were incompatible with assuming adult obligations. See Joseph Kett, *Rites of Passage: Adolescence in America, 1790 to the Present* (New York: Basic Books, 1977); Kathleen C. Hilton, "Growing Up Female: Girlhood Experiences and Social Feminism, 1890–1929" (Ph.D. diss., Carnegie Mellon University, 1987).

of age. Furthermore, they presumed adults would adopt the practices modeled by corn and canning club members. This flexibility with regard to age accentuates the Extension Service's steadfast reluctance to cross gender and race lines.

Until 1921 the Office of Extension Work South remained a separate administrative unit in which program formulation reflected distinctive patterns of race relations and gender roles.[4] Under the auspices of the Smith-Lever Act of 1914, a centralized administrative bureaucracy disseminated guidelines and held state directors accountable for the activities of specialists and male and female demonstration agents who were jointly hired and funded. The Office of Extension Work South, however, added race hierarchy to the national pattern of gender hierarchy and conducted three separate programs, one for each of its constituencies: white males, white females, and blacks. Like the Office of Extension Work North and West, the southern office intended the national economy and rural social fabric to be the ultimate beneficiaries of all categories of work, but its conceptualization of the populations to be served distinguished southern work from that carried on elsewhere.

Federal Extension Service administrators articulated the USDA's fundamentally conservative public policy goals in prescriptive national guidelines that described farming and homemaking as discrete occupations coinciding with public and private realms of activity. Provisions of the Smith-Lever Act, which authorized nationwide funding after 1914, permanently divided men's and women's programs. Both before and after 1914, when administrative channels linked specific USDA projects to land-grant college departments of agriculture or home economics, the Office of Extension Work South deliberately chose a gender-segregated pattern for the work. The choice was not an unanticipated by-product of bureaucratic logic or local academic politics.[5] Methods and tasks consistently reflected the USDA's determination to revolutionize agriculture but maintain male control of gender relations within rural society.

4. Secretary Wallace to Extension Service directors, Circular No. 574, September 20, 1921, Circular Letters, March 1908–June 1944, States Relations Service, Miscellaneous Records, NA.

5. See Margaret W. Rossiter, *Women Scientists in America: Struggles and Strategies to 1940* (Baltimore: Johns Hopkins University Press, 1982), chap. 3, especially 65–70.

For black and white women, the USDA's restrictive methods differed significantly from its expansive approach to men. Farm demonstration agents related to men as constituents in need of scientifically based agricultural practices to generate larger incomes. Agents demonstrated for both black and white farmers the economic benefits of crop rotation, diversification, and mechanization. The USDA used bank deposits, farm implements or buildings added, yields per acre, and earned cash to measure farmers' success. Agents also encouraged innovative collective purchasing and marketing strategies to increase farmers' economic leverage within regional and national markets.[6] Departmental goals for rural females were decidedly less ambitious.

Bradford Knapp, who replaced his father as head of the southern extension work office in 1911, consistently mandated an exclusively task-centered approach to all women's work. Even within the safety of the kitchen, prescriptive guidelines stressed this pattern. An extension circular issued in 1928 explained: "The thing to do is to help the housewife to learn how to can and preserve vegetables and fruits, to feed her family better, to clothe herself more tastefully or economically. If she learns the scientific principles that govern successful canning, well and good, but the essential thing is for her to learn to do the job." Although demonstration guidelines in general, and directives for work with black farmers in particular, emphasized practical results, only guidelines for working with women carried explicit injunctions against "useless" meetings and discussions of scientific bases for procedures for women's work.[7]

White agents who deviated from Knapp's prescriptive guidelines risked sharp rebukes. One state director, so intent on initiating canning club work that he permitted a male agent to give instructions, received an irate letter reminding him that men could not do women's work. The reverse was, predictably, too inconceiv-

6. John B. Pierce, supervisor of black demonstration work in Virginia from 1909 until his death in 1942, was credited with spreading "a clearer insight into farming as a business rather than as a mere occupation." William A. Aery, "A Hampton Agricultural Missionary: J. B. Pierce," Student Records, HA.

7. Warburton, *Interpretation of the Smith-Lever Act,* 9. O. B. Martin to E. Parrott, September 15, 1915, South Carolina Extension Service Correspondence, NA, reveals the resistance of the Washington, D.C., officials to an emphasis on regular gathering.

able to have become an issue. Women presented different problems. Knapp adamantly insisted that only the Department of Agriculture could decide which tasks were appropriate for women and angrily accused some female agents of jeopardizing the work in 1919. He claimed they had "gone too far . . . [from] . . . home industries within the sphere of women's proper influence on the farm."[8]

A few home demonstration agents established women's market garden clubs without crossing prescribed boundaries. These small groups were deemed acceptable because they facilitated a woman's supplemental economic role within the rural household. Agents in charge of club work with white youths expressed satisfaction with their efforts to inculcate appropriate economic behavior at an early age. The elder Knapp reported: "Corn-club work has given many boys a new view of agriculture as a profession. Canning and poultry clubs have been established for the girls, so that . . . they may have some means of making money which, being girls, they will use in the improvement of their homes." The Department of Agriculture's relentless preoccupation with rural women's "affairs within and about the home" emerged, in part, from fears that, by teaching anything other than isolated tasks, "home economics extension work might very seriously create a discontented home." Showing women how to improve family diets and living quarters would, in contrast, make rural life more attractive to an adequate base of capable, scientific farmers.[9]

8. O. B. Martin to L. N. Duncan, September 29, 1913, Alabama Extension Service Correspondence, NA; Bradford Knapp, "Home Demonstration Work in Peril," Circular No. 287, July 11, 1919, NA. On the topic of men doing women's work, see Martin to All Agents, Circular No. 67, January 18, 1915, NA. Others expressed concerns on the topic as well: "Women's Institutes in North Carolina," *Journal of Home Economics* 1 (April 1909): 162; M. Creswell to L. P. Dowdle, April 17, 1918, Georgia Extension Service Correspondence, NA.

9. Quoted in a summary of S. A. Knapp's remarks, in William A. Aery, "The Hampton Farmers' Conference for 1911," typescript in Extension Department Collection, HA; B. Knapp to W. W. Long, July 16, 1914, South Carolina Extension Service Correspondence, NA; "Woman's Part in Farm Life," *Hampton Bulletin* 9 (April 1913): 14. This remained an overriding concern of the department as well as various correspondents. Secretary of Agriculture David E. Houston to Mr. Steiner, November 19, 1913, Rural Organization Service Correspondence, RG 16, NA; Secretary of Agriculture Henry C. Wallace to Herbert Myrick, December 15, 1923, Bureau of Home Economics, RG 16, NA; "Report

Home demonstration agents, the chief source of USDA mandates on acceptable activities for most women, prescribed similar food-preparation and housekeeping tasks for both black and white females between 1907 and 1929. The first projects for girls required them to grow tomato plants and then can the produce for home consumption. Agents also encouraged planting year-round vegetable gardens, canning a variety of vegetables and meats, preserving fruits, making bread, and raising poultry.[10]

Some prescribed tasks took women away from the garden and the stove. Installing window screens, building sanitary privies, and constructing home water systems all fell within women's purview according to USDA guidelines. Agents also promoted yard beautification and household furniture arrangements that reflected home economists' scientifically derived ideals. Females were urged to undertake these projects to improve family health and increase the aesthetic pleasures of rural life for household members. All program activities reminded white participants that the separate spheres of white men and women were uncontestable. Race was the only factor powerful enough to attenuate the boundaries.[11]

The department stopped short of prescribing gender-neutral work roles for black men and women but at least tacitly approved of practices condemned in white work. One anecdote describing a black farmer's response to President Woodrow Wilson's wartime appeal for increased food production clearly reveals the separate standard. The farmer in question was plowing with a mule when the proclamation was read to him. According to the reporting agent, about ten days later he "had turned the mule over to his wife

---

of the Secretary," in *Annual Reports of the Department of Agriculture for the Year Ending June 30, 1914* (Washington, D.C.: Government Printing Office, 1915), 10–11; Report of 1923 Hampton Farmers' Conference, 7, Extension Department Collection, HA.

10. Poultry raising seems to have been an area in which gender lines mattered far less than in most farm tasks. Some circulars explained why it was a good task for women and children, but others gave directions for men. Of the nineteen projects conducted within the state of Virginia in 1922 and 1923, the poultry project was the only one to have both male and female specialists. John R. Hutcheson, "Annual Report of the Director of Extension Work in Virginia," June 1923, Burruss Papers, VPI&SU.

11. Program schedules for short courses conducted by Extension Service and correspondence between men and women at the upper levels of administration consistently reveal dichotomous assumptions.

and had bought a horse for himself, and they were both in the field, each with a plow, and working in earnest."[12] This farm couple's actions indicate the existence of alternative distributions of rural work. More instructively, the agent's recounting the incident as a "success story" suggests that African American agents and farm families frequently crossed gender lines without interference from USDA administrators. John B. Pierce, who supervised black work in several states, knew better than to report anything USDA administrators did not want to hear.

In practice, black and white Extension Service agents translated the USDA's prescriptive guidelines into programs that altered female labor patterns. Crop diversification and mechanization undoubtedly changed the rhythm of farm life and altered tasks performed by wives and daughters of both races who worked in the fields,[13] but Extension Service sources document the impact of home demonstration projects on "women's work" as they defined it. Shifts occurred gradually and unevenly, making it difficult to do more than identify dominant trends in new work roles, innovative approaches to traditional tasks, and the changing environment in which women labored.[14] Data clearly suggest, however, that USDA efforts to make the South self-sufficient in food reached growing numbers of white and black women and girls.

White girls and women were much more likely to receive instruction in a club setting, but canning and poultry raising, two prominent home demonstration projects, added new tasks to participants' daily routines regardless of race. Pierce reported that farm wives had shifted from their custom of preserving fruit to

12. George J. Davis to George P. Phenix, December 31, 1917, Phenix Papers, HA.

13. One change involved the switch from growing Spanish peanuts, which women and children had to shake with their hands to harvest, to runner or bunch peanuts. In 1918, 90 percent of the farmers in Prince George County grew Spanish peanuts; by 1953 over 95 percent grew those more easily harvested. W. H. George, "History of Extension Work in Prince George County, 1918 to 1953," Advisory Board Materials, Virginia State University Extension Office files, Virginia State University, Petersburg, hereinafter cited as VSUEO.

14. As one indication of how slowly some changes occurred, Hattie P. West noted, in her summary of "Extension Work in Nansemond County, 1947–1963," p. 5, Advisory Board Materials, VSUEO, that by 1963 farm wives no longer cooked cabbage a half-day over wood stoves as they had when she began serving the county in 1947.

canning, saving money, time, and fruit that was formerly wasted. Women may or may not have shared his delight that "some canning is done every day without interferring [sic], but very little, with the other duties of the home." Enthusiastic about their ability to fit one more task into the day or not, both the numbers of females involved and their output grew. In Virginia, 124 black women and girls canned 8,306 quarts of fruit in 1911; 1,000 canned 19,000 quarts of fruits and vegetables in 1915. The following year local district agent Lizzie Jenkins reported that longtime participants continued to value help while others "who have been standing out against the work" were gradually choosing to become involved.[15]

Ella Agnew and her agents reported a similar expansion of canning club work among white girls in Virginia. The state's 495 enrolled members canned 44,912 containers in 1912; 1,149 produced almost 100,000 containers in 1915. Agents demonstrated improved methods as they learned them, but the primary change in women's work patterns came as farm wives and daughters chose to add raising vegetable gardens and canning the produce to their repertoire of tasks, thereby introducing year-round supplies of several vegetables to family menus.[16]

Care of poultry flocks, the other major addition to women's work roles, was actually presented as a task appropriate for either males or females; but many women assumed responsibility for selecting and breeding birds. Even for farm wives who had previously tended flocks, demonstration methods significantly altered the nature of the process. Five years after black agents introduced the work, one of the Hampton leaflets contained the following lament: "As one travels through the country one cannot help being impressed by the scarcity of pure-bred poultry. The majority of farmers . . . are apparently more anxious that the birds shall have different colors and shapes, than that they shall lay eggs." The remainder of the leaflet and much of an agent's time was spent teaching farm family members to improve their flocks and results. White agents also reported the culling practices of farmers and

15. John B. Pierce, 1911 Annual Report to Hollis B. Frissell, Frissell Correspondence, HA; Pierce, *Southern Workman*, February 1915; Lizzie Jenkins, 1916 Annual Report and 1917 Annual Report, Extension Department Collection, HA.

16. Ella G. Agnew, *Hand Book for the Use of County Agents' Home Demonstration Work in Virginia*, July 1916, Bulletin No. 7, p. 15, VPI&SU.

their wives who discarded valuable fowl and saved colorful hens in the 1920s. Although their previous practices must have been functional, albeit disconcerting to the agents, women and girls who followed agents' instructions were pleased with their new poultry-tending skills and markedly increased egg supply.[17]

Poultry record-keeping would have been another new task had women fully complied with departmental guidelines. To agents' dismay, figures beyond flock size were difficult to establish. In 1924 the white agent in charge of Virginia poultry work noted that a few women had begun to keep records. Agent Lizzie Jenkins explained that because black women exchanged the eggs and poultry for groceries and dry goods and did not receive any money for the transactions, record keeping seemed burdensome. As a new task, however, poultry work was financially significant even to those who kept no records. Jenkins recounted her conversation with a York County farmer's wife. "[She] told me that the family cow died during the past winter. Since then she had raised and sold enough chickens to buy another cow."[18]

Canning and poultry projects added novel tasks, but most home demonstration work taught women new methods for accomplishing familiar duties within their homes. Agents who conducted cooking demonstrations insisted on cleanliness and exact measurements regardless of the food being prepared. One woman remarked that since observing a bread-making demonstration, "I have not had my hands in my bread bowl. I just feel that the old method is everything but sanitary."[19]

17. Pierce, 1911 Annual Report to Frissell; Gammach, "Poultry Raising in the South," *Hampton Leaflets,* vol. 7, no. 6, p. 4; Lizzie Jenkins, "Home Makers' Clubs," *Hampton Leaflets,* vol. 7, no. 8, p. 8; Jenkins, 1917 Annual Report, Extension Department Collection, HA; Extracts from County Agents' Reports, July–August 1923, and April–May 1924, Burruss Papers.

18. Jenkins, 1916 Annual Report and 1917 Annual Report, Extension Department Collection, HA. The Poultry Husbandry Department head reported that a few white ladies were keeping records. Virginia Annual Report, 1924, 7, Burruss Papers. Ironically, the USDA itself worked to prevent any shift in women's attitude about their economic dependence; however, farm wives' resistance is probably more adequately explained as added evidence of women's emphasis on exchange and reciprocity, noted by Nancy Grey Osterud, *Bonds of Community: The Lives of Farm Women in Nineteenth-Century New York* (Ithaca: Cornell University Press, 1991), especially 142 and chap. 9.

19. Extracts from County Agents' Reports, April–May 1924, Burruss Papers.

Labor-saving devices similarly altered women's work patterns. Both black and white agents demonstrated the construction of fireless cookers, a heated stone placed in an insulated container, but economic class influenced the way the proud owners used the equipment. African American women who owned one could cook a hot dinner while they worked in the fields. Although this was a welcome change, the white James City agent's report suggests the greater relative advantages that the device had for women who could afford not to do field work. She recounted a white woman's enthusiastic praise. "My fireless cooker is splendid. . . . Why didn't you make me make one when you first came to the county. Think of the time I have lost. I made my little girl a dress yesterday while my chicken and vegetables cooked themselves."[20] Most black women had to turn to their sewing after a day in the fields. The differing benefits are substantial, and they underscore the fact that a broad socioeconomic spectrum of rural women adopted practices the agents recommended and found them helpful.

Finally, home demonstration projects altered the material and social context in which black and white rural women worked. Thousands of women improved physical conditions as they built sanitary privies, screened windows, and placed flytraps in their family homes.[21] The very presence of women who had achieved expert status and uncommon visibility within the rural South as

Jenkins reported purchases of measuring cups and similarly altered work patterns in her 12th Annual Report, 1923, and 13th Annual Report, 1924, Burruss Papers. J. B. Pierce also included the changes in his "Brief History." White specialists and agents insisted on precision with girls' club members, but they introduced adult women who joined home demonstration clubs to more convenient kitchen arrangements. Women who were suddenly finding themselves without servants valued step-saving floor plans. Edith A. Roberts, "Kitchens," *Bulletin*, No. 49, Virginia A & M College and Polytechnic Institute, February, 1919, VPI&SU.

20. I. O. Schaub, *Agricultural Extension Work: A Brief History*, Extension Circular No. 377 (Raleigh: North Carolina Agricultural Extension Service, 1953), 28; Extracts from County Agents' Reports, April–May 1924, Burruss Papers. Most annual reports mention demonstrations of the cookers and give numbers constructed.

21. Jenkins reported 224 barns built and 1,182 outhouses as "Miscellaneous" home improvements, 1917 Annual Report. Black and white reports both listed these additions consistently; for parallel years, see Hutcheson, "Annual Report for 1922–23," 23, Burruss Papers, and Report of 1923 Hampton Farmers' Conference, 2, Extension Department Collection, HA.

agents also modified the social environment in which young women learned housekeeping tasks. Home demonstration agents served as forceful role models, opening new horizons for girls in canning and homemakers' clubs. Many club members attended school, earned home economics degrees, and went on to become agents themselves. For white girls, though not for blacks, this route sometimes led to positions as specialists or state administrators. Whether the young women elected to pursue careers or not, as club members, they were provided with new links to other females. Some agents with whom they came in contact belonged to regional and national women's organizations, potentially broadening all participants' support networks.[22]

Involvement in demonstration work also altered adult women's sense of their importance outside their own homes. County and state fairs, usually but not always segregated, provided public forums for displaying women's accomplishments. Many rural women regarded government initiatives suspiciously, but, once involved, some interpreted federal attention as tangible evidence of the significance of their labor. Jenkins reported, "Two old women, exslaves, told of their joy to know that the government was considering Negro women and girls of sufficient importance to send an agent among them." Displaying Food Administration window cards gave others a similar sense of pride.[23]

Demonstration projects lent added status to women's work, but the USDA's conservative goals precluded radical shifts in women's actual leverage. In both black and white households, dominant patterns of family financial resource allocation gave priority to farm equipment rather than to household renovations. Getting running water into the kitchen or purchasing electrical appliances, both of which would have significantly altered the physical context in which they worked, remained major accomplishments for rural women.[24] Floyd Stokes, a farmer from Gloucester County, reported

22. M. M. Davis to J. D. Hutcheson, "Annual Report of White Home Demonstration Work, 1922," Burruss Papers, mentions a district agent's attendance at an American Country Life Association meeting in New York. Her visit to the State Federation of Women's Clubs was a more typical kind of affiliation for agents. Ella Agnew and Lizzie Jenkins belonged to other organizations as well.

23. Jenkins, 1917 Annual Report.

24. O. B. Martin, *A Decade of Negro Extension Work, 1914–1924*, Miscella-

purchasing "sheds for housing the farm tools when not in use" and had spent about forty-five hundred dollars to purchase forty acres of land since 1906. After twenty years of marriage and seventeen years of successful farming, he began to remodel his house in 1923. The Stokeses had spent part of that year's two thousand dollar net income on electric lighting, and he planned to install a water system the following year. The Stokeses were actually ahead of most Virginians on both counts. In adverse circumstances, when black women had no access to cash and men refused to spend family funds on household improvements, Jenkins reportedly purchased window screens, which she and farm wives considered important.[25]

Because home demonstration projects concentrated on gender-defined roles, the program offered similar kinds of information to all rural women; however, the data reveal significant class- and race-based contrasts. For all but the poorest white participants, agents stressed joining formal women's organizations and acquiring expert status through scientific approaches to housekeeping, often using urban norms as a touchstone. Geography and region, rather than class, largely determined a white female's access to demonstration agents; however, in marked contrast to patterns in other regions, once agents in Virginia had made a contact, they conscientiously tried to meet the individual's needs.[26] For young

---

neous Circular No. 72 (Washington, D.C.: Government Printing Office, 1926), 17–18; Pierce, 1916 and 1918 Annual Reports, and Report of George J. Davis, January 1919, both in Extension Department Collection, HA; "Outstanding Farm Family" narratives, VSUEO. In 1915, 5 percent of farm homes in the state had running water, and by 1939 the figure had reached only 20 percent. Fewer than one thousand rural Virginia homes had electricity in 1910; seventy thousand did in 1938. J. R. Hutcheson, *Extension Work in Virginia, 1907–1940: A Brief History* (Blacksburg, Va.: Alpha Gamma Chapter of Epsilon Sigma Phi, 1941), 27.

25. Charles Elliott, interview by author, Lynchburg, Va., March 8, 1990, tape in possession of author.

26. T. O. Sandy, director of Extension Work for Virginia, reported that it was difficult to introduce demonstration work in areas where farmers made a comfortable living from naturally rich soil. Sandy to B. Knapp, Burkeville, Va., June 12, 1911, Virginia Extension Service Correspondence, NA. Class surfaced as a factor in men's work, usually either as complaints that agents were ignoring the poorer farmers or as agents' reports that they were serving all classes. Knapp to Sandy, March 8, 1913; Jesse M. Jones, March 15, 1915, both in

white women who worked in the fields, sometimes that meant teaching them to read and write, ostensibly so they could complete report forms properly. Participation in home demonstration projects gave women from more prosperous households access to cash income from prize money or profits on fresh and canned goods not needed for home consumption. Personal income, at least potentially, increased women's independence in making household decisions; some enthusiastically took advantage of the change.

The context in which African American farm wives performed their domestic tasks also changed, but the new reality differed from that of the white farm wives because white and black families rarely shared a common starting point. A high proportion of black females initially came in contact with agents as their families worked to escape the vicious economic cycles associated with tenantry. Better farming practices permitted the couples to purchase land. Then, gradually, windowpanes, whitewashed homes, clean kitchens, and sewing skills radically altered the physical surroundings in which these homemakers provided for their families.[27]

In her annual report for 1924, Jenkins listed physical home improvements and then vigorously defended them in a tone that makes the diverging standards of progress between black and white participants unmistakable.

> There may be persons who do not consider that the 7 wash-tubs
> and 12 ordinary smoothing irons reported should be classed under

---

Virginia Extension Service Correspondence, NA; Pierce, 1916 and 1917 Annual Reports. Class rarely emerged as an issue for women agents in the South. Even the incongruously class-conscious comments of Specialist in Home Economics Lulu Walker reveal the broad range of rural women served by female agents (Report, December 1922, Burruss Papers). The USDA was primarily concerned that they have a "rural" viewpoint and not be likely to threaten the status quo of gender relations within the rural community. On another region, see Joan Jensen, "Canning Comes to New Mexico: Women and the Agricultural Extension Service, 1914–1919," *New Mexico Historical Review* 57, no. 4 (1982): 361–86, and Mary C. Neth, *Preserving the Family Farm: Gender, Community, and the Foundations of Modern Agribusiness, 1900–1940* (forthcoming).

27. Pierce, 1916 Annual Report, and Jenkins, 1917 Annual Report; Report of 1923 Hampton Farmers' Conference, p. 2, Conferences RG, HA; Agnew, "Summary of Home Demonstration Work Done in Virginia for the Year Ending December 30, 1915," RG 25, and "Extension Work in Virginia in 1926," RG 26, VPI&SU.

labor-savers. They may not be such, strictly speaking, but they are certainly time savers, because in many homes . . . time must be consumed in going sometimes more than half a mile to borrow tubs or irons. We feel that it is absolutely necessary to acquaint people with the ownership of the simple equipment before they are ready to spend money on higher-priced things.

Because of the needs of those she served, the "wood and water lady," as Jenkins was known to blacks throughout Virginia, spent most of her time helping women perform basic tasks with less wear and tear on themselves.[28]

Race mildly altered prescriptive patterns and the implementation of comparable projects, but minimal federal and state commitment to black work permitted the emergence of distinctive programs marked primarily by the diverging meanings that participants assigned to gender roles. Within the white program, gender clearly functioned as a divisive category. Even when no female agent was available, administrators refused to approve of a white male agent entering the female sphere. In *A Decade of Negro Extension Work, 1914–1924,* O. B. Martin, who had personally rebuked white agents, excused this very practice. He attributed violated gender lines in adult work to economic constraints faced by the African American community. Since few counties could afford both men and women agents, "the men agents do more home work and the women agents more farm work."[29]

White-written accounts like Martin's, however, invariably couched such irregularities in reassuring terms of progress toward white norms. Martin happily noted that "in field-crop activities the enrollment of negro girls has been very small." He applauded this "disposition for the boy to do the farming and the girl the home making" and predicted that more agents would ensure adult conformity to gender-specific work patterns as well.[30] However, the participants whom the Office of Extension Work South defined as "Negro" saw gender as a less divisive attribute than race.

28. Jenkins, 13th Annual Report; clipping from *Petersburg Journal and Guide,* June 2, 1945, in Jenkins's Student Records, HA; T. W. Allen, "High Lights in Fifteen Years of Extension Work in King and Queen County" (talk presented at State Advisory Board Meeting, September 7, 1950), mimeograph in Advisory Board Materials, VSUEO.
29. Martin, "A Decade of Negro Extension Work," 7, n. 11.
30. Ibid., 23.

For black agents and rural farm families, gender served as one of several meaningful categories within the context of cohesive family and community units.[31] In marked contrast to white patterns, it seems that black agents readily acknowledged the vital contributions of women to the economic survival of rural black families. While less dramatic than the World War I "success story" about the wife plowing with the mule, J. B. Pierce's annual report for 1915 included a revealing comment from agent J. F. Wilson about his work in Charlotte County. "A few days ago a demonstrator's wife told me that before we began demonstration work with them, they were making not more than a peck of peas per year. This year they made 10 bushels." Although Wilson and Pierce considered increased production of cowpeas the salient point of this exchange, both the wife's awareness and the agent's willingness to cite her as an authority are remarkable. During the war another agent noted, "Wives and daughters will never get the credit they have earned in the field . . . they came forward like men."[32]

These attitudes flowed naturally from assumptions shared by Virginia's black community leaders. Hampton Institute sponsored a number of extension programs and trained students to be of service to their communities. Pierce, Jenkins, and many of the agents they supervised had gone to Hampton to obtain preparation for offering needed assistance. Launching to Rescue, the motto of Jenkins's class, suggests the motivating force behind black farm

31. Cynthia Neverdon-Morton, *Afro-American Women of the South and the Advancement of the Race, 1895–1925* (Knoxville: University of Tennessee Press, 1989), assesses the separate women's sessions held at Hampton Farmers' Conferences as evidence of an "invisible wall assumed to exist between men's and women's duties" which "kept the two groups from working together," 113. While structures mattered, the "wall" was much more easily crossed by black agents than by white Extension Service agents in the South.

32. J. B. Pierce, Annual Report, 1915, and George J. Davis, Report to Dr. James E. Gregg, January 20, 1919, both in Extension Department Collection, HA. Nancy Grey Osterud, "'She Helped Me Hay It as Good as a Man': Relations among Women and Men in an Agricultural Community," in *"To Toil the Livelong Day": America's Women at Work, 1780–1980,* ed. Carol Groneman and Mary Beth Norton (Ithaca: Cornell University Press, 1987), 87–97, presented evidence of a similar reference from a New York farmer; but I have found nothing comparable from white males connected with the Extension Service. One midwestern state 4-H Club director dismissed girls' ability to win prizes during the war as a phenomenon attributable to boys' responsibilities for men's work.

and home demonstration work. These agents' "rural uplift" efforts centered on the welfare of the African American community; race, rather than gender, supplied the primary focal point.[33]

Black organizations institutionalized workers' community centered approach. The Hampton Farmers' Conference gathered men and women annually beginning in 1897. Virginia county farmers' organizations, which included women and children, actually outnumbered men's organizations. In 1917 the 49 black farmers' clubs had a membership of 785, and 225 community farmers' clubs enrolled 4,225 men, women, and children.[34]

In 1926 Pierce, Jenkins, and other extension leaders organized the Negro State Agricultural Board of Virginia as a forum for coordinating USDA Extension Service programs. Each county with either a male or female black extension agent formed a board "to assist the Extension Worker in developing and carrying out a program of Agriculture and Home Making that will benefit all of the people in the county." The constitution and bylaws specified that women be members of each county board and that each county send one farmer, one farm woman, and the local male or female agent as delegates to State Advisory Board meetings. The board established a competitive Live at Home Program with a family-centered orientation that encouraged individual farmers to give gender secondary status as an organizing principle.[35]

Extension Service agents also benefited from existing commu-

33. H. B. Frissell, principal, "Address at Unveiling of Class Motto," January 1, 1902, reprinted in *Class Souvenir Book,* Hampton Institute; Neverdon-Morton, *Afro-American Women of the South,* 31–32; L. A. Jenkins to scholarship donors, February 2, 1900, and May 15, 1902, Student Records; J. B. Pierce, Script of Address at General Assembly, December 7, 1923, Student Records— all in HA. Elsa Barkley Brown has offered *womanism* as a useful term to describe women's simultaneous consciousness of race, sex, and class in their political activity. "Womanist Consciousness: Maggie Lena Walker and the Independent Order of Saint Luke," *Signs* 14, no. 3 (Spring 1989): 610–33. The rural black community's approach to work roles reflects this orientation. Program, Annual Hampton Farmers' Conference, June 28 and 29, 1927, HA; Laura R. Daly, "A Happy Helper for Rural Homes in Virginia," *Alumni Journal* (Hampton Institute), July 1932, 7–8.

34. J. B. Pierce, 1917 Annual Report, Extension Department Collection, HA.

35. Blanche D. Harrison, "The Negro State Advisory Board (An Evaluation)" (talk presented at Negro State Advisory Board of Virginia Conference, 1956), original typescript in possession of Mrs. Frank Hart, Richmond, Va.

nity institutions. Religion, which kept white home demonstration work out of some counties, united African American communities and muted the significance of gender as a category. Extension Service agents seem to have taken the initiative in convincing rural pastors that collaboration would be beneficial. Once persuaded, ministers preached on the importance of farm and home demonstration work and offered their congregations as captive audiences. Lizzie Jenkins reported that one minister insisted that she speak before his sermon, "while the people were fresh." On another occasion she was taken to a funeral that lasted so long she left to make other calls. Before the mourners dispersed, however, the minister sent for her. She returned and talked to an audience of three hundred.[36] Extension workers realized that a minister's approbation helped them gain credibility within rural communities; ministers, in turn, valued the contributions of extension agents to improved rural conditions.

Within the three-tiered program of the Office of Extension Work South, participation in home demonstration work was a distinctive experience for Jenkins and the agents she supervised. Administratively, black agents constituted a "district" within each state. In Virginia, after Extension Service headquarters relocated from Burkeville to Virginia Polytechnic Institute, the land-grant college in Blacksburg, J. B. Pierce reported directly to state director J. D. Eggleston rather than to the Office of Extension Work South in Washington, D.C. After some discussion, however, officials in Washington and Eggleston apparently decided that Lizzie Jenkins should report to Pierce, not to Ella Agnew, who had assumed responsibility for white home demonstration work in the state.[37]

Jenkins, in the most privileged of black female positions, received a lower salary than white agents, covered much larger territories throughout her career, and had difficulty gaining access to resources. A series of letters documents Jenkins's efforts to obtain franking privileges, which were readily available to white agents.

36. Ayres, "Report of 1912 Negro Farmers' Conference," Conferences RG; Jenkins, 1916 Annual Report; Jenkins, 1917 Annual Report; Report of R. E. F. Washington, Charles City County, 1917; J. L. B. Buck, "Report of the Director of Extension Work to the Principal," 1923—all in Extension Department Collection, HA.

37. J. D. Eggleston to Jesse M. Jones, August 11, 1915, and Jones to Eggleston, August 16, 1915, both in Virginia Extension Service Correspondence, NA.

She was actively excluded from meetings of state home demonstration leaders. Even when J. D. Eggleston, as state director, lobbied for Jenkins's attendance at a meeting of home demonstration administrators, department officials in Washington, D.C., refused to permit it.[38]

Racism explains most of the discrimination by state and national officials; sexism diminished Jenkins's leverage within the black program. In 1920 W. B. Mercier from the Washington office and J. B. Pierce exchanged letters about an upcoming meeting. Mercier claimed, "I was under the impression that there were no leaders of [women's] work in your group of states." Pierce's reply made no mention of Jenkins or any other women who should attend. Given Jenkins's heavy work load, Pierce's intervention a few years later probably cost her even more than his previous silence. Hampton officials supported her request for another female agent until Pierce said she did not need one.[39] White state home demonstration agents could appeal directly to the Washington, D.C., administrators in charge of their work. Lizzie Jenkins, however, had no direct recourse to other women, because within the organizational structure, she and her agents were categorized as blacks rather than females.

Administrators' obsession with gender-appropriate tasks and separate spheres notwithstanding, race and gender hierarchies both forcefully shaped the directives for revitalizing rural life that emanated from USDA Extension Service offices between 1907 and 1929. Gender served as the preeminently critical factor in the implementation of this public policy initiative, but only among white females and males. Federal and state administrators and black agents themselves adopted a much more flexible posture toward

38. J. M. Jones to J. D. Eggleston, July 1, 1915; Eggleston to C. K. Graham, Hampton, July 26, 1915; M. V. H., general assistant, to Jenkins, May 29, 1914; Eggleston to B. Knapp, November 24, 1915; Knapp to O. B. Martin, December 1, 1915; Martin to Eggleston, December 4, 1915—all ibid.

39. W. B. Mercier to J. B. Pierce, March 31, 1920, ibid.; Neverdon-Morton, *Afro-American Women of the South,* 119, suggests that the refusal came from white female administrators. Actually, J. L. B. Buck, director of extension programs for Hampton relayed Jenkins's request to Gregg, principal, but later penciled in a marginal comment "Please Disregard this—Mr. Pierce thinks it inadvisable." Report of Mr. Buck to Gregg, 1925–26, Extension and Demonstration folder, Extension Department Collection, HA.

discrete gender roles among rural blacks. Benign neglect, the most lavishly generous label one could assign to official attitudes toward the black program, tended to preserve the status quo in southern race relations and often compounded rural black women's hardships. Few women, for example, would have vied for an opportunity to plow with a mule, unless the alternative was to plow without one.

In another sense, however, racist policies that made black women's work a subset of "black" work rather than of "women's" work had advantages. African American agents enjoyed remarkable latitude to shape a practical program that increased land ownership and raised living standards. Lizzie Jenkins told farmers what they needed to do for their wives in a way that neither Ella Agnew nor her successors would have dared to. All female participants acquired added tasks, learned new methods for familiar chores, and enjoyed home improvements and the moral support agents offered. For African American women, however, participation in this public policy initiative, constructed around a matrix of unbreachable, appropriate gender roles, was an experience which differed significantly from that of their rural white counterparts.

"Go Ahead and Do All You Can"

Southern Progressives and Alabama Home Demonstration Clubs, 1914–1940

LYNNE A. RIEFF

At the beginning of the twentieth century, southern Progressives embarked on a reform movement to remedy the "neglect of rural life" in the South. These advocates of reform valued the rural way of life and hoped to improve its quality. They believed that the pervasive backwardness of the South—created and frozen in place by the one-crop economy, the tenant system, isolation, racism, and ignorance—retarded the region's progress. While the New South Creed had been ballyhooed for decades, its call for economic diversification, modernization, and improved race relations had remained mostly rhetoric.[1] Progressives argued that the South needed to "develop" in order to feed all its citizens, to eliminate poverty and inequality, and to secure economic independence.[2] Since the region was still predominantly rural, reformers were determined to

1. Frederick T. Gates, "The Country School of Tomorrow," *World's Work* 24 (August 1912): 461, quoted in Dewey W. Grantham, *Southern Progressivism: The Reconciliation of Progress and Tradition* (Knoxville: University of Tennessee Press, 1983), 336; Paul Gaston, *The New South Creed: A Study in Southern Mythmaking* (Baton Rouge: Louisiana State University Press, 1970), 7, 189–90; C. Vann Woodward, *Origins of the New South, 1877–1913* (Baton Rouge: Louisiana State University Press, 1951), ix–x; George B. Tindall, *The Emergence of the New South, 1913–1945* (Baton Rouge: Louisiana State University Press, 1967), ix–x.

2. Jack Temple Kirby, *Rural Worlds Lost: The American South, 1920–1960* (Baton Rouge: Louisiana State University Press, 1987), 118–19. Kirby cites economist Dudley Seers in suggesting that "development" is "the realization of the potential of human personality."

revitalize and modernize community life by building better schools, churches, and roads; advocating diversified agriculture, scientific farming, and improved homemaking practices; and supporting rural health clinics and traveling libraries. Progressives believed these reforms would instill in rural people a spirit of unity that would impel them toward economic opportunity, material progress, and ultimately, regional uplift. With southern rural communities assuming their responsibilities in the region's development, a Progressive South would emerge to take its place in national and world affairs.[3]

Despite their optimistic outlook and plans for the region's development, Progressives allowed certain "paradoxical combination[s]" as part of their agenda.[4] Because these reformers were unwilling to abandon certain beliefs and institutions that retarded the South's progress, they were ambiguous in their rhetoric and actions, simultaneously advocating tradition and modernization. For example, Progressives perpetuated race, class, and gender divisions while promoting unity and consensus. They urged blacks, poor whites, and women to participate in reforms, but only if they adhered to their proper roles in the region's development. With white supremacy, distrust of poor whites, and women's domestic sphere dominating southern thinking, Progressives viewed education as an "instrument for [effecting] material progress" and a means of social control for instructing various groups in their duties to their communities.[5]

Progressives held other conflicting positions. Because of the cataclysmic 1890s, reformers advocated stability in southern society, yet they refused to confront the cause of much of the Populist unrest, the agricultural labor system of tenancy. Instead of addressing the labor problem and offering solutions, Progressive leaders treated only the conditions of tenancy. By their refusal to confront such a deeply rooted, exploitive institution, Progressives furthered the South's economic and social disintegration. The Progressives, then, looked both backward and forward, articulated conservative and liberal views, and supported tradition and modernization. These contrasting positions and the Progressives' unwillingness fully to

3. Grantham, *Southern Progressivism*, xvi–xvii, 336.
4. Woodward, *Origins of the New South*, 373.
5. Grantham, *Southern Progressivism*, xvi–xvii, 200.

embrace change led to what Dewey W. Grantham called "a politics of cultural conflict rather than cultural consensus."[6]

The Cooperative Extension Service, established by the 1914 Smith-Lever Act, was one means Progressive reformers devised to revitalize the nation's farms and rural communities. Extension Service personnel—home demonstration agents and agricultural agents— were the individuals who taught rural people ways to improve their standard of living.[7] An examination of the home demonstration program in one state, Alabama, from 1914 through 1940, offers an opportunity to explore the work of African American and white home demonstration agents who worked with rural women. It highlights the cultural conflict that emerged as agents pursued reforms, and reveals that the home demonstration program, during its formative years, adopted and maintained ambiguities that characterized and weakened the larger southern Progressive movement. With the mixed message home demonstration agents received, physical and attitudinal barriers to reform impeded them from organizing, and rural women from joining, home demonstration clubs. As Extension Service reform efforts shifted during the 1920s and 1930s from revitalization to emphasis on efficiency and production, the Extension Service maintained its ambiguous positions. Rather than dismantling the barriers erected prior to 1920, the Extension Service leaders allowed them to remain in place.[8]

Agents organized home demonstration clubs early in the extension program as they realized the clubs' potential for effectiveness over individual contacts. The clubs served as a forum, giving women opportunities to ask questions and discuss problems; in return, agents had an audience for their demonstrations in improved home-

6. Ibid., 337, 346; Kirby, *Rural Worlds Lost,* 49; Grantham, *Southern Progressivism,* 410–11, 421.

7. *An Act to Create the Agricultural Extension Service in the United States [Smith-Lever Act], U.S. Statutes at Large* 38 (1914): 372–74; *U.S. Code,* vol. 1, sec. 341 (1977); United States Department of Agriculture, *Home Demonstration under the Smith-Lever Act, 1914–1924,* Circular No. 43 (Washington, D.C.: Government Printing Office, 1929), 10–11; Thomas M. Campbell, "Narrative Summary of Negro Extension Work in the Southern States, 1934," Reports, 1934, file, box 2, Thomas M. Campbell Papers, Tuskegee University Archives, Tuskegee, Ala., hereinafter cited as TMC Papers.

8. Tindall, *Emergence of the New South,* 224; Mary S. Hoffschwelle, "The Science of Domesticity: Home Economics at George Peabody College for Teachers, 1914–1939," *Journal of Southern History* 57 (November 1991): 668–69.

making practices. In club meetings agents addressed topics in the areas of nutrition, health, sanitation, sewing, and home improvements. Agents hoped that by organizing clubs, members would adopt suggestions, share ideas with other rural women, and persuade them to join. Clubs also encouraged socialization of rural women and their families.[9]

While home demonstration agents faced a daunting task, the Extension Service only partially equipped them with fiscal resources to meet the people and conditions that awaited them. Furthermore, gender and race divisions within the Extension Service raised the first barriers to reform. As employees of the Alabama Cooperative Extension Service, male agricultural agents received preference over home demonstration agents in financial support. With segregation embedded in southern society, funding for extension work among whites far surpassed money appropriated for work among African Americans. White male favoritism began in 1914 and continued. As an example of the preference shown agricultural work, total funds for one year (from federal, state, and local sources) to provide salaries, supplies, and travel for Alabama extension agents were: $398,396 for white agricultural work; $281,487 for white home demonstration work; $86,144 for black agricultural work; and $62,020 for black home demonstration work. Funds available for white home demonstration work were twice those appropriated for all black extension work. Individual salaries followed this trend, with white agricultural agents receiving the highest salaries, followed by white home demonstration agents, then black agricultural and black home demonstration agents.[10] Differentials in salaries between men and women and

9. J. F. Duggar, "Report of the Director of the Extension Service of the Alabama Polytechnic Institute: 1914–1915, Organization and Work under the Smith-Lever Act of Congress," U.S. Department of Agriculture, Records of the Federal Extension Service, RG 33, Annual Reports of Extension Service Field Representatives, National Archives, microfilm T-845, roll 1, hereinafter cited as NARS T-845; P. O. Davis, *Guide Book for Alabama Extension Workers* (Auburn: Alabama Polytechnic Institute Extension Service, 1947), 37.

10. Alabama Polytechnic Institute, "Proposed Budget of Income and Expenditures, July 1, 1940, to June 30, 1941," file 75, box 3, L. N. Duncan Papers, Auburn University Archives, Auburn, Ala., hereinafter cited as Duncan Papers; L. N. Duncan, "Proposed Budget of Income and Expenditures, July 1, 1944–June 30, 1945," file 79, box 3, Duncan Papers. Annual salaries for white county agricultural agents ranged from $3,400 to $5,160; white county home

black and white agents created tension and frustration and contributed to turnover. Moreover, the Extension Service prohibited
women from marrying and retaining their jobs but permitted men
to do so. At some time between her engagement and marriage,
extension officials expected a woman to resign her position. Both
county officials and the state Extension Service considered married women undesirable because county officials feared married
agents' contacts with rural constituents would give their husbands
impetus to seek elected office. State leaders feared agents' husbands and children would distract them from their work. Moreover, the Extension Service retained the prerogative to transfer
agents to other counties. State leaders thought it would be difficult
to uproot agents whose husbands' occupations tied them to a
particular locale.[11]

Counties that employed white agents had to provide local funds
to supplement federal and state payments for salaries and supplies.
In Alabama, local boards of revenue and education each appropriated money to pay percentages of the salaries of white home demonstration and agricultural agents.[12] When local funds could support only one white extension worker, the agricultural agent became
the preferred employee. Since agricultural agents taught, advised,
and consulted with farmers, county officials deemed the economic
effects of their work more important than the effects of work done
among women and girls. Some counties, however, employed only
white home demonstration agents for a period, either because
they could not support the salary of an agricultural agent or because an agent was unavailable.[13] In times of economic hardship

---

demonstration agents' salaries ranged from $2,650 to $3,740. African American
agents were paid the least: agricultural agents received from $1,860 to $2,460,
while black home demonstration salaries ranged from $1,380 to $1,920.

11. "Proceedings of the Conference on Negro Extension Work," State
A & M College, Orangeburg, S.C., January 26–28, 1927, Agents' Conference,
1927, file, box 4, TMC Papers; Etna McGaugh, "Annual Report of the State
Home Demonstration Agent, 1941," box 196, RG 71, Records of the Alabama
Cooperative Extension Service, Auburn University Archives, Auburn, Ala.,
hereinafter cited as ACES; Mildred Maxwell, interview by author, Talladega,
Ala., August 28, 1990. Tape of interview is in author's possession.

12. Madge J. Reese, "Report of Home Demonstration Work in Alabama,
1916," box 107, ACES.

13. Mary Wigley, "The Wind Is from the East," Mary Wigley Harper Collection, Auburn University Archives, Auburn, Ala., 362; J. F. Duggar, *A Year of*

and declining county revenues, availability of local funds and preference given to white agricultural agents became obstacles to
home demonstration work.

The African American extension force in Alabama, headquartered
at Tuskegee Institute, operated only on federal and state funds. Consequently, only counties with the largest black populations, such as
those in the Black Belt, had African American home demonstration
and agricultural agents. For rural blacks outside this area, Tuskegee
Institute's "Movable School of Agriculture," as it was called, provided
periodic contact. Movable schools of agriculture were traveling extension schools operated from, initially, horse-drawn wagons (for
example, the Jesup Agricultural Wagon) and, later, trucks (the
Knapp Agricultural Truck and the Booker T. Washington School on
Wheels). An agricultural agent, home demonstration agent, and
rural nurse operated the schools, which carried various kinds of
equipment and materials needed for demonstrations. Agents advertised in advance that the movable school would be in a particular area. Upon arrival, agents set up demonstrations in a church or
school yard, country store, crossroads, or private home—anywhere
agents thought they could attract a crowd. Demonstrations covered a wide range of topics in farming, homemaking, and health
care. Men, women, and children were urged to attend.[14]

Segregation and racism not only affected support given black
extension work but gave some county officials reason to think they
could intimidate and manipulate black extension workers. Mildred
Maxwell, a black agent in Lowndes County from 1932 through

Extension Work, Alabama Polytechnic Institute Extension Service Circular
No. 44 (Auburn: Alabama Polytechnic Institute Extension Service, 1930), 120.

14. L. C. Hanna, "Annual Report of State Agent for Negro Women, State of
Alabama, December 31, 1928," box 356, ACES; W. B. Hill, "A Brief History of
Extension Work with Negroes in Alabama," box 360, ACES; Rosa Jones, "Sup-
plement to the Annual Report of Agricultural Extension Work among Negroes
in Alabama," December 31, 1927, NARS T-845, roll 24; Thomas M. Campbell,
The Movable School Goes to the Negro Farmer (Tuskegee, Ala.: Tuskegee
Institute Press, 1936), 117, 152–54; Linda O. McMurry, *George Washington
Carver: Scientist and Symbol* (New York: Oxford University Press, 1981), 124–
27; Deborah Waldrop Austin, "Thomas Monroe Campbell and the Development of Negro Extension Work, 1883–1956" (master's thesis, Auburn University, 1975), 56–57; Allen W. Jones, "The Role of Tuskegee Institute in
the Education of Black Farmers," *Journal of Negro History* 60 (April 1975):
262–65.

1934, related how the white county school superintendent extorted money from black public school teachers. Black teachers earned approximately forty dollars per month in Lowndes County, whereas Maxwell, as a home demonstration agent, received ninety dollars each month. Claiming that she was "bringing too much money into the county for him not to get a cut," the superintendent demanded a portion of Maxwell's salary, as he had done with school-teachers. When she refused, the superintendent called the director of the Alabama Cooperative Extension Service at Alabama Poly-technic Institute (later Auburn University) and claimed that Max-well was not doing her job adequately. The director, in turn, called Thomas M. Campbell at Tuskegee Institute, who was the black field representative from the United States Department of Agricul-ture and oversaw black extension work in seven southern states. When Campbell visited Maxwell, his investigation revealed, not surprisingly, that the superintendent's corruption, not Maxwell's work, was the problem. Officials at Tuskegee Institute and Ala-bama Polytechnic Institute resolved the situation by transferring Maxwell to Talladega County in eastern central Alabama. Her re-placement, a young woman who had been a mathematics major in college, had no experience with extension work. Presumably, cor-ruption and intimidation continued in Lowndes County.[15]

This episode exemplifies the tribulations a black home demon-stration agent faced in rural Alabama and indicates the precarious-ness of black extension work in Alabama and the rest of the South. Although Tuskegee Institute had a well-deserved reputation as a pioneering institution in extension work, the black extension force operated under the auspices of the Alabama Cooperative Exten-sion Service, headquartered at Alabama Polytechnic Institute. Fed-eral and state funds for work were channeled through Alabama Polytechnic, which dispersed them to Tuskegee. Major decisions regarding black extension work and personnel received approval from white administrators.[16] The Alabama Cooperative Extension Service hired black agents on the basis of their competency, their ability to be models for their race, and their agreement not to say or

15. Maxwell, interview.
16. Campbell, "Duties—Campbell," box 20, TMC Papers; "Professional Ethics in Extension Work and County Personnel Relationships," in "Report of Workshop of Alabama Extension Agents, Tuskegee Institute, August 4–15, 1947," Workshop, Alabama, Tuskegee, file, box 8, TMC Papers.

do anything to challenge the relegated position of blacks in southern society. The black extension force in Alabama served at the pleasure of white administrators in Auburn and Washington, D.C., and the ruling class of white landowners. Therefore, Tuskegee extension workers were careful to appear positive and nonthreatening in their relationship with whites.[17]

At first, though, black home demonstration agents and other black extension workers faced resistance from white landowners. Some believed that, in permitting black government workers to hold meetings and organize clubs, "something [might] be done in secrecy to destroy the peace and contentment of plantation life." Others argued that black agents would be used to build a political machine to work in the "interest of Northern political groups." Some landowners relented when they heard of the extension workers' ties with Tuskegee Institute. As one white farmer who previously had vigorously opposed black extension work said: "I know about the work of Booker T. Washington's school and if that is the kind of work you are talking about, go ahead and do all you can. You have my hearty support."[18] Campbell and other black extension leaders at Tuskegee recognized the potential for confrontation between Tuskegee's extension force and the white public. When problems arose, such as the incident involving Maxwell, they worked to defuse the situation and reconcile the two sides.

The Extension Service perpetuated class divisions as well as those of gender and race. Both home demonstration and agricultural agents sought the support and approval of the white landowning class. Consequently, in their work, they did not challenge the prevailing system of tenancy and sharecropping. Instead, they

17. Campbell, "Annual Report of Negro Extension Work Containing Narrative Statistics for the States of Georgia, Florida, Alabama, Mississippi, Louisiana, Oklahoma and Texas—1925," 1925-Reports file, box 1, TMC Papers; "Professional Ethics in Extension Work and County Personnel Relationships," box 8, TMC Papers; Cynthia Neverdon-Morton, *Afro-American Women of the South and the Advancement of Race, 1895–1925* (Knoxville: University of Tennessee Press, 1989), 132.

18. J. C. Hyman, "Interprets Rural Negro to White Diocese," Reports file, box 3, TMC Papers; Campbell, "A Supplement to the Annual Report of the Agricultural Extension Service as Performed by Negroes," December 31, 1919, Annual Reports, 1919–20, file, box 1, TMC Papers; Maxwell, interview; Campbell, "A Supplement to the Annual Report of the Agricultural Extension Service as Performed by Negroes."

addressed the conditions in which rural people lived. For home demonstration agents responsible for ministering to needs of all rural women of their respective race, this constituency created a broad spectrum of diverse needs that agents found overwhelming.[19] Although agents commonly had rural backgrounds and knew about abysmal living conditions, their familiarity with rural life quickly became inadequate as they confronted constituents' various problems. Home economics courses technically prepared agents for teaching homemaking practices but did not give them experience or insight into "putting their work over" with rural people. A high illiteracy rate limited agents' courses of action. Pamphlets, brochures, and other printed material intended to supplement agents' work often proved useless. Members of home demonstration clubs expected agents to attend their monthly club meetings and confer with individuals between meetings. Although visiting clubs throughout the county each month consumed time and energy, agents realized the necessity of direct contact, because as one agent remarked, "They don't read[;] they must hear [and see]."[20]

When home demonstration agents arrived in counties to assume their appointments, they had little more to guide them in working with different socioeconomic groups than their consciences and the Extension Service's mandate that they acquaint as many rural women as possible with home demonstration work. Increasingly after 1920, demonstrations and lessons emphasized new technology and household management, subjects of limited interest for women whose families lived at a subsistence level.[21] Agents discovered rural women often lacked, and could not afford, basic supplies and equipment used in demonstrations (cooking utensils, stoves, sewing needs, garden implements). One African American agent lamented, "I was convinced that we were simply revealing to the people the things that they might do if they had access to the equipment such as we were carrying[;] the lessons taught for the most part would be remembered more or less as a dream after [we] departed from the community." In northern Alabama a white agent

19. Duggar, "Report of the Director of the Extension Service of the Alabama Polytechnic Institute: 1914–1915," NARS T-845, roll 1.

20. Mary Segers, "Annual Report of Home Demonstration Work, Escambia County, 1926," box 127, ACES; "Proceedings of the Conference on Negro Extension Work," Agents' Conference, 1927, file, box 4, TMC Papers.

21. Hoffschwelle, "The Science of Domesticity," 668.

wrote of the plight of rural families in her county: "The ladies have so little money . . . I often think how hopeless is the situation. . . . One of my clubs [is] so remote that there are not three homes among club members that have any screens or any kind of toilet. About the most we have done in this project is to have heart to heart talks at our club meetings along the lines of simple improvements and sanitation."[22]

Some agents, such as these, remained sensitive to their constituents' needs and circumstances. They improvised and searched for solutions. Others, reflecting common prejudicial attitudes, ignored the poor or grudgingly worked with them. Given the choice of groups to work within a large constituency, china and silver selection, giving teas, and teaching crafts proved far more pleasant topics for demonstrations than building sanitary privies, culling chickens, or educating people about hookworm and pellagra. A clubwoman from Montgomery County expressed her sentiments about the poor and how they should be treated: "The indigent must always be cared for by the government. . . . For the great mass of rural people the government will serve as big brother to guide [and] direct."[23] Unfortunately, some agents shared this woman's condescension. Agents' affirmation of such prejudice also suggests the paternalism that the Extension Service promoted and how agencies had the opportunity to use education and assistance as means of social control.

Rural people sensed the paternalism. Black and white agents regularly confronted people skeptical of their motives or overcome with a sense of failure. Some rural people found it difficult to accept that agents wanted to assist them and expected nothing in return. Others distrusted agents because the government employed

22. Harry Sims to Thomas M. Campbell, December 12, 1922, Harry Sims file, box 6, TMC Papers; Ila Deane Griffin, "Annual Report of Home Demonstration Work, Limestone County, 1923," box 120, ACES.

23. Mamie C. Thorington, "Annual Report of Home Demonstration Work, Montgomery County, 1937," box 168, ACES. Other agents expressed similar sentiments or made reference to these more frivolous activities in their reports. See Meta Grace, "Annual Report of Home Demonstration Work, Tallapoosa County, 1936," box 164; Annette S. Breeden, "Annual Report of Home Demonstration Work, Dallas County, 1930," box 140; Harriett Plowden, "Annual Report of Home Demonstration Work, Talladega County, 1936," box 164; Carrie Threaton, "Annual Report of Home Demonstration Work, Geneva County, 1939," box 180—all in ACES.

them or feared that landowners had sent agents to spy on them. Even though some whites shared these fears, African Americans frequently believed that "no good could come from suggestions made from someone, colored though he [or she] may be, who [is] paid by the government and by white people to do this work."[24]

A sense of failure or apathy prevented other rural women from joining home demonstration clubs. Feelings of low self-esteem and acceptance of poverty as their lot in life led many to believe that "times were hard and could not be made easy." Tenants often responded by withdrawing. "[We] ain't got nothin and don't want nothin; [we] just want to be left alone" became a common reply to agents' efforts. Others saw home demonstration clubs as social gatherings that they did not have time to attend. Furthermore, most clubs met in rural homes because of the unavailability of central meeting places.[25] Tenant women, self-conscious about the poor state of their homes, hesitated to invite visitors. Some tenants, though, became interested in joining a club and getting involved with home demonstration work but resisted because their families moved frequently. One sharecropper emphatically stated that "the safe plan was to grab as much as possible [because a] stay was only temporary." Others wanted to take agents' advice and make modifications in their homes but did not because landowners refused to compensate them. Tenants understandably resisted adding to their debts when improvements benefited the landowner by increasing property values.[26]

24. Campbell, "Fifty Years of Progress in Agriculture," n.d., Fifty Years of Progress in Agriculture file, box 47, TMC Papers; Maxwell, interview; "Rural Extension Work among Negroes in the Southern States," n.d., Beginning of Extension Work file, box 3, TMC Papers.

25. L. E. Fry, "A Preliminary Statement on Rural Housing," March 1938, Reports file, box 3, TMC Papers; Regina Matlock, "Annual Report of Home Demonstration Work, Perry County, 1926," box 123, ACES; Mabel Feagin, "Annual Report of Home Demonstration Work, Bullock County, 1929," box 135, ACES.

26. H. F. Wilson, "The Present Negro Extension Problem," *Southern Workman* 58 (October 1929): 471; Zelma G. Jackson, "Annual Report of Home Demonstration Work, Chambers County, 1924" box 122, ACES; Mary Segers, "Annual Report of Home Demonstration Work, Escambia County, 1923," box 120, ACES; Wayne Flynt, *Poor but Proud: Alabama's Poor Whites* (Tuscaloosa: University of Alabama Press, 1989), 88–89; Wilson, "The Present Negro Extension Problem," 471; Jackson, "Annual Report of Home Demonstration Work, Chambers County, 1924."

In addition to persuading tenants to join home demonstration clubs, agents became frustrated over getting different socioeconomic groups to cooperate. Rural white women with higher class status included those from families of cash renters and small landowners as well as large farmers. Some members of this class graciously welcomed anyone interested in home demonstration work to join. Others who viewed tenants as inferiors proved difficult and tenacious. Clara Hall, a white agent in Sumter County, discovered that landowning women resisted home demonstration work because they did not want to be identified as "hardworking Farm Women." Hall wrote that these women, mostly college educated, considered themselves cultured and sophisticated with backgrounds superior to hers. Sumter County, located in western Alabama, had a substantial number of tenants. Hall, responsible for involving as many white women as possible in the work, determined that large landowners, because of their status in the county, needed to be involved in the clubs as well. After the organization of a club, members ultimately concluded that home demonstration work benefited them and deserved their support. Although agents like Hall diverted time and effort toward such women when great need existed elsewhere, they realized their acceptance by county leaders and well-established individuals was imperative. Agents' livelihood and the survival of the Extension Service depended on gaining and maintaining ruling-class support.[27]

African American agents also needed ruling-class support, but fortunately they did not face the barrier of different socioeconomic groups creating cleavages in the black community. Black home agents found the majority of their constituents engaged in some form of tenancy. The 1940 census reported over 78 percent of Alabama's black farm operators were sharecroppers, tenants, managers, or wage laborers. In contrast, the census reported 50.1 percent of all white farm operators were landowners.[28]

The limitations of white southern society trapped most African Americans in a life of poverty, and restricted socioeconomic diver-

27. Clara J. Hall, "Substitute Agent's Report, Status of Work," in "Annual Report of Home Demonstration Work, Sumter County, 1930," box 140, ACES.

28. *Statistical Abstract of the United States, 1941* (Washington, D.C.: Government Printing Office, 1942), Table 642, p. 689; J. C. Ford, "Annual Report of the Coordinator of Negro Work, Alabama Extension Service, 1941," box 356, ACES.

sity. Yet in such abysmal circumstances, black home demonstration agents enjoyed one advantage over their white counterparts: the shared poverty and burden of living in a discriminatory society created a more cohesive spirit among African American home demonstration club members. This advantage meant that black home demonstration agents did not expend time or energy cajoling particular groups. Yet the fundamental "backwardness" and prejudices of southern society continued to impede the overall success of African American home demonstration agents.

To some rural women, home demonstration agents represented elitist attitudes and criticisms of "country" ways and traditions. The Extension Service employed and sent out home demonstration agents as professionals to teach country women to stay at home and to better care for their families, keep house, and maintain the domestic sphere; yet the home demonstration agent's example was that of a single, independent, college-educated, professionally employed woman. Moreover, some rural women doubted the ability of an unmarried professional woman and resented her recommendations for their households.[29]

While agents dared not challenge the entrenched traditions of a distinct domestic sphere, segregation, and tenancy, they decried as backward other customary ways relating to farming, homemaking, and general practices of living. When black and white agents met with clubs and visited individuals, they affirmed changes women had made in their homes and appearances. While charged to implement change and encourage progress, agents did little to blend country people's attitudes and identities with reforms. The implication was that "country" was inferior to "town" and that rural women should emulate and conform to town ways in their appearance, behavior, and life-style. Discussions of rural women's personal appearance indicated this attitude. Agents instructed women that their "clothes [should] compare very favorably with any of the town women's wardrobes," and "when you see a car drive into town 'country' [should] not [be] stamped on the manner or appearance of the occupants."[30]

29. Hoffschwelle, "The Science of Domesticity," 665–66; Hall, "Substitute Agent's Report, Status of Work."

30. Mrs. Frank Daugherty, "What the Past Year's Project, Clothing, Has Meant to the Club Women as a Community," in "Annual Report of Home

Home demonstration agents espoused another mixed message in advocating the town model. The home demonstration program taught farm women that they could become self-sufficient and should live at home.[31] Agents urged women to plant gardens and orchards; to raise cows and chickens to produce milk, butter, eggs, and meat; to sew and renovate clothes; to recycle materials for various uses; and to sell any surplus products for additional family income. Agents emphasized producing as many necessities as possible so that families would spend less money and incur less debt. However, the Live-at-Home Program conflicted with the credibility given the town model and with the emphasis and attention agricultural agents gave commercialized farming. Town people were consumers, not producers. With commercialized agriculture becoming dominant in the rural economy, farmers produced cash crops, not necessities, so that they, too, were becoming consumers. By encouraging rural women to use consumers as models, agents sent another ambiguous message to rural women that contributed to conflict. Furthermore, by holding the town as the model, agents stifled rather than encouraged rural women's ingenuity in finding solutions to resolve their situation. Rural people were made to feel that to prosper they must adapt their way of life to the town.[32]

In examining African American and white enrollments in Alabama's home demonstration clubs, it is clear that black agents, despite indignities and disabilities suffered because of racial and sexual discrimination, were more successful in overcoming barriers than were their white colleagues. By the 1940s, enrollment for black and white clubs had peaked. In 1940, black home agents served in 32 of Alabama's 67 counties and reported that 13.7 percent of rural African American women in the state belonged to a home demonstration club. In contrast, white agents serving in all 67 counties (with 24 counties employing assistant home agents)

Demonstration Work, Limestone County, 1929," box 136, ACES; Victoria C. Lingo, "Annual Report of Home Demonstration Work, Barbour County, 1925," box 122, ACES.

31. Ruth Dobyne, "Annual Report of Home Demonstration Work, Autauga County, 1926," box 127, ACES.

32. Diana B. Williams, "Annual Report of Home Demonstration Work, Etowah County, 1929," box 136, ACES; Sallye Hamilton and Florence Farish, "Annual Report of Home Demonstration Work, Calhoun County, 1929," box 135, ACES.

reported just 17.4 percent of rural white women had joined a club.[33] What these figures do not relate is the perception that women had of agents who assisted them outside of clubs. Agents worked with relief efforts such as community canning centers. Home agents supervised the management of these centers, which aided thousands of rural families during the Great Depression. The Agricultural Adjustment Agency sponsored a Mattress Making Program that was designed to assist low-income families (income below four hundred dollars annually) and utilize surplus cotton. Agents established mattress-making centers where they provided training. They also helped organize soup kitchens, "Opportunity Literacy Schools" for adults, and curb markets for selling farm products and country crafts; and they assisted county health departments and the Red Cross. Through informal social networks, individual visits, and association with relief work, agents helped women outside the clubs and made them aware of the home demonstration program's purpose.[34]

Through home demonstration clubs and agents assisting individuals and their families in various capacities outside the clubs, by 1940 the Alabama home demonstration program ranked as a well-known and established division within the Alabama Cooperative Extension Service. Created in 1914 to teach women and girls how to improve living conditions in the rural South, the home demonstration program in Alabama and other states was intended to assist in revitalizing the South's farms and rural communities. As an objective of the southern Progressive movement from 1914 until 1920, teaching better homemaking became part of the trend of

33. McGaugh, "Annual Report of the State Home Demonstration Agent, 1939," box 181, ACES. Actual numbers reported were as follows: 182,180 rural white families residing in Alabama with 31,761 white home demonstration club members; 76,958 rural African American families residing in the state with 10,536 black home demonstration club members. Club enrollments peaked by the late 1940s and early 1950s. White clubs peaked at 42,253 club members in 1948; black clubs reached their maximum enrollment in 1953 with 16,875 members. See Lillie M. Alexander, "State Supervisory Narrative Report, 1948," box 239, ACES; W. B. Hill, "Combined Annual Narrative Report of Negro Supervising Agents, 1953," box 357, ACES.

34. Erin Rowe, "Annual Report of Home Demonstration Work, Morgan County, 1933," box 153, ACES; Cecile Hester, "Annual Report of Home Demonstration Work, Lauderdale County, 1940," box 187, ACES; Flynt, *Poor but Proud,* 301–5.

"business progressivism." Home demonstration agents attracted large numbers of rural women into clubs, and membership grew steadily after 1914. Yet the large number of rural women who did not join in home demonstration work overshadowed the relative success agents enjoyed in persuading women to join clubs and modify their living conditions.

Leaders in the program did not recognize or acknowledge the paradoxical positions they and other Extension Service leaders held. Nor did they recognize the conflict that came from those positions. Rather than resolving the paradoxes characteristic of southern Progressivism, the home demonstration program and the Extension Service perpetuated them. Consequently, physical and attitudinal barriers arose among agents and rural women.

The experience of the home demonstration program in Alabama suggests that revitalization and rural reforms fell short largely because the leadership in the Alabama Cooperative Extension Service refused to embrace fully the changes that the Progressive spirit engendered. Instead, southern Progressives and Extension Service leaders pursued those reforms that could be reconciled with southern customs. Home demonstration agents, therefore, lacked clear direction in their work, and the most serious problems that retarded Alabama's and the South's development remained unaddressed. While the program ultimately failed in its goal of revitalizing rural communities in Alabama, many black and white Alabamians affirmed the changes agents made in their communities. Reforms the agents succeeded in making, despite ambiguities, conflicts, and barriers, are testimony to their commitment and ingenuity.

RACIAL COOPERATION
AND
REFORM MOVEMENTS

"A Melting Time"

Black Women, White Women, and the WCTU in North Carolina, 1880–1900

GLENDA ELIZABETH GILMORE

On a hot July day in 1886, several white women in Winston, North Carolina, rose early to pack picnic baskets full to the brim with ham, cake, pickles, and candy. Baskets in one hand and flowers in the other, they resolutely left their homes and headed out for a long-awaited rendezvous. The women were members of Winston's newly organized Woman's Christian Temperance Union (WCTU). Their destination: the jail. There eight prisoners awaited them, two white and six black men. Mustering the courage of their convictions, the women marched in and announced to the jailer that they had arrived to convert the inmates to temperance. Nervous at first, the women were soon leading the prisoners in song and prayer; afterward, everyone crunched pickles and savored ham biscuits. The visit represented an emotional turning point for the women, and they said they felt so close to the prisoners that it seemed as if "the power of the Holy Spirit rested upon all," white and black,

I wish to thank Karl Campbell, Karen Leathem, Jacquelyn Dowd Hall, and Nell Irvin Painter for their comments on earlier versions of this essay. Alfred Epstein, librarian at the Frances E. Willard Memorial Library, provided invaluable assistance, and Leslie Dunlap of Northwestern University graciously shared her research and ideas. An Archie K. Davis Grant awarded by the North Caroliniana Society facilitated the research. This essay is taken from my forthcoming book, *Gender and Jim Crow: Black Women and the Politics of White Supremacy in North Carolina, 1896–1992,* to be published by the University of North Carolina Press.

male and female. One woman recalled, "We all felt . . . good to be there." Then she added, "It was a melting time."[1]

In the 1880s and 1890s, the North Carolina WCTU undertook a novel experiment in interracial contact. In encounters such as the one just described, white women interacted with black men and came to care for their souls. Then, within the WCTU itself, black and white women worked as members of separate chapters within a single statewide organization, the first statewide biracial voluntary organization in North Carolina.[2] Under the heat of temperance fever, racial boundaries "melted" ever so slightly.

Both black and white women understood temperance to be a woman's problem, because drunkenness threatened family support systems. White women envisioned interracial cooperation as both races working together, with the women they referred to as "our sisters in black" participating in a segregated structure that reported to white women. For black women, however, temperance represented not just a woman's issue, but a race issue as well, and their work in the WCTU drew upon their doubled consciousness.[3]

1. *Greensboro Anchor* 2, no. 4 (July 1886): 5.
2. In 1884 the southern Independent Order of Good Templars also accepted separate black chapters. Daniel Jay Whitener, *Prohibition in North Carolina, 1715–1945* (Chapel Hill: University of North Carolina Press, 1945), 22–28. On the context of temperance reform in the United States, see Jack S. Blocker, *American Temperance Movements: Cycles of Reform* (Boston: Twayne Publishers, 1989), and Barbara Leslie Epstein, *The Politics of Domesticity* (Middletown, Conn.: Wesleyan University Press, 1981).
3. My thinking on black women's activism and feminism owes a debt to scholars who have explored the dual consciousness of black women. Among the works that inform my analysis are the following: Elsa Barkley Brown, "Womanist Consciousness: Maggie Lena Walker and the Independent Order of Saint Luke," *Signs* 14, no. 3 (Spring 1989): 610–33; Patricia Hill Collins, "The Social Construction of Black Feminist Thought," *Signs* 14, no. 4 (Summer 1989): 745–73; bell hooks, *Feminist Theory: From Margin to Center* (Boston: South End Press, 1984); Hazel Carby, *Reconstructing Womanhood: The Emergence of the Afro-American Woman Novelist* (New York: Oxford University Press, 1987); Gloria T. Hull, Patricia Bell Scott, and Barbara Smith, *All the Women Are White, All the Blacks Are Men, but Some of Us Are Brave: Black Women's Studies* (Old Westbury, N.Y.: Feminist Press, 1982); Paula Giddings, *When and Where I Enter: The Impact of Black Women on Race and Sex in America* (New York: Bantam Books, 1984); Evelyn Brooks Higginbotham, *Righteous Discontent: The Women's Movement in the Black Baptist Church, 1880–1920* (Cambridge: Harvard University Press, 1993); Bonnie Thornton

To black and white women in the WCTU, sisterhood was power-ful. In the post-Reconstruction South, the founding of a biracial organization, even one separated internally, took courage and a vision of the future that differed from the male perspective. In starting the WCTU, white women recognized gender as a binding force that mitigated racial difficulties. Black women hoped that through white women's recognition of common womanhood they could forge a structure that allowed racial interaction on a more egalitarian basis.

But sisterhood was not all-powerful. White women thought that if they formed one biracial WCTU, its power relations could mirror the racial hierarchy of society at large. Black women found this assumption contradictory on its face. If all WCTU members were temperance women, they must be equally worthy. To be called sisters meant that all were one in the family of God. Because their temperance work involved both women's and racial goals, African American women refused to trade equality for interaction. Trying and failing to attain leadership in the interracial WCTU, black women withdrew in 1889 to promote temperance through a sepa-rate organization, the WCTU No. 2.

After secession, the two organizations continued to cooperate, as temperance women operated in a highly charged political arena. Formal electoral politics crafted the nature of the WCTU's commu-nity work and influenced the organization's internal structure and activities. Because African Americans were still political actors in North Carolina in the 1880s and 1890s, the effort to ratify prohibi-tion pushed the WCTU to manipulate social convention. After a white supremacy campaign in 1898, African American votes disap-peared, white women lost the impetus for interracial cooperation, and ties between black and white women snapped.

A short exegesis of the term *interracial cooperation* helps bring into focus the biracial WCTU's significance. African Americans and whites used the term to signify working across racial lines to

Dill, "The Dialectics of Black Womanhood," *Signs* 4, no. 3 (Spring 1979): 543–55; Aida Hurtado, "Relating to Privilege: Seduction and Rejection in the Sub-ordination of White Women and Women of Color," *Signs* 17, no. 4 (Summer 1989): 833–55; and Rosalyn Terborg-Penn, "Discontented Black Feminists: Prelude and Postscript to the Passage of the Nineteenth Amendment," in *Decades of Discontent: The Women's Movement, 1920–1949,* ed. Lois Scharf and Joan M. Jensen (Westport, Conn.: Greenwood Press, 1983), 261–78.

solve common problems. Most white women understood inter-racial contact in the WCTU not as an effort to achieve understanding between the races but as coalition politics in the fight for prohibition. Black women undertook interracial cooperation without illusion, because racial progress depended on it as long as whites controlled southern institutions. Nothing about the term implied a common commitment to civil rights, to racial equality, to working together cheerfully, or even to working together with civility.

There was never a point in the two decades of interracial cooperation in the WCTU when white women could not be characterized as "racist." Yet such a characterization reveals little about actual practice and obscures a more important truth: racism is never a static phenomenon. It waxes and wanes in response to a larger social context, sometimes perniciously defining the contours of daily life, sometimes receding as behavior and speech challenge racial constructions. Black and white women in the WCTU accepted difference, and for a brief period their behavior outdistanced the racial conventions of their time.[4]

The roots of the African American temperance movement took hold in North Carolina during Reconstruction when several black lodges joined the Independent Order of Good Templars (IOGT), a temperance organization. Headquartered in Great Britain, the IOGT already had active white chapters in North Carolina. When the newly formed black chapters petitioned the state organization for official recognition, however, the white members refused them a charter and would not even divulge the secret Templar password. Stung by this exclusion, the black Templars forged ahead and formed lasting ties with other white and black chapters throughout the world.[5]

4. My analysis of the relationship between electoral politics, social practice, and the changing construct of racism was strengthened by Lawrence Goodwyn's argument in "Populist Dreams and Negro Rights: East Texas as a Case Study," *American Historical Review* 76 (December 1971): 1435–56, and by Jacquelyn Hall's reading of this essay.

5. Templars material, file 1818–1885, box 1, Charles N. Hunter Collection, Manuscript Department, Perkins Library, Duke University, Durham, N.C.. For a discussion of the Good Templars and prohibition in the period, see Whitener, *Prohibition in North Carolina*, 55–57. On the IOGT and race, see John H. Haley, *Charles N. Hunter and Race Relations in North Carolina* (Chapel Hill: University of North Carolina Press, 1987), 27–30.

Black North Carolinians joined in great numbers. The Raleigh chapter boasted two hundred members, and its officers included men and women.[6] The African American Templars recruited women as full members, elected them to office, and applauded their speeches at meetings. At an African American IOGT meeting in Fayetteville in 1875, the keynote speaker recognized "the power of the females, and their duty in exercising it" in the organization. Black women gained experience and self-confidence through their work in the IOGT, and men came to admire their forcefulness and courage. When Sarah McLaurin gave a rousing speech to the Cape Fear Lodge on New Year's Day in 1888, a male listener reported that "[s]he addressed the house with as much bravery as did some of our modern heroes." In the IOGT, African American women took leadership roles in temperance work that predated their involvement in the WCTU.[7]

While black men and women worked together as Templars, the monumental statewide prohibition referendum of 1881 set the stage for the WCTU's entry into the state. In the midst of the 1881 prohibition campaign, Frances Willard, president of the national WCTU, visited Wilmington to organize white women into a local chapter.[8] Willard worried about the way that southern white women might receive a northern woman, but her nervousness did not prevent her from advocating temperance work among African Americans.

6. Mainly News and Editorials file, box 16, Hunter Collection; clipping from *The Banner of Temperance,* n.p., n.d., in file 1833–1879, and clipping "Temperance," Raleigh, N.C., November 20, 1871, file 1833–1902, both in box 13, Scrapbooks (xerox copies), Hunter Collection.

7. *Fayetteville Educator,* February 5, 1875; *Charlotte Messenger,* January 7, 1888; Whitener, *Prohibition in North Carolina,* 31–32, and David M. Fahey, ed., *The Collected Writings of Jessie Forsyth, 1847–1937: The Grand Templars and Temperance Reform on Three Continents* (Lewiston, N.Y.: Edwin Mellen, 1988).

8. Whitener, *Prohibition in North Carolina,* 60–80; Frances E. Willard Diary, March 11, 12, 13, 14, 1881; *Wilmington Morning Star,* March 12, 1881; *Charleston News and Courier,* March 15, 1881; *Our Union* (May 1881), 10—all in Willard Scrapbook 1881, Frances E. Willard Memorial Library for Alcohol Research, Evanston, Ill. On the racial politics of the 1881 election, see Helen Chesnutt, *Charles Waddell Chesnutt, Pioneer of the Color Line* (Chapel Hill: University of North Carolina Press, 1952), 29; Eric Anderson, *Race and Politics in North Carolina, 1872–1901: The Black Second* (Baton Rouge: Louisiana State University Press, 1981), 96–98; clipping from the *Daily Record,* April 28, 1881, file 1880–1886, box 13, Hunter Collection.

To Willard's surprise, southern white women embraced her suggestion with enthusiasm. She observed, "Everywhere the Southern white people desired me to speak to the colored."[9]

White support for Willard's speeches to African American audiences demonstrates the importance of black men's votes and black women's political influence. Willard's appeal to black political power was not unique, and North Carolina white women sought to organize black women during the election in 1881. For example, when a "ladies' prohibition club" met at a Methodist church in Concord, the members reported that "the galleries of the church were set apart for our colored friends."[10]

Statewide prohibition failed in North Carolina in 1881, and many whites blamed blacks, despite the nearly unanimous endorsement of the black press. Reports from across the state declared that African Americans voted overwhelmingly in favor of whiskey, probably because many blacks kept small shops in which liquor sold briskly and the Republican party supported the "wets." White prohibitionists, mostly Democrats, charged that liquor interests bought black votes to tip the election. After 1881, temperance strategy centered on local option elections, and the WCTU attempted to win prohibition town by town, county by county.[11]

Realizing black political power, white women determined to work with African American women. In 1883, Frances Willard returned to North Carolina and brought the existing WCTU chapters into a statewide organization. The state structure made Work Among the Colored People one of six departments and subordinated all

9. Frances E. Willard, *Glimpses of Fifty Years: The Autobiography of an American Woman* (1889; reprint, New York: Source Book Press, 1970), 373. On Willard's first southern trip, see Ruth Bordin, *Woman and Temperance: The Quest for Power and Liberty, 1873–1900* (Philadelphia: Temple University Press, 1981), 76–78; Willard, *Glimpses of Fifty Years,* 373–74. On her visit to Georgia, see Lulu Ansley, *History of the Georgian W.C.T.U., 1883–1907* (Columbus, Ga.: Gilbert Publishing Company, 1914).

10. *Concord Temperance Herald,* June 16, 1881.

11. Ibid.; Whitener, *Prohibition in North Carolina,* 70, 58, 61–80, 87, 102. One-fourth of the liquor dealers at a convention called to fight the referendum were African American, according to Whitener, 70. Most blacks voted against prohibition. In Charlotte, for example, Ward 2 was three-fifths black. Of 331 voters, only 95 voted for prohibition. In Ward 3, three-fifths of the voters were black, and 74 voted for prohibition, according to the *Charlotte Messenger,* June 9, 1888.

black chapters to the white female department head.[12] Despite the separate chapters and the reporting structure, the biracial WCTU was a dramatic departure from the past. Unlike the white male Templars, white women hoped that a single voluntary organization could contain both races. Women temperance leaders realized that membership in one WCTU would necessitate interracial contact, and they foresaw interracial cooperation in local option elections and in social service projects.

The white women who volunteered to organize black WCTU chapters were already involved in interracial educational and religious work. Rosa Steele, wife of Wilbur Steele, the white president of Bennett College, an institution for African Americans, headed the statewide Work Among the Colored People department. Steele bridged two worlds, and she had already earned a reputation among blacks as a "zealous" woman. When the African American editor of the *Messenger* went to visit his daughter at Bennett College, he and his wife had dinner with the Steeles. Apparently Rosa Steele preached and prayed during the dinner, impressing the editor with her piety and enthusiasm. A Methodist and a native New Englander, Rosa Steele, together with her husband, regularly dined with African American friends, a practice that earned Wilbur Steele the designation in the press of "Social Equality Steele." Rosa Steele found support for the Work Among the Colored People department among other white women connected with African American educational institutions. In Concord, for example, she turned to the wife of the white president of Presbyterian Scotia Seminary for black women. Soon Scotia organized campus temperance activities as well as a local African American WCTU chapter.[13]

White women such as Steele saw temperance work among Afri-

12. Anastatia Sims, "'The Sword of the Spirit': The W.C.T.U. and Moral Reform in North Carolina, 1883–1933," *North Carolina Historical Review* (October 1987): 395; Bordin, *Woman and Temperance,* 78; Lou Rogers, "The W.C.T.U. in North Carolina," *We the People* 3 (August 1945): 22–23; Sims, "The Sword of the Spirit," 398.

13. *Charlotte Messenger,* June 24, 1887; Wilbur Daniel Steele, clipping, *Greensboro News,* September 23, 1924, in North Carolina Collection Clipping File through 1975, vol. 139, p. 711, North Carolina Collection, Wilson Library, University of North Carolina at Chapel Hill; Whitener, *Prohibition in North Carolina,* 82, 85; *Minutes of the Second Convention of the W.C.T.U. of the State of North Carolina* (Greensboro: Thomas, Reece & Co., 1884), 16; *Greensboro Anchor* 1, no. 8 (November 1885): 6.

can Americans as missionary labor, uplifting for the white women as well as the black women. She reminded the white women that "God's soul diamond in a black casket is as precious in His sight as the one in the white casket." Clearly Steele used the WCTU as a way to promote her own agenda—interracial understanding—but strictly under white direction. The fact that some black chapters formed and functioned without the supervision of white women worried her. "They have many workers of their own and many teachers doing this temperance work among them," Steele noted, but added that white women must take the lead supervising chapters.[14] While her belief in the superiority of white leadership indicated the racial distance she perceived between herself and blacks, Steele's racial attitudes represented those of the most liberal white women in the South. Southern white communities generally ostracized white women who promoted black education, yet the WCTU accepted and used their talents in order to achieve its goals.[15]

Steele's exhortations inspired white women who had never attempted interracial work to try to organize black WCTU chapters in their hometowns. They often complained that when they tried to approach African American women, "they were looked upon suspiciously by those whom they desired to help." The racial dynamics baffled white women who could not fathom black women's reactions. African American women drew upon their long experience in temperance, and they chafed at the patronizing, missionary approach of whites. The white women who wanted to bring African Americans to the temperance cause were not able to recognize black women's capabilities. The black women were understandably resentful, and the gap between the two groups was difficult to breach. To make matters worse, most white women worked with black women during the annual local option elections and neglected the work the rest of the year. Steele admonished white women not to view blacks opportunistically or to cultivate them just for political purposes. Temperance would succeed if

14. *Minutes of the Fifth Annual Convention of the W.C.T.U. of North Carolina* (Greensboro: Thomas, Reece & Co., 1887), 51; *Minutes of the Third Annual Convention of the Woman's Christian Temperance Union of North Carolina* (Greensboro: Thomas, Reece & Co., 1885), 29–30.

15. *Minutes of the First Convention of the Woman's Christian Temperance Union of the State of North Carolina* (Greensboro: Thomas, Reece & Co., 1883), 7; *Greensboro Anchor,* 2, no. 4 (July 1886): 2.

whites showed a "real live interest in the colored man, not born of a disire [sic] to win his vote at election time," Steele argued.[16]

In many cities and towns, however, no white woman would come forward to head the Work Among the Colored People department, and black women organized their own WCTU chapters. The experience of Mary Lynch and the Charlotte chapter illustrates how African American women came to the temperance cause and built their own statewide organization. A student at Scotia Seminary in Concord during the prohibition campaign of 1881, Lynch was caught up in the fever of the biracial ladies' temperance meetings and influenced by her teachers' participation in the WCTU.[17] Upon graduation, when she moved to Charlotte to teach in the graded school, she joined a sixty-member WCTU chapter that had formed independent of white sponsorship. That year, the Charlotte African American chapter sent delegates to the state convention and addressed the assembled women of both races.[18]

Once a town had black and white chapters, WCTU women occasionally launched joint ventures in community welfare that proved the WCTU's cooperative potential. For example, in the final months of 1886, white and black women united to build a hospital for African Americans in Charlotte. The white chapter held an art exhibition to raise funds for the cause, and the black chapter passed the hat at community meetings. At the hospital's opening, the president of the white WCTU acknowledged, "We greatly appreciate the work of the (colored) W.C.T.U. in their co-operation with the White W.C.T.U."[19] The Charlotte white women realized the importance of black management in the hospital, and they pledged that African Americans would retain control of the work. Despite everyone's good intentions, funds ran out quickly, and both chapters struggled to support the hospital. Ultimately the cooperative hospital failed, and a separate group of white women, with funding

---

16. *Minutes,* 1887, 51; *Greensboro Anchor,* 2, no. 2 (May 1886): 6.

17. *Charlotte Messenger,* June 17, 1882; April 8, 1883.

18. *Minutes,* 1887, 29; *Charlotte Messenger,* August 7, 1886; August 14, 1886; *Greensboro Anchor* 2, no. 5 (August 1886): 2; *Minutes of the Fourth Annual Convention of the Woman's Christian Temperance Union of North Carolina* (Greensboro: Thomas, Reece & Co., 1886), 37, 63.

19. *Charlotte Messenger,* December 18, 1886; February 19, 1887; April 16, 1887.

from the northern Episcopal church, opened a larger facility for blacks under white women's management.[20]

In 1888, after five years of appealing to white women to organize black temperance chapters, Rosa Steele tried a new tactic that produced extraordinary results: she invited Sarah Jane Woodson Early to North Carolina. Early, an African American woman who was superintendent of Colored Work for the South for the national WCTU, spent five weeks in the state. Early entered the local prohibition battles raging in Raleigh and Concord and encouraged African American women to join the campaign.[21] One African American woman from Concord lobbied hard for black male votes after Early's visit and felt sure that Christians would "vote as they pray." Early's African American audiences financed her trip, and by the time that she left the state, fourteen WCTU chapters stood on solid ground.[22]

The next year, building on Early's organizing campaign, African American WCTU leaders seceded from the state organization. Black women resented being relegated to a subordinate department under white direction. Steele reported to the remaining white women that African Americans "wanted to attain their full development and this can best be done in an independent organization . . . with the department work under their own control." The new African American WCTU would report directly to the national WCTU and achieve organizational status equal to that of the white group. The black women named their organization the WCTU No. 2 and announced, "We cautiously avoided using the word colored . . . for *we* believe *all* men equal."[23]

Black women across the South replicated North Carolina's ex-

20. Ibid., April 7, April 28, May 19, 1888.

21. *Minutes of the Sixth Annual Convention of the Woman's Christian Temperance Union of North Carolina* (Greensboro: Thomas Brothers, 1888), 41. On Early, see Lawson Andrew Scruggs, *Women of Distinction: Remarkable in Works and Invincible in Character* (Raleigh: L. A. Scruggs, 1893), 71, and Ellen N. Lawson, "Sarah Woodson Early: Nineteenth-Century Black Nationalist 'Sister,'" *UMOJA* 2 (Summer 1981): 22–23.

22. Annie L. Harrington to the Editor, *Charlotte Messenger,* June 2, 1888; *Minutes,* 1888, 40.

23. *Minutes of the Seventh Annual Convention of the Woman's Christian Temperance Union of North Carolina* (Greensboro: Thomas Brothers, 1889), 17; *Chicago Union Signal,* November 27, 1890, quoted in Sims, "The Sword of the Spirit," 398.

perience. Prior to the organization of the National Association of Colored Women's Clubs in 1896, the WCTU represented the principal interdenominational voluntary association among black women. In addition to creating flourishing northern and western statewide WCTU organizations, black women managed statewide unions in five southern states. Southern African American women traveled to national and international temperance conferences, published newspapers, and learned skills of self-presentation that they took back to their churches and women's clubs.

Black women temperance workers seceded from white-led WCTUs because they believed that the organization failed to meet their goals. Their decision to secede illustrates the different meanings that temperance held for black and white women and the divergent expectations that black and white women brought to an interracial statewide organization. In the process of reclaiming the context of the temperance movement and its role in women's empowerment in the nineteenth century, historians have argued that the WCTU's chief attraction for women was its critique of the drunken father and husband, and that its activism sprang from a conviction of "feminine moral superiority." White female temperance activists linked drinking with male profligacy, domestic physical abuse, and women's economic dependence. They drew on the doctrine of separate spheres to confer on women moral authority in family matters, even if the exercise of that power necessitated a temporary foray into the public sphere. Thus among whites, temperance became increasingly a woman's issue, an expression of, in historian Nancy Cott's phrase, "female consciousness," or women's "shared sense of obligation to preserve and nourish life."[24] But most treatments of temperance reform and the WCTU focus on white women and neglect black women's participation.[25] The se-

24. Sims, "The Sword of the Spirit," 394; Cott, "What's in a Name? The Limits of 'Social Feminism'; or, Expanding the Vocabulary of Women's History," *Journal of American History*, 76, no. 3 (December 1989): 826–27.

25. An exception is Anne Firor Scott, *Natural Allies: Women's Associations in American History* (Urbana: University of Illinois Press, 1991), 99–103. Scattered references include the following: Jean E. Friedman, *The Enclosed Garden: Women and Community in the Evangelical South, 1830–1900* (Chapel Hill: University of North Carolina Press, 1985), 124; Dorothy Salem, *To Better Our World: Black Women in Organized Reform, 1890–1920* (Brooklyn: Carlson Publishing, 1990), 36, 37; Cynthia Neverdon-Morton, *Afro-American*

cession of the WCTU No. 2 suggests that black women brought another agenda to temperance work.

While African American women understood the women's issues embedded in the movement, participation in the WCTU folded into the cause of "racial uplift."[26] Before the institutionalization of segregation in the South, black women worked to build a society that recognized African American dignity, industriousness, and citizenship. Since many whites predicted that the absence of the "civilizing" influence of slavery would result in the extinction of the black race, drunkenness among blacks evoked a constellation of emotionally laden condemnations in the white community. When white southern tobacco farmers went to town to tie one on, no one suggested that their drinking sprees foretold the racial degeneracy of Anglo-Saxons. But a drunken black man staggering home from a saloon could inspire an editorial in the local white newspaper predicting that the black race would be extinct by the turn of the century.[27] Thus black women temperance activists worried not just about the pernicious effect of alcohol on the family but about the progress of the entire race. For them, temperance activities bolstered African Americans' contested claims on full membership in the polity.

Black women also hoped that the WCTU would provide an opportunity to build a Christian community that could serve as a model for interracial cooperation. For African American women,

---

Women of the South and the Advancement of the Race, 1895–1925 (Knoxville: University of Tennessee Press, 1989), 206–7; Beverly Guy Sheftall, *Daughters of Sorrow: Attitudes toward Black Women, 1880–1920* (Brooklyn: Carlson Publishing, 1989), 22; Mrs. N. F. Mossell, *The Work of the Afro-American Woman* (Nashville: Fisk University Press, 1894), 177–78.

26. For educated black women, the term *uplift* represented the class presumptions inherent in their approach to community work. Black women WCTU members used the term without question. On *racial uplift*, see Evelyn Brooks Higginbotham, "African-American Women's History and the Metalanguage of Race," *Signs* 17 (Winter 1992): 271.

27. Sims, "The Sword of the Spirit," 394–415; C. Vann Woodward, *Origins of the New South, 1877–1913* (Baton Rouge: Louisiana State University Press, 1951), 352; Joel Williamson, *The Crucible of Race: Black-White Relations in the American South since Emancipation* (New York: Oxford University Press, 1984), 115–16, 120. Williamson fixes 1915 as the year by which whites became convinced that blacks were not dying out but actually increasing in numbers, 461.

the WCTU represented a place removed from the pressures of capitalism and politics where women might see past skin color to recognize one another's divinity. One source of black women's optimism sprang from Frances Willard's family background. As a child, her abolitionist family opened their home as a stop on the Underground Railway, and her father was a Free-Soiler. She had the confidence of Frederick Douglass and William Lloyd Garrison, both members of an older generation of abolitionists.[28]

Throughout the 1890s in North Carolina, the WCTU No. 2 continued under African American women's direction. The career of Mary Lynch, the young Scotia Seminary graduate who joined the Charlotte WCTU, reveals the work's expansion after secession. In 1891, Lynch moved from Charlotte to teach at Livingstone College, a coeducational college operated in Salisbury under the auspices of the African Methodist Episcopal Zion church. The campus branch of the Young Woman's Christian Temperance Union (YWCTU) languished, but Lynch immediately revitalized it and invited North Carolina author Anna Julia Cooper to speak.[29] Cooper had recently written *A Voice from the South* and was then one of the most famous African American women in the country. From her post at Livingstone, Lynch threw herself into temperance work; within five years, she formed connections with the nation's leading African American women. At the founding meeting of the National Association of Colored Women's Clubs (NACWC), delegates adopted a resolution commending the work of the WCTU; and the following year, Mary Lynch delivered an address at the national NACWC convention entitled "Temperance Reform in the Twentieth Century." By 1899, Lynch had organized numerous chapters, served as president of the WCTU No. 2, and attended the national WCTU convention in St. Paul, Minnesota.[30]

Meanwhile, the group that Lynch had formed at Livingstone

28. "The Position of the National Woman's Christian Temperance Union of the United States in Relation to the Colored People," February 6, 1895, Willard Memorial Library.

29. *Living-stone* 8, no. 3 (September 1891): 44; 8, no. 4 (October 1891): 63; 8, no. 6 (December 1891); 8, no. 7 (January 1892): 145.

30. Charles Harris Wesley, *The History of the National Association of Colored Women's Clubs: A Legacy of Service* (Washington, D.C.: National Association of Colored Women's Clubs, 1984), 43, 45; *Star of Zion,* September 7, 1899. *A.M.E. Zion Quarterly Review* nos. 1–2 (1899): 100.

flourished. One of Lynch's protégées was Annie Kimball, a classics major. Kimball led the YWCTU in early morning prayer meetings on Sundays. Peer pressure to join must have been strong, for an observer reported, "Every girl, without exception, [who was a] boarder in the school . . . has signed the pledge and become a member." Each year, the group visited the almshouse, bringing box lunches, tracts, hymnbooks, and Bibles. A male classmate marveled, "Young women who at first were too embarrassed to lead a prayer meeting can do so now with all of the earnestness necessary."[31]

Kimball brought both racial and female consciousness to temperance work. She argued eloquently that where whites found black degeneracy, she found hope. The only trait becoming extinct among African Americans, she charged, was "the spirit of unmanly and unwomanly servility and fawning." Kimball exhorted her female classmates to lift "[t]he banner of purity . . . around every home," and she predicted that the "dram-shop and all other places of ill-repute" would soon fall to "school houses, and churches of the living God." Then, she predicted, those whites who "maligned and slandered" blacks would be "utterly put down by a more enlightened and healthy public sentiment." On a May day in 1894, Annie Kimball graduated as salutatorian of her class, gave the commencement address in Latin, and that afternoon married an AME Zion minister named George Clinton. They made their home in Charlotte, where she became state president of the YWCTU.[32]

When Annie Kimball Clinton moved to Charlotte, she joined a statewide network of African American women who had been active in the cause for over a decade. She could have become a member of any of several black chapters in the city. In a single week in September 1897, one group met at the Congregational church, another met at the Seventh Street Presbyterian Church, and the chapter at the Grace AME Zion Church kicked off its annual oratorical contest. The meetings at churches were not exclusively for church members; the public was invited to all of them. A "bicycle entertainment" raised almost one hundred dollars for "caring for the sick and needy and burying the dead." To coordinate the

31. W. F. Fonvielle, *Some Reminiscences of College Days* (Raleigh: privately published by the author, 1904), 119–21.
32. *Living-stone* 8, no. 1 (May 1891): 3; *Star of Zion*, June 15, 1899, 1. Annie Kimball died six years after her marriage.

separate groups, the citywide officers of the local union met every Monday afternoon at a private home. Chapter activities included contemplative meetings, fund-raising, and outreach work among the intemperate at the jail and the hospital.[33]

When the WCTU No. 2 seceded, the white organization initially realized that its original approach to black members should be replaced by cooperation with the officers of the African American chapters. It dropped the Work Among the Colored People department from its letterhead and appointed a committee to cooperate with the black women.[34] But within two years, the white women were back at work, this time with the department of Home and Foreign Missionary Work Among and Through Afro-Americans. Did the switch to "Afro-Americans" exemplify increased sensitivity, or was it a marketing ploy, now that white organizers competed with the WCTU No. 2? Did "Among and Through" result from some sort of committee fight over whether to recognize black leaders by working "through" them? Whatever promise the new name held, by 1895 "Through" and "Afro-American" had disappeared from the title, and the department became Home and Foreign Missionary Work Amongst the Colored People.[35]

Although white women knew about black women's activities, apparently they refused to recognize black women's authority and competed with them to organize new African American WCTU chapters under local white control.[36] White women cryptically

33. *Star of Zion*, September 9, 1897; April 14, 1898; August 26, 1897; September 2, 1897; September 23, 1897; October 7, 1897; October 21, 1897; March 4, 1897.

34. *Minutes*, 1889, 17.

35. In 1892, the national WCTU abolished the Work Among the Colored People department and gave black WCTU chapters equal organizational status. Mrs. J. E. Ray, the director of Home and Foreign Missionary Work Among and Through Afro-Americans for North Carolina asked that the state's white WCTU retain this department on a trial basis. Ray replaced Steele when she moved with her husband to Denver, Colorado. *Minutes of the Eleventh Annual Convention of the Woman's Christian Temperance Union of North Carolina* (Greensboro: C. F. Thomas, 1893), 68–74. On the title Home and Foreign Missionary Work Amongst the Colored People, see *Minutes of the Thirteenth Annual Convention of the Woman's Christian Temperance Union of North Carolina* (Greensboro: C. F. Thomas, 1895), 70.

36. *Minutes*, 1893, 68; *Minutes of the Tenth Annual Convention of the Woman's Christian Temperance Union of North Carolina* (Greensboro: Thomas Brothers, 1892), 4.

reported in 1895 that the "'sisters in black' have an Independent Union in Charlotte, well officered and doing good work." The new white state superintendent noted, "Naturally we look for co-operation among the colored women under auspices of Unions controlled by them and this gives us an open door of helpfulness in many ways." Black women must have resented white women who looked for cooperation, yet devalued black women's work. The white women's efforts found some success among African American youth, through the schools and prisons, all captive audiences, but only rarely did they form an organization of adult black women under white control.[37]

Why did white women continue to try to establish black chapters under their control when they knew that the WCTU No. 2 existed? Why did they refuse to recognize the leadership of that organization and respond cooperatively? There are at least two reasons. Except for a few leaders like Rosa Steele, most white women knew very little about, and discounted the abilities of, educated black women. Hence, they presumed that a black union would do better work under white leadership. Most important, the white women wanted very much to control the politics of the black temperance workers. They were not altogether sure that African Americans, because of their political allegiance to the "wet" Republican party, could be trusted to vote for prohibition. Moreover, they believed that blacks proved easy prey for corrupt politicians and sinister forces. For example, after the formation of the WCTU No. 2, the new white superintendent of the Work Among the Colored People department of the white WCTU announced an imminent Catholic peril. She reported that Catholics, the arch-nemeses of prohibitionists, had spread out, "propagating Catholicism among the *blacks* of the *South*." She asked, "Is it to *save souls* this new movement is made to Catholicise the negroes, or is it that he has a *vote* and now, that he is free, can aid in extending papal dominion in the United States?"[38] White women reasoned that, left on their own, black women might not be counted as political allies in local prohibition elections.

Despite the distance between the white and black organizations, flawed but important interracial contacts between women con-

37. *Minutes,* 1895, 71; 1893, 71; 1895, 71–72.
38. *Minutes,* 1893, 69.

tinued until the turn of the century. For example, when the black women met in statewide convention in Salisbury in 1896, the local white WCTU members attended a session and heard the white state president speak. Elected president of the WCTU No. 2 at that meeting, Mary Lynch attended the white convention the following year as a delegate from the WCTU No. 2. Black women must have continued to hope for interracial cooperation between the two branches. They referred to the white group as the WCTU No. 1, and in 1896 they reorganized themselves as the Lucy Thurman WCTU, honoring the black national organizer. They eschewed any term that would denote racial exclusivity.[39]

The racial issues experienced on a local level in North Carolina also surfaced in the national WCTU. In the 1890s, growing numbers of Catholic and southern European immigrants threatened prohibition, and the Spanish-American War inspired an upsurge of popular imperialism.[40] Despite her abolitionist legacy, Willard sought to avoid disruptive fights over the WCTU's racial policies. A new generation of African American leaders, for example, Ida Wells-Barnett, criticized Willard for tolerating segregation.[41]

Willard's laissez-faire policy put black WCTU members in the difficult position of weighing divided loyalties. At the 1893 national convention in St. Louis, black women delegates found themselves seated at a separate banquet table. Staging an impromptu protest, the African American women refused the segregated seating, dispersed, and sat at the tables assigned to their respective state organizations. The white leadership asked them to return to their separate table, but instead the black women rose and walked out. Rather than risk the consequences of secession of the national black WCTU, the white women hurried out after them and "had enough good sense and Christianity to call them back and treat them like sisters."[42]

Reflecting the national mood, party politics impinged upon the

39. *Star of Zion,* August 6, 1896; *Minutes of the Fifteenth Annual Convention of the Woman's Christian Temperance Union of North Carolina* (High Point: Enterprise Book and Job Print, 1896), 20.

40. James H. Timberlake, *Prohibition and the Progressive Movement, 1900–1920* (Cambridge: Harvard University Press, 1966), 115–21.

41. Dorothy Sterling, *Black Foremothers: Three Lives* (New York: Feminist Press, 1988), 90–91.

42. *A.M.E. Zion Quarterly Review* 3 (April 1893): 417.

continuing interracial contact between the North Carolina WCTUs. A black-supported coalition of Republicans and Populists won control of state government in 1896, and African Americans gained their greatest political voice since Reconstruction. Retaliating two years later, the Democratic Party mounted a white supremacy campaign that used gendered rhetoric to introduce violence and extralegal intimidation into politics. Women joined the White Government Unions and exhorted white men to protect them by ending black participation in politics.[43]

Temperance, which had once held such promise for interracial understanding, now served white supremacy in North Carolina. In 1896, at the height of black political power in the state, Belle Kearney, a white Louisianian with North Carolina roots, gave a speech at the North Carolina white WCTU convention entitled "Why the Wheels Are Clogged." Mary Lynch sat in the audience as a delegate from the WCTU No. 2 and listened to Kearney tell the delegates that prohibition would never pass while 250,000 blacks voted in the South.[44] Quickly white women's local temperance strategies reflected the racial hysteria of the moment. Temperance workers actually held mock elections for whites only to demonstrate that prohibition would pass if blacks could not vote.[45] In 1898, the state's white WCTU abolished its Work Among the Colored People department forever, and delegate exchanges between

43. On the white supremacy campaign in North Carolina, see the following: Helen Edmonds, *The Negro and Fusion Politics in North Carolina, 1894–1901* (Chapel Hill: University of North Carolina, 1951); Paul D. Escott, *Many Excellent People: Power and Privilege in North Carolina, 1850–1900* (Chapel Hill: University of North Carolina Press, 1985), 247–61; J. Morgan Kousser, *The Shaping of Southern Politics: Suffrage Restriction and the Establishment of the One-Party South, 1880–1910* (New Haven: Yale University Press, 1974); Henry Leon Prather, Sr., *We Have Taken a City: Wilmington Racial Massacre and Coup of 1898* (Rutherford, N.J.: Fairleigh Dickinson University Press, 1984); Anderson, *Race and Politics in North Carolina, 1872–1901*. On white women and white supremacy, see Williamson, *The Crucible of Race*, 124–30; George Fredrickson, *The Arrogance of Race* (Middletown, Conn.: Wesleyan University Press, 1988), 178; Jacquelyn Dowd Hall, *Revolt against Chivalry: Jessie Daniel Ames and the Women's Campaign against Lynching* (New York: Columbia University Press, 1974); Glenda Gilmore, "Gender and Jim Crow: Women and the Politics of White Supremacy, 1896–1920" (Ph.D. diss., University of North Carolina, 1992), 188–243.

44. *North Carolina White Ribbon* 6, no. 1, July 1, 1896.

45. Whitener, *Prohibition in North Carolina*, 121.

the WCTUs ended. Two years later, after North Carolina whites disfranchised blacks by state constitutional amendment, Belle Kearney returned to the state WCTU convention to peddle copies of her book, *A Slaveholder's Daughter,* which painted a romantic portrait of bondage.

A few months before disfranchisement, Mary Lynch set sail for the international WCTU convention in Edinburgh, Scotland. She spoke to the assembled women, visited London, and spent time in the countryside. While there she must have heard the news that North Carolina had robbed its African American citizens of the right to vote.[46] Lynch's journey is a metaphor for the problem of knitting gender ties across racial lines. After the white supremacy campaign, she had to travel across the Atlantic in order to discuss shared concerns with white women; she could no longer work with white women in her hometown. Race had one meaning in Salisbury, where organizing for temperance brought up issues of political power, and another in Edinburgh, where white women could recognize Lynch as a missionary working fervently for a women's issue.

It was a force beyond the control of women—party politics—that obliterated interracial contact in North Carolina's WCTU. Temperance was above all a political issue, and the WCTU solicited prohibition votes. When the white supremacy campaign at first discouraged black voting and then disfranchised African Americans, white women's concern with black temperance ended, and they readily recast their former WCTU allies as part of the "Negro problem." While the experience of the WCTU points up the difficulty of transcending difference, as long as African Americans had political rights, women's interaction continued because black votes mattered.

Disfranchisement profoundly reordered society and had a powerful impact upon the lives of those normally cast as the group with the least direct involvement in the political process—women. After two decades of interaction, the Democrats' white supremacy campaign caused black and white WCTU members to enter the Jim

46. Marcus H. Boulware to Mrs. M. J. Bahnsen, May 12, 1974, in the North Carolina Collection Clipping File through 1975, vol. 91, p. 725, North Carolina Collection. On the international work of the WCTU, see Ian Tyrrell, *Woman's World, Woman's Empire: The Woman's Christian Temperance Union in International Perspective* (Chapel Hill: University of North Carolina Press, 1991).

Crow era more estranged than ever before. North Carolina white women severed ties with black women, and they henceforth chose not to see them, making black women's temperance work invisible to the white community.

What began as a novel experiment in coalition politics based on gender solidarity ended in a lesson in the limits of sisterhood. Yet this failure left a heritage of struggle that affords precious glimpses of "melting times"—century-old parables of empowerment for all southern women, black and white. In the debris of southern society, women conceived a new kind of politics, a biracial attack on a single issue that affected all women. They formed a grass-roots organization that defied some racial conventions and left others in place.

The experience of the North Carolina WCTU suggests that class and racial divisions operate powerfully in daily life, isolating women with shared concerns from one another and providing fertile ground for political demagoguery that obscures commonality. Maximizing dichotomy in 1990 engenders false hierarchies—and produces racism—as easily as it did in 1890. Such social constructions mean that feminists of all races have to travel, as Mary Lynch did, across metaphorical oceans to reach one another.

"We'll Take Our Stand"

Race, Class, and Gender in the Southern Student Organizing Committee, 1964–1969

CHRISTINA GREENE

In response to the black freedom movement that swept throughout the South in the early 1960s, increasing numbers of southern whites, particularly students on predominantly white college campuses, became civil rights activists.[1] Some of these white southerners organized the Southern Student Organizing Committee (SSOC) in the spring of 1964 with the primary goal of mobilizing other young, white southerners to join the freedom movement. In its second year, SSOC established a biracial leadership and attempted to organize African American students from historically black campuses in the South. During its brief existence (from 1964 to 1969), SSOC was a persistent voice in the South against racial oppression, poverty, and the Vietnam War, and was an advocate for university reform and women's liberation.[2]

For comments on several earlier versions of this essay, I would like to thank Betty Brandon, Leslie Brown, William H. Chafe, Kirsten Fischer, Jacquelyn Dowd Hall, Maya Hasegawa, Charles Payne, and Tim Tyson.

1. The *Southern Patriot,* a publication of the Southern Conference Education Fund that was edited by Carl and Anne Braden, reported numerous instances of growing civil rights activism on white campuses between 1962 and 1964. *Southern Patriot:* 22 (February 1964): 1; "White Students Challenge Segregation" and Vivien Franklin, "Campus Report: Renaissance in Texas," 20 (May 1962): 2, 4; Marion Barry, "Knoxville Movement Unites Negro and White," 21 (May 1963): 4; Sam Shirah, "Visit to Birmingham: White Youth Seek Liberation," 21 (November 1963): 4 and "Student Citizens at Work," 21 (December 1963): 1; Sue Thrasher, "A Campus Victory: White Students Move," 22 (February 1964).

2. "Proposal of Organization," box 2, folder 25; "Southern Student Organiz-

Significantly, the emergence of civil rights activity on predominantly white southern campuses occurred *prior* to the massive influx of northern white students to the South in 1964. Any study of the civil rights movement must acknowledge that it was primarily a struggle by and for African Americans. Yet historians of the civil rights and student movements have almost entirely overlooked white southern student activism.[3]

SSOC's formation in the spring of 1964 was the result of the sometimes sporadic, frequently unconnected activity of students on white campuses throughout the South in the early 1960s. During those years, a small number of white southern students were formulating, often in cooperation with black students from other colleges, their own distinctively southern solution to racial injustice in their region. Sometimes there was only a handful of whites in largely black-initiated and black-organized protests. These white participants were not "Yankee transplants" but were white southerners responding to racial oppression in their homeland. Some had become active in local civil rights groups. Many had been moved to their "apostasy" by religious convictions. Others were motivated by a sense of shame and even horror, particularly after the 1963 Birmingham church bombing that killed four little black girls. Although SSOC became the major catalyst for organizing white southern students after 1964, in the early 1960s, white activists such as Bob Zellner and Sam Shirah were funded by the Southern Conference Education Fund to recruit whites on southern campuses for the Student Nonviolent Coordinating Committee (SNCC).

---

ing Committee, Funding Proposal by Ron Parker and David Kotelchuck," box 2, folder 25; "We'll Take Our Stand—Nashville, April 4, 1964," box 1, folder 4—all in Southern Student Organizing Committee Papers, Martin Luther King Center for Social Change, Atlanta, Ga., hereinafter cited as SSOC Papers. For a good organizational history of SSOC, see Bryant Simon, "Southern Student Organizing Committee: A New Rebel Yell in Dixie" (honors essay, History Department, University of North Carolina at Chapel Hill, 1983), in North Carolina Collection, Wilson Library, University of North Carolina at Chapel Hill.

3. SSOC activities and members are briefly discussed in Clayborne Carson, *In Struggle: SNCC and the Black Awakening of the 1960's* (Cambridge: Harvard University Press, 1981); Anthony J. Lukas, *Don't Shoot—We Are Your Children!* (New York: Random House, 1971); Sara Evans, *Personal Politics: The Roots of Women's Liberation in the Civil Rights Movement and the New Left* (New York: Random House, 1979). Kirkpatrick Sale, *SDS* (New York: Random House, 1973).

Where students did organize at predominantly white southern schools, the pattern was typical. On recently desegregated campuses in Florida and Arkansas, for example, protests erupted over campus housing, dining, and athletic policies that continued to exclude blacks. And in college towns from Texas to Tennessee, students and community protesters joined together to picket local restaurants that refused to serve blacks.[4]

The experiences of Nan Grogan (now Nan Orrock) and Sue Thrasher, two white women prominent in SSOC, were representative of those of many young white southerners who found their way into the movement. Grogan described herself as "a typical southern white female student from a middle-class background, small town upbringing, parents from Georgia and Tennessee, you know, real decidedly southern roots." During the summer of 1963, Grogan went to Washington, D.C., where she worked "for the first time with black people" and "was encouraged to go to the march [the 1963 March on Washington] by people in the office that I worked with." At the demonstration, Grogan discovered how widespread the civil rights movement had become and that it had even touched the small towns in Virginia near her college. When she returned to Mary Washington College, she became involved in the movement through the campus YWCA and then volunteered in the 1964 Mississippi Summer Project, where she met Sue Thrasher. That winter, Grogan participated in an SSOC Christmas project in Laurel, Mississippi, where she was arrested. Following her graduation, she became involved in an innovative and highly successful voter registration project in several black counties in the Southside region of Virginia.[5]

Sue Thrasher, who was from a working-class family in Savannah, Tennessee, was one of the SSOC founders and served as its first executive secretary. Like Grogan, Thrasher initially hesitated to move from college social life to social activism at Scarritt College, a Methodist missionary school in Nashville. But several racial incidents changed her mind, including an episode in which her roommate, a woman from the Fiji Islands, was refused service at a local restaurant. As Thrasher explained, "These painful reminders

4. See *Southern Patriot* 20 (September 1962): 3; 21 (February 1963): 1, 4; 21 (May 1963): 1.
5. Nan Orrock (formerly Nan Grogan), interview by author, Atlanta, Ga., February 27, 1989; Stanley Wise, interview by author, Atlanta, Ga., February 26, 1989.

resulted in an evaluation of our feelings as well as a deep questioning into the Christian student's role in social change."[6]

Although the racial intolerance in the surrounding community deeply disturbed her, she was uncertain about how to respond. First, she introduced a rather mild resolution at the Student Council that called for universal Christian "brotherhood" but never mentioned race. In retrospect, Thrasher thought the statement seemed "completely wishy-washy," yet it stirred rancorous debate on campus and she was suddenly cast as a radical troublemaker. As she recalled, "I was terrified. . . . It was the first time I'd gone against a major part of whatever group I belonged to." She soon began working with a local Southern Christian Leadership Conference (SCLC) affiliate. In 1963, Thrasher helped to establish an intercollegiate coalition that included a large number of white faculty and students to protest the segregationist policies of a local restaurant in Nashville.[7]

Most whites, of course, including students, remained largely indifferent or hostile to the civil rights movement. Even for those few who were concerned, and especially for the still smaller number who were willing to become involved, it was difficult. As Thrasher explained: "White students didn't know, for one thing, how to get involved in the civil rights movement. They couldn't very well go across town and find an SNCC meeting and join up. And also there was a reluctance. People got involved very slowly, from doing one thing and getting more pulled in."[8]

For white southerners like Sue Thrasher, there was a feeling of cultural isolation in becoming active in the civil rights movement. Most of the freedom workers in the early 1960s were either blacks or northern whites. (Among women, however, the reverse was true, for the majority of white women in the movement prior to 1964 were southerners.) Not only did southern whites risk the dangers confronting all freedom workers, but unlike northern whites, they also risked more immediate ostracism from friends and family, and a resulting sense of displacement in their homeland.[9]

6. *Southern Patriot* 21 (May 1963): 1.

7. Lukas, *Don't Shoot—We Are Your Children!*, 144–47. At this time, SNCC and SCLC were almost indistinguishable in Nashville.

8. Sue Thrasher, telephone interview by author, Amherst, Mass., April 8, 1989.

9. Evans, *Personal Politics*, 35. For recent discussions of northern whites in the black freedom movement, see Mary Aiken Rothchild, *A Case of Black*

College and university officials often used disciplinary action to discourage southern white students from becoming active. For example, Bob Zellner, a white student who was an early SNCC worker and the son of an Alabama minister, was subjected to cross burnings by the Ku Klux Klan, was summoned to the state attorney general's office, and was then asked by his college president to withdraw from school. In another incident, four southern colleges in succession expelled one of Zellner's white friends because of "his integrationist beliefs," and his family suffered violent reprisals, including the kidnapping and police beating of his younger brother. Both Sue Thrasher and Nan Grogan were followed by the Klan in Mississippi and Virginia. But usually the intimidation was more subtle than these examples suggest. As Zellner explained: "One should not get the impression that these situations occur each day in the South. The fact is that these fascist attacks are seldom necessary because the majority, in the deepest levels of their unconscious minds, understand that there are certain areas of life and ideas into which they are not to venture."[10]

And so white students were isolated, afraid, and discouraged by families, including those who considered themselves moderate or liberal, who told them to "stay out of this integration mess." Even students who were "capable and desirous of participation in the integration movement" felt threatened by both real and imagined reprisals from white authorities.[11]

In response to such fear and isolation, forty-five students gathered the weekend of April 3, 1964, in Nashville "to talk about common problems and goals as [we] seek to create a better Southland." Mostly white southerners, but including a number of black students as well, they came from ten southern states: Alabama, Florida, Kentucky, Georgia, Louisiana, Mississippi, North Carolina, South Carolina, Tennessee, and Virginia. According to Sue Thrasher:

> **Our initial instinct was to just find other people like ourselves who were white and were southern and who had gotten somewhat in-**

---

and White: Northern Volunteers and the Southern Freedom Summers, 1964–1965 (Westport, Conn.: Greenwood Press, 1982), and Doug McAdam, *Freedom Summer* (New York: Oxford University Press, 1988).

10. Bob Zellner, "Repression Keeps White Students Silent," *Southern Patriot* 22 (January 1964): 1; Zellner, "Visit to Ole Miss: 'Creative Minority' Is Emerging," *Southern Patriot* 20 (December 1962): 1; Orrock, interview.

11. Zellner, "Repression," 4.

volved in the civil rights movement; and [we were] feeling that there could be more people involved if there was a support network established. . . . [w]e sort of knew who those people were by word of mouth and [we] pulled that group together to see about the possibility of forming a Southwide organization.[12]

One of the first tasks the new organization undertook that weekend was to formulate its vision of a new South. The SSOC manifesto, "We'll Take Our Stand," pointed out the irony of southern poverty amidst American prosperity while a southerner (President Lyndon Johnson) sat in the White House. It described its southern homeland as the "leading sufferer and battleground of the war against racism, poverty, injustice and autocracy." Like their agrarian forebears, SSOC activists railed against the evils of industrialization and urbanization that had cast a blight upon their region. They vowed to begin a movement that would start on southern campuses but would spread to communities throughout the South "to tell the Truth that must ultimately make us free." They urged their region to be "an exemplar of the national goals we all believe in rather than a deterrent to them." Specifically, the writers called for "an end to segregation and racism" and "to personal poverty and deprivation" as well as the eradication of "'public poverty' that leaves us without decent schools, parks, medical care, housing and communities." SSOC advocated "a democratic society" to replace "manipulation by vested elites" and "a place where industries and large cities can blend into farms and natural rural splendor to provide meaningful work and leisure opportunities." They closed their manifesto with a ringing call to fellow southerners to join in the creation of a new South: "We, as young Southerners hereby pledge to take our stand together here to work for a new order, a new South, a place which embodies our ideals for all the world to emulate, not ridicule. We find our destiny as individuals in the South in our hopes and our work together as brothers."[13]

The closing statement revealed not only youthful idealism but also a certain defensiveness regarding their southern identity. Moreover, their use of the term "brothers" indicated a male-centered

12. "Proposal of Organization," SSOC Papers; Thrasher, interview.
13. "We'll Take Our Stand—Nashville, April 4, 1964," SSOC Papers; Sue Thrasher, "SSOC Defended," *Great Speckled Bird,* June 30, 1969, 7; *New Rebel,* May 27, 1964.

perspective that manifested itself not simply in language but through-out the organization.

The SSOC proclamation was written primarily by Robb Burlage, a Texan who was a graduate student in economics at Harvard. Burlage was also a member of Students for a Democratic Society (SDS) and had been one of the principal authors of the Port Huron Statement, produced by an early meeting of SDS students in Ann Arbor, Michigan, in 1962.[14] In many ways, the SSOC manifesto reflected the same idealism as the Port Huron Statement, partic-ularly its belief that social democracy could be achieved peacefully by reforming rather than abolishing existing economic and politi-cal structures.

At the conclusion of the founding meeting in Nashville, it was clear to the students that there was "a great deal of activity on [southern] campuses, ranging from moderate to radical" and that a number of issues concerned southern students, among them civil rights, peace, academic freedom, civil liberties, capital punishment, and unemploy-ment. Echoing one of SNCC's central organizing principles, the founders decided that SSOC's purpose would be to aid local campus groups in efforts that the groups themselves would determine.[15]

Despite SSOC's radical agenda, its vision and ideology were problematic from the organization's inception. The SSOC mani-festo, "We'll Take Our Stand," was an explicit and self-conscious appeal to a tradition of indigenous white southern radical dissent. The title was drawn from another manifesto, *I'll Take My Stand,* written thirty-five years earlier in Nashville by twelve southern white agrarian radicals who called themselves the Fugitives.[16] Like their predecessors, SSOC members hoped to build a redemptive new South based upon an agrarian anti-industrialism and the ide-als of participatory democracy, social justice, and pride in southern identity (often referred to as "southern consciousness"). This time, though, SSOC hoped to transform the racism and white supremacy

14. James Miller, *"Democracy Is in the Streets": From Port Huron to the Siege of Chicago* (New York: Simon and Schuster, 1987), 122–25; *New Rebel,* May 27, 1964.

15. Ron Parker and David Kotelchuck, "Southern Student Organizing Com-mittee," SSOC Papers. SSOC later voted to become a membership organiza-tion and to organize SSOC chapters and affiliates on southern campuses.

16. Twelve Southerners, *I'll Take My Stand: The South and the Agrarian Tradition* (New York: Harper and Brothers, 1930).

that marred the vision of the Nashville enclave. In SSOC's vision, blacks and whites would be participants together in the struggle.

A contradiction existed, however, between SSOC's appeal to southern consciousness (or southern nationalism) and members' efforts to mobilize white southerners on behalf of racial harmony in their homeland. The disjuncture constituted the Achilles' heel of the organization: how could a movement of white southerners reclaim white southern tradition as a basis for social change when so much of that heritage was mired in centuries of economic, racial, and sexual oppression? More to the point, SSOC drew on symbols of the Confederate South rather than on an explicitly anti-racist, southern white tradition (represented, for example, by the abolitionist Grimké sisters and even by some of the early Populists) as strategies for re-creating a new southern identity and for building a southern white progressive movement. The first title of its newsletter, the *New Rebel,* and the SSOC logo, a Confederate flag with a black hand and a white hand clasped over it, signified this contradiction. During its first year, SSOC abandoned both the newsletter title and the logo as insensitive to blacks, but the SSOC logo reappeared in 1967 and again in 1969, shortly before the organization's dissolution. Not insignificantly, the logo resurfaced well after SSOC had ceased to recruit students on historically black campuses and also after the Black Power Movement had emerged.[17]

Even SSOC's more strategic use of southern consciousness was problematic. For example, the Days of Southern Secession, an organizing strategy devised by SSOC in 1968 to attract white southern students to the antiwar movement, was created "in the tradition of the poor and progressive southerners who seceded from the Confederate States rather than fight in the rich man's war for slavery and in the tradition of other southerners and southern movements that have resisted Yankee imperialism whether directed against South Vietnam or our own South."[18] Yet the creators of this

17. After the appearance of only two publications, the title of SSOC's newsletter, *The New Rebel,* was changed to the rather innocuous *SSOC Newsletter* and finally became the *New South Student* in 1965. The disagreement over the SSOC logo still prevails, for some former SSOC members continue to defend the use of the symbol. Gene Guerrero, interview by author, Atlanta, Ga., February 26, 1989; Thrasher, interview.

18. Lyn Wells and Tom Gardiner, "Southern Students Mobilize," *Student Mobilizer,* April 15, 1968, 2.

strategy also acknowledged that southern secession had a "more widely accepted Confederate usage" than the one they hoped to evoke. In effect, the contradictions of organizing southern whites to forge an interracial "beloved community" created a dilemma that significantly worsened after 1964, when the role of whites in the movement was becoming ever more problematic and the vision of an integrated society was slowly fading before exhortations of black autonomy and black power.

It is important to remember, however, that SSOC was formed in April of 1964, several months before the massive influx of northern white civil rights workers to the South and prior to the Democratic National Convention in August, when the biracial Mississippi Freedom Democratic Party delegation was denied seating—two events that raised deep suspicion among black activists regarding the role of whites in the civil rights movement. Thus, before adjourning the April meeting, SSOC selected a subcommittee that included Sue Thrasher and two white male SNCC members, Ed Hamlett and Sam Shirah, to present its program proposal to SNCC. The decision of SSOC members to seek SNCC's approval for their new organization signaled an understanding on the part of SSOC that it was part of a larger movement. Similarly, the decision to form fraternal ties with SDS, with the latter agreeing not to organize SDS chapters in the South, suggests that while SSOC may have been perceived as more moderate by some than SNCC or SDS, SSOC members clearly saw themselves as linked to radical and militant student protest groups.[19]

A number of SNCC members were highly supportive of SSOC and appreciated the difficult task the organization faced—organizing white southerners to join the southern freedom movement. Not surprisingly, the most vocal SNCC supporters of SSOC were among the first SNCC people to articulate the concept of black power— Courtland Cox and Stokely Carmichael, in particular. As Thrasher remembers the exchange:

19. Sue Thrasher to SSOC, May 25, 1964, box 1, SSOC Papers; Parker and Kotelchuck, "Southern Student Organizing Committee," SSOC Papers; Carson, *In Struggle,* 102; SDS president Todd Gitlin to SSOC, May 7, 1964, SSOC Papers; "A Resolution Concerning SDS's Role in the South and the Relationship between SDS and the Southern Student Organizing Committee," May 29, 1964, Students for a Democratic Society Files (Glen Rock, N.J.: Microfilming Corp. of America, 1977), series 2A, reel 9; American Friends Service Committee, Report No. 14, November 25, 1964, in author's possession.

I used to think about it as being sort of a preliminary discussion around the whole issue of the role of whites, because it was a hot discussion in that SNCC Executive Committee. . . . [W]ere we creating an alternative, a competitive organization? Was there a need for two organizations? Could we just do the work we wanted to do inside the organization [SNCC]? And we felt pretty strongly that there needed to be a separate organization . . . but [we] always saw ourselves as being linked to SNCC. . . . it was never our intention to create a competitive organization, but to create an organization that would in some ways be part of SNCC, if not directly.[20]

Although the debate over SSOC's relationship to SNCC was intense and even somewhat heated at times, according to Thrasher, it was "always a friendly discussion." SSOC members presumably did not pose the same problem for SNCC that other whites in the movement did. With southern whites in their own organization, SNCC did not have to worry about them undermining the autonomy and leadership of black activists, as often happened after large numbers of northern whites joined the movement. Moreover, SSOC was geared primarily toward organizing whites and students, whereas SNCC was focusing more of its energy in black communities. Thus the two groups worked cooperatively for several years, and SNCC even provided financial support to the fledgling SSOC in its first year. At the same time, it appears that at least to some SNCC members SSOC was an aberration. According to SNCC executive secretary Stanley Wise: "There was another prevailing view in the organization [SNCC]—that we were wasting time in the white community, that to participate with whites and encourage that kind of group . . . was just unrealistic. . . . these were not the people in the white community. This was a diversion which we could not explain; that is not *the* white community."[21]

Although most SSOC members were white, the organization included a small number of blacks and other students of color. The

20. Dorie Ladner Cherne, interview by author, Washington D.C., June 13, 1989; James Forman, interview by author, Washington D.C., June 14, 1989; Courtland Cox, interview by author, Washington D.C., June 14, 1989; Sue Thrasher to Ruby Doris Smith, May 23, 1964, Student Non-Violent Coordinating Committee Papers, 1959–1972 (Sanford, N.C.: Microfilm Corp. of America, 1982), reel 44; Carson, *In Struggle,* 22, 102; Thrasher, interview.

21. Thrasher, interview; Carson, *In Struggle,* 103; Sue Thrasher to SSOC, May 25, 1964, SSOC Papers; Wise, interview.

presence of African American students in SSOC is an interesting phenomenon, especially given the presence of SNCC in the South. Black students may have joined SSOC because by 1964 SNCC was focusing little of its energy in campus organizing. The perception that SSOC was less radical than SNCC may have also attracted some black students to SSOC. Stanley Wise worked closely with some of the SSOC students in Virginia in 1964 and 1965 and has suggested another more controversial explanation—one that might not have been articulated in the wake of the Black Power Movement—for the presence of black students in SSOC. Wise described the sense of elation that he and other black students felt at discovering white students, especially white southern students, who shared their commitment and dream of an interracial community. "I could understand very easily how a [black] person would choose to work with SSOC rather than SNCC because it was just such a powerful psychological and emotional experience, unlike experiences that you've had, and [that] you really didn't expect to have."[22]

Not only did SSOC deliberately elect a biracial leadership (all male) in 1965, but the newsletter included a number of articles, written mostly by African American SSOC members, that addressed issues of particular concern to black students. Several pieces explored the appalling conditions at historically black colleges and universities in the South; and in 1966, SSOC published a special issue on black power, edited by SSOC member Bob Dewart, a black student from Virginia. Nevertheless, black students in SSOC appear never to have numbered more than 5 percent of the total membership, and by 1967 most had left the organization. Several, such as Laly Washington, who joined SNCC, became part of the Black Power Movement. In 1969, Howard Spencer, former SSOC vice-chairman, became a victim of an FBI frame-up that was part of an effort to crush black militancy in Jackson, Mississippi. Howard Romaine, a white student who was part of SSOC's biracial leadership along with Spencer, later claimed that black membership was largely tokenism and that SSOC was an organization primarily of and for southern whites.[23]

22. Wise, interview; Cox, interview; Forman, interview.
23. "The Black Power Controversy," *New South Student* 11 (December 1966); *Southern Patriot* 28 (May 1969): 5; Howard Romaine, telephone interview with author, Nashville, Tenn., April 8, 1989. Articles by black SSOC

At the same SNCC Executive Committee meeting in 1964 in which SSOC sought SNCC's approval for its new organization, the three SSOC members also presented a proposal for SNCC to fund a white students' project. The committee agreed, and under the auspices of the Council of Federated Organizations 1964 Summer Project, SSOC organized a white community project in Mississippi—known as the White Folks Project.[24]

The project was designed to attract new allies in the white community to the civil rights movement. Despite noble intentions, most participants deemed the project a failure. Yet it also spurred endless discussions within SSOC regarding the feasibility of organizing poor southern whites and of organizing any whites separately from blacks. The issue was further complicated for SSOC by the emergence of the Black Power Movement. In a 1966 memo to the organization, Anne Braden, a white veteran civil rights worker from Alabama who served as an informal advisor to SSOC, made this comment about the Mississippi project: "People say the poor white people of Mississippi cannot be reached—but how do we know? Suppose all the human energy that has been poured by white people into reaching Negro Mississippians had been put into reaching white Mississippians? What would have happened? We'll never know."[25]

Braden went on to outline some of the dangers she saw in SSOC's efforts to organize whites separately from blacks. Arguing against the concept of white consciousness, which was usually termed southern consciousness or southern nationalism within SSOC, she urged that teams of white and black organizers be created. If SSOC failed to do this, she warned, it risked creating a "Frankenstein." SSOC must be ever-vigilant about combating racism, particularly when organizing among whites, Braden insisted. Racism was combated not by logical arguments but by new experiences; thus SSOC must look for situations in which whites could recognize the strength that would come from alliances with blacks, and whites must initiate these alliances. In a 1968 SSOC newsletter

students, all in *New South Student,* include Herman Carter, 2 (December 1965): 17–18; "The Church in Mississippi," 3 (January 1966): 15; and Janet Dewart, 3 (December 1966).

24. Carson, *In Struggle,* 102; Guerrero, interview; Thrasher, interview.

25. Memo, Anne Braden to SSOC, 1966, Student Non-Violent Coordinating Committee Papers, 1959–1972.

article, Braden again urged the formation of biracial coalitions initiated by whites. Because too many southern white student radicals lacked the experience of working jointly with blacks, they had the dangerous illusion that they could "accomplish something in a movement of their own. They can't," she insisted. Instead of fearing black power, radical whites ought to see it as a sign of hope, Braden concluded.[26]

The issue of southern consciousness or southern nationalism was a tricky one for SSOC. Although its precise meaning was elusive and ambiguous, it was debated widely within the organization and in 1969 became a factor in SSOC's demise. Despite the ambiguity of the phrase, southern consciousness was based on the notion that the South shared a collective historical experience that was fundamentally distinct from that of other Americans. Much of the (white) South's "exceptionalism," as it was termed, lay not simply in its advocacy of slavery and its defeat in the Civil War but in its historic exploitation by "Yankee" imperialists (and their white southern counterparts). The exploitation and oppression of both poor whites and blacks made the South akin to a Third World colony, the argument went.

In other respects, SSOC's appeal to southern consciousness seemed to be strategic. SSOC hoped to counteract the charge that the problem of racism in America was due largely to southern "rednecks," or "white trash," as white southerners, especially the poor, were derogatorily labeled. The accusation belied the institutional basis of racism and provided a convenient scapegoat for northern liberals who preferred to point a finger at the South, meanwhile ignoring similar manifestations of racism and poverty in their own communities. SSOC correctly recognized that an effective white southern progressive movement could not be based on guilt. Rather, southern consciousness was seen as an antidote to white guilt and as a way to rally white southerners by appealing to a tradition that was not simply marred by slavery and racism but that also contained elements that were both good and worth preserving. In an early SSOC newsletter, one member wrote: "We must ask ourselves what part of the southern tradition do we wish to

26. Anne Braden, "A Continuing Quest," *New South Student* 5 (February 1968): 13–15. See also Anne Braden, "Black Power and White Organizing," *New South Student* 3 (December 1966): 17–20.

emulate? That of compassion, of the heroism of thousands of southerners in working for a better world through the labor movement
and now the civil rights movement—or the dark tradition of the
KKK, the citizens councils and assassination."[27]

Five years later, another SSOC member defined southern consciousness as "the positive cultural expression of identity with
one's people and regional roots."[28] Although SSOC always saw
itself as linked to the larger national radical movement, such expla-
nations sought to justify SSOC's regional approach to organizing a
radical movement in the South.

For some SSOC members, southern consciousness and the goal
of mobilizing white southerners gave them a sense of purpose and
identity, particularly in the wake of the Black Power Movement.
According to Gene Guerrero, SSOC's first chairman, "Even as the
whole Black Power thing was raised, we never felt uncomfortable
about it because we had our place, whereas a lot of the northern
whites felt uncomfortable, because what was their place . . . all
along?"[29]

But not all SSOC members felt the same sense of belonging. For
these young white southerners, black power only served to increase the sense of isolation that southern apostasy had forced
upon them. As Howard Romaine commented:

> I didn't really understand the kind of deep feelings of identity black
> people had toward their own schools, the need to work together.
> Most white people didn't understand that. We didn't understand a
> lot of things. . . . the blacks who were our peers didn't want to be
> with us; they wanted to be doing their own thing. [I]t was a pretty
> devastating and lonely feeling. Because in some sense a lot of us
> had left our families . . . the movement had become our families
> and it's like getting kicked out of your family. So it was kind of
> frightening and strange.[30]

27. Jim Williams, "These Are the Times . . . That Challenge the South,"
New Rebel 1 (October 1964): 3.

28. Lyn Wells, *SSOC: On Southern Liberation,* position papers written by
staff and members of SSOC (Nashville: SSOC, 1969), 5, in Lyn Wells Papers,
State Historical Society of Wisconsin, Madison, hereinafter cited as SHSW. See
also "The South: A Search for Meaning," a special issue of SSOC's *New South
Student* 4 (March 1967).

29. Guerrero, interview.

30. Romaine, interview.

For Romaine, southern consciousness did not serve as a refuge from the alienation he felt. He went on to say:

> But I always had ambiguous feelings about that [southern consciousness] because to me . . . the most salient thing about the southern experience was racism. Racism was the official ideology and it didn't seem to me the thing you could organize people around. It was what you wanted to organize them against. . . . I didn't ever feel comfortable organizing just white students. In fact, the deal I thought we cut with SNCC before they reneged on it was that they would organize in the community. . . . And we would organize just on campuses. And we'd channel people into the SNCC projects in the Black Belt.[31]

Other SSOC members were also skeptical about southern consciousness. According to SSOC staffer Jody Palmour, southern white culture provided a poor basis for organizing a new South, for it was mired too deeply in "depravity and racism." SSOC member Ed Hamlett, who had worked with the Southern Conference Education Fund and SSOC on the White Folks Project, cautioned, "Raising the banner of Southern Nationalism is both difficult and dangerous for one who advocates a New South."[32] But even SSOC members' denunciations of southern consciousness were often ambivalent. In a 1967 special issue of the *New South Student* entitled "The South: A Search for Meaning," Palmour and Hamlett had this to say about southern consciousness:

> As a systematic attempt to suggest answers or even define the questions surrounding the meaning and political possibilities of working and living in the South, it is easily judged a failure. We think it does succeed, however, as an effort to legitimize the discussion of major issues of personal identity, political strategy and organizational alliances within the context of our own experience in the Movement in the South and within the context of the historical experience of the South as a whole.[33]

As some in SSOC recognized, there were a number of problems with SSOC's appeal to southern consciousness. Perhaps the appeal's greatest flaw, as the concept was often articulated in SSOC,

31. Ibid.
32. Jody Palmour, interview with author, Washington D.C., August 12, 1989; *New South Student* 3 (December 1966): 25.
33. Jody Palmour and Ed Hamlett, "About This Issue: To Build the Ark," *New South Student* 4 (March 1967).

was that the southern tradition it evoked referred largely, if not exclusively, to white southerners, thereby rendering black southerners invisible. One early SSOC member, Archie Allen, insisted that SSOC's emphasis should be on southern traits, not whiteness. The 1966 SSOC Constitution did refer to "valuable traditions in both white and black cultures, which will enable Southerners to make a unique contribution to a truly democratic America." Yet "southern consciousness," as SSOC most often used the term, was implicitly white.[34] The problem was perhaps unavoidable given SSOC's goal of organizing and appealing to whites and given the rise of the Black Power Movement, which made interracial organizing difficult if not impossible. But the emergence of southern consciousness was also an ironic and disturbing outcome in light of the organization's effort to create an interracial and antiracist South.

SSOC hoped to draw on, and educate its members about, a truly antiracist, progressive, southern white tradition, but by its own admission, it fell short. For example, the 1969 Radical Southern History Conference, SSOC's first organized attempt to "reveal the true history of struggle in the South," apparently featured no "speakers who talked specifically about the contributions of black southerners to the struggle for change or about the particular experience of blacks as a colonized people."[35]

SSOC's own ambivalence and defensiveness about southern consciousness left it open not only to charges of racism but also to attacks concerning southern exceptionalism. SDS argued, and some inside SSOC agreed, that the problems the South confronted— racism, poverty, the war—were not regional but national and even international. Thus, why the need for a separate southern organi-

34. *New Rebel* 1 (December 1964): 2; "Constitution of the SSOC (adopted June 1966)," Social Action Collection, vertical file, box 45, SSOC folder, SHSW; *SSOC Handbook* (Spring 1969), Harry Boyte Papers, box 17, folder 5, Duke University.

35. David Simpson, Jim Skillman, Lyn Wells, "Dare to Struggle . . . Dare to Win," *New Left Notes,* May 13, 1969, 2. Both Wells and Simpson were SSOC members, and all three authors were also SDS members; this piece was written in response to Howard Romaine's article "Movement South" in the *Great Speckled Bird,* April 28, 1969, which held SDS factionalism responsible for splitting SSOC. Here Wells contradicts her appeal to southern consciousness, written that same year in "SSOC: On Southern Liberation."

zation? Of course, this argument surfaced as SDS launched an attack on SSOC, and many suspect that the critique of southern consciousness was based less on principled analysis than on opportunism and ideological schisms within SDS. Still, SSOC's own ambivalence left it vulnerable both to outside attacks and to internal squabbling concerning its vision and mission, a weakness that resulted in SSOC's destruction in 1969.

Although the White Folks Project drew SSOC into an endless debate concerning southern consciousness and race and class politics in the South, a far more successful effort was the student-labor coalition in North Carolina. The project attracted large numbers of students who assisted union organizing drives, strikes, and boycotts of nonunion stores and products. The action was so effective in reaching North Carolina students that it resulted in the creation of nearly sixty SSOC chapters throughout the state, making North Carolina an SSOC stronghold after 1967 and providing a model for similar efforts in other states. SSOC had hoped not only to build its student base through student-labor coalitions but also to help forge a biracial labor movement in the South. In 1966, SSOC members Cecil Butler, a black student from North Carolina A & T University, and Gene Guerrero helped to organize a student-labor conference at the historically black North Carolina College in Durham. The following year, SSOC launched a summer project on racism and poverty in North Carolina to educate poor and middle-class whites about racism, black power, and poverty. Once again, however, SSOC was criticized by some for reinforcing white workers' racism by appealing to southern consciousness; and Bob Dewart, one of the few African Americans in SSOC after 1967, criticized SSOC's efforts to work with organized labor in the South. He believed the effort was misguided because organized labor was reactionary, evidenced by AFL-CIO head George Meany's endorsement of the Vietnam War.[36] By 1969, SSOC had officially abandoned attempts to organize southern poor and working-class whites, presumably because the organization needed a larger student base. However,

36. Harlon Joye, "Dixie's New Left," *Transaction* 7 (September 1970); *New South Student* 4 (February 1967). For information on the North Carolina project and organizing poor whites in Durham, see Harry Boyte and Richard Landerman, "Poor Whites on the Move!," n.d., box 1, ACT folder, Boyte Papers; and Anne Braden, "Durham's ACT: A Voice for the South's Poor," *Southern Patriot* 27 (March 1969).

SSOC continued to urge students to actively support the struggles of workers, and at the March 1969 SSOC conference, a number of student-labor actions were reported among SSOC chapters in West Virginia, Tennessee, and Mississippi. (In Laurel, Mississippi, SSOC students supported black and white strikers at a masonite plant.)[37]

If the politics of race and class proved difficult for SSOC, the dynamics surrounding gender relations, though more elusive, were no less problematic and contradictory. Sara Evans has described SSOC's inability to create an atmosphere in which the concerns of women could be addressed. It is true, as Evans asserts, that women in the early SSOC did not talk much about women's issues even among themselves, although several SSOC women later reported that they had been subjected to discrimination within the organiza-tion. Despite SSOC's unequal treatment of women, during the early years, women were more prominent than after 1967. Accord-ing to Evans, SSOC did not and could not provide a seedbed for feminist consciousness because 1) it was a predominantly white organization and thus members could not confront racism directly as did women in SNCC, who made the link between racism and sexism, and 2) most SSOC members had come into the southern freedom movement after it had been well established and thus did not face the same historic isolation that white women in early SNCC experienced. Men always outnumbered women in SSOC, but women were campus travelers and staff members and held posi-tions on both the Continuations Committee and the Executive Committee. According to Nan Grogan, Sue Thrasher had "created a space there for women" and set "a whole different tone."[38] Except for Thrasher, however, there were no women officers during SSOC's brief existence. Still, women were included in SSOC's early at-tempts at creating a representative structure for the organization, and a number of women had visible and important positions.

Charlotte Bunch posed an interesting hypothesis regarding the treatment of women in SSOC. Bunch, who later became a leading lesbian-feminist activist and theorist, participated in civil rights

37. *New South Student* 2 (February 1965): 2; 3 (April 1966): 12; 4 (April 1967): 5–15; Carol Stevens, "Students, Labor Form an Alliance," *Southern Patriot* 24 (May 1966): 1; Simon, "SSOC: A New Rebel Yell in Dixie," 65–66; Steve Wise, "Southern Consciousness," *Great Speckled Bird,* March 17, 1969, 12; Jim Gwin, "The South Moves," *Great Speckled Bird,* March 31, 1969, 7.

38. Evans, *Personal Politics,* 45–47; Orrock, interview.

work in North Carolina in the 1960s and worked with some SSOC people through her role as president of the United Christian Movement. She suggested that perhaps because of the relative isolation of white progressives in the South, southern white radical men could not afford to ignore like-minded white women. Thus southern white women may have had a somewhat easier time than did women in northern radical groups such as SDS. This is not to suggest that southern white men were not sexist, Bunch added, but if they had come out of the black freedom movement, then they, as well as white women, "were very clear that leadership came from the Black Movement. . . . So, maybe having accepted that, they [white men] weren't quite as domineering. . . . I didn't feel them to be quite as oppressive [or] as egotistical . . . as I experienced a lot of SDS leaders to be." Lyn Wells, a member of SDS as well as a SSOC program secretary and campus traveler, echoed similar sentiments. "SSOC doesn't have as many problems with women as SDS or other groups." In contrast to Bunch and Wells, however, Sara Evans reported that a number of SSOC men had reputations for the "frequency of their sexual conquests" and for "their verbal condescension to women."[39]

Like the women in SNCC and SDS, most notably in the Economic Research and Action Projects (ERAP), SSOC women were especially prominent in community-organizing projects. Women like Rhonda Stilley and Laly Washington, one of the few black women in SSOC, formed a biracial team to set up a community project in north Nashville. Cathy Cade and Cathy Barrett helped initiate the Community Action Project (CAP) in New Orleans. Nan Grogan was active in a community project in Southside Virginia, one of the most successful biracial projects in the South. This project was notable particularly for involving black and white Virginia students rather than bringing in northern whites; moreover it demonstrated the possibility for campus-based community organizing close to home and belied the necessity for students to venture into the Deep South to engage in civil rights work.[40]

39. Charlotte Bunch, interview with author, Washington, D.C., June 14, 1989; Evans, *Personal Politics,* 194; Lyn Wells to "Dear Folks," ca. 1968, Wells Papers; Evans, *Personal Politics,* 46, 194.

40. See articles in the *Southern Patriot* describing these projects: "Experiment in Virginia," 23 (September 1965): 1; "Louisiana Students Organize in

Community organizing constituted an arena in which the skills of listening, negotiation, and personal contact were crucial for success. Because of socialized gender roles, such traits also tended to be more developed in women than in men. Despite the success of some of these projects, and perhaps indicative of the subordinate role of women in the organization, SSOC never fully developed the community-organizing aspect of its work. As SSOC moved from its early focus on civil rights and community organizing to a greater emphasis on the Vietnam War, women's influence and visibility seemed to recede. However, SSOC was never a very centralized organization. Policy, ideology, and even direction were often loosely constructed, and broad organizational trends always had exceptions.[41]

In other, more subtle ways, SSOC discouraged the participation of women. Because SSOC placed greater emphasis on modes of organizing more often employed by men, such as public demonstrations, other efforts received less support. For example, SSOC staff member Anne Romaine created a highly effective organizing strategy in the Southern Folk Tour, an integrated group of folk, gospel, blues, and country singers, many nationally renowned, that appeared at both historically black and predominantly white campuses throughout the South. The tour was designed to utilize both black and white musical expressions of traditional southern culture with the hope of inspiring southerners to become involved in the freedom movement. According to one male staff member, Jody Palmour, the idea of the tour was "strategically brilliant," but it was not treated seriously enough within SSOC or given the support it deserved largely because it did not conform to traditional—that is, male—notions of organizing, such as antiwar protests.[42]

Slums," 24 (March 1966): 1; "North Nashville Project Begins Community Work," 24 (August 1966): 4. The SSOC newsletter, the *New South Student,* also ran reports on these community projects between 1965 and 1966.

41. Former SSOC member Maya Hasegawa, conversation with author, Chapel Hill, N.C., May 29, 1992; Maya Hasegawa to author, June 20, 1992.

42. *New South Student* 3 (January 1966): 5; Palmour, interview. See also *New South Student* 3 (March 1966) and 3 (December 1966), for information on the Southern Folk Tours. For a discussion regarding women's community organizing styles and the critical role of women, particularly black women, in organizing drives, see Charles Payne, "Men Led, but Women Organized: Movement Participation of Women in the Mississippi Delta," in *Women in the*

Not only men in the organization supported traditional notions of gender. In 1966, a female SSOC member from North Carolina wrote a newsletter article on how to organize people over thirty years old, which was later distributed as an SSOC pamphlet. Under "Do's and Don't's" she advised, "Don't ask a man to do busy-work until he is thoroughly committed. And even then, try to make the best use of his talents." She continued, "When you ask a man to do something, try to let him do it his way, if that is not going to defeat your cause." Sue Thrasher offered these retrospective comments concerning SSOC's insensitivity toward women: "Women's issues were neither addressed nor articulated very well in those years in SSOC. . . . I think that women had a dual role. They were sometimes in leadership positions and sometimes in equal positions; on the other hand, it was a very sexist movement and there were just a lot of sexual issues. . . . So it was a difficult time for women."[43]

Despite the barriers women confronted, SSOC did sometimes attempt to address the issue of women's liberation. For example, the 1968 Constitution made the commitment to "racial and sexual equality" a requirement for membership. And in the fall of 1967, Nan Grogan spoke at Mary Washington College (the women's college in Virginia from which she had graduated) about the southern freedom movement, emphasizing "the role of women in the movement." The *Fall 1968 SSOC Speakers Guide* listed several women who were available to serve as organizing consultants or to speak on women's liberation. The guide included Anne Braden and SSOC member Ann Johnson; Sara Evans, who helped found the Charlotte Perkins Gilman group in Durham, North Carolina; Karen Mulloy from the Southern Conference Education Fund; Charlotte Bunch Weeks; and Judith Brown. Brown was active in civil rights and in SDS at the University of Florida in Gainesville. She was coauthor in 1968 with Beverly Jones of an SDS paper entitled "Towards a Female Liberation Movement," known as the "Florida Paper." It ar-

Civil Rights Movement: Trailblazers and Torchbearers, 1941–1965, ed. Vicki L. Crawford, Jacqueline Anne Rouse, Barbara Woods (New York: Carlson, 1990); Karen Sacks, "Women and Grassroots Leadership," and Cheryl Gilkes, "Building in Many Places: Multiple Commitments and Ideologies in Black Women's Community Work," in *Women and the Politics of Empowerment,* ed. Ann Bookman and Sandra Morgen (Philadelphia: Temple University Press, 1988).

43. Elizabeth Tornquist, "Over 30 . . ." *New South Student* 3 (March 1966): 5–6; Thrasher, interview.

gued for an independent women's liberation movement and proclaimed that all men were the enemy. Brown also was cofounder with Carol Giardina of the first women's liberation group in the South, Gainesville Women's Liberation, in the summer of 1968, though during the same summer, two other women also started a women's liberation group in Durham, North Carolina. SSOC's literature list included a bibliography and several pieces on women's liberation, including the Jones and Brown essay as well as a piece written by Roxanne Dunbar entitled "Female Liberation as the Basis for Social Revolution." Dunbar was a New Left activist from California who later founded the Southern Female Rights Union and the New Orleans Female Workers' Union.[44]

Regardless of such gestures, the position of women in SSOC seemed to deteriorate during its later years. The number of women staff visibly declined and by the time the organization dissolved, Lyn Wells was the only female staff member listed in the SSOC newsletter. After 1967, men wrote almost all the newsletter articles; an April 1968 article on a wildcat strike by women workers (written by one of the women strikers) was one of the few references made to women at all. Even this piece did not discuss the problems specific to women workers. Other articles referred to food boycotts by "disgruntled housewives" in Nashville and described a similar boycott by black women in Washington, D.C., as a "ladycott." An anonymous poem appearing in October 1967 was chilling in its misogynist language. Likening America to a mother and wife who had seduced and then betrayed the writer, the poem ended with a threat of violence: "Goddamn your eyes / But I'm sharpening my razor / You bitch you better get ready / For some cutting." The poem elicited no response in future editions of the newsletter.[45]

44. "Constitution of the SSOC," August 1968, box 17, folder 5, Boyte Papers; *New South Student* 3 (November 1967): 16. *Great Speckled Bird,* March 3, 1969, 7; Alice Echols, *Daring to Be Bad: Radical Feminism in America, 1967–1975* (Minneapolis: University of Minnesota Press, 1989), 62–64, 166; Evans, *Personal Politics,* 211; *SSOC Speakers Guide* (Fall, 1968); "Women's Liberation Bibliography," n.d., box 16, folder 1, Boyte Papers.

45. The anonymous poem was entitled "A Grrreat Society," *New South Student* 4 (October 1967): 15. See also Dave Nolan, "Ladies Boycott," *New South Student* 3 (November 1966): 5–6; Brenda Mull, "The History of the Levi Strauss Strike: Blue Ridge," *New South Student* 5 (April 1968): 18–22.

Many of the young southern white women who joined SSOC after Sue Thrasher and Nan Grogan lacked their predecessors' experiential base in the black freedom movement—the ingredient Evans claims was crucial to the first stirrings of feminist consciousness among white women. Yet women's experience within SSOC and in activist groups at southern colleges and universities propelled many of these younger women toward women's liberation. By the fall of 1968, SSOC women had begun organizing consciousness-raising groups. In November 1968, Lyn Wells (who had been active in the civil rights movement since high school, thus fitting Evans's model) and two other SSOC members, Ann Johnson and Maggie Heggen, sent a letter to over eight hundred women at fifty southern colleges and universities inviting them to attend a conference on women's liberation. The opening paragraph indicates the burgeoning interest in women's issues among women activists on southern campuses: "In response to increasing discussion and concern about women's problems, in society and in the movement, many women, actively working for social change on southern campuses, have expressed interest in coming together to further the dialogue."[46]

For some reason, the SSOC newsletter never mentioned the southern women's conference, not even to announce it. Yet one month before the conference, in one of the last issues of the SSOC newsletter, Judith Brown wrote an article that detailed the oppressive conditions that women, especially southern women, faced on campuses. In the article, she called for women students to adopt "self-consciously organized adversary political behavior." Judith Brown was an advocate for what Alice Echols terms the "feminist" position among early women's liberationists—the belief that men were the primary enemy and that women should organize separately from the Left. The "politicos," in contrast, believed that capitalism as well as male supremacy oppressed women and that separate women's groups should be part of the larger radical movement. There is some evidence that the feminist-politico split was a

---

46. Evans, *Personal Politics,* 46–47; Lyn Wells, Ann Johnson, and Maggie Heggen to "Dear Sisters," December 18, 1968, Wells Papers. The three initially mailed a similar letter in November to women on thirty campuses throughout the South. The second mailing was the December letter. Wells, Johnson, and Heggen to "Dear Sisters," November 20, 1968, Wells Papers.

concern to the planners of the SSOC women's conference and that Lyn Wells, in particular, was concerned about Brown's influence.[47]

The conference was organized specifically for women students, but the planners hoped it would be broad enough to attract community activists and women who were "not yet involved with women's liberation." Between 120 and 180 women from eleven southern states met in Atlanta from February 7 through 9, 1969, for the first southern meeting on women's liberation. The conference featured sketches and narratives about some of the South's unsung heroines, including the abolitionist Grimké sisters, Populist organizer Rebecca Felton, labor activist Mother Jones, and civil rights activist Anne Braden.[48]

According to Anne Braden, who attended the conference, the participants were all white and almost entirely middle class. SSOC had considered making the conference interracial, and a preliminary conference program had included SNCC member and singer Bernice Reagon speaking about Sojourner Truth. Apparently, the organizers revised their initial plans after talking with "some radical black women" and deciding that black women would not attend.[49] But by attempting to include African American women as invitees rather than as conference organizers, the conference reflected the same racial insensitivity that had marred the August 1968 Sandy Springs conference. At that meeting, in which a group of twenty white women planned the first national women's liberation conference, which took place in November of 1968, a similar discussion regarding the role of black women in women's liberation emerged. The issue was presumably resolved by deciding to contact Elizabeth Sutherland, a member of New York Radical Women

47. Judith Brown, "The Coed Caper," *New South Student* 6 (January 1969): 6; Lyn Wells to Bernadine Dohrn, January 24, 1969, Wells Papers; Echols, *Daring to Be Bad,* 51–101.

48. The Southern Woman Conference Agenda, Southern Student Organizing Committee file, Wells Papers; Anne Braden, "Southern Women Talk Freedom," *Southern Patriot* 27 (March 1969); Marilyn Salzman Webb, "Southern Women Get Together," *Guardian,* February 22, 1969.

49. Braden, "Southern Women Talk Freedom," 6–7. A similar pattern was evident at the Southern Female Liberation Meeting in May 1970 in Mississippi. Organized by the New Orleans–based Southern Female Rights Union, the conference attracted over two hundred women, but fewer than ten were African Americans. Jan Hilligas, "Women Organize," *Southern Patriot* 20 (May 1970): 3.

and a former SNCC member, and Kathleen Cleaver of the Black Panther Party to plan a conference on black women and women's liberation. The conference never materialized.[50]

Like many of the women at Sandy Springs, the SSOC conference organizers implicitly defined women's liberation as white. Thus, issues and agendas were set in terms of white women's interests and needs, perhaps not deliberately but out of the conviction that black and white women's problems were too different for mutual consideration across racial lines—a belief shared by many African American women as well. And yet Anne Braden, who never ceased to be wary of the implications of organizing solely among whites, commented: "That may be so for now [that black and white women's interests were dissimilar]. But I have always found that the experiences black and white women share as women are more powerful than the ones that divide them. I doubt we'll ever build a movement strong enough to free us all until this truth is recognized—on both sides of the barrier." According to Braden, the women talked about class differences among women, and the film *Salt of the Earth* led to a discussion of how such differences might be bridged. "There was less talk about their whiteness, although everyone was aware of it," she observed.[51]

The conference highlighted women's liberation activities among white women in the South. Organized women's groups from Durham, North Carolina; Gainesville, Florida; the University of Georgia; and Atlanta reported on their activities and provided suggestions for future work. Workshops on women as sex objects and consumers seemed to be particularly popular. (Two of the sessions were entitled "Pussy, Belle, Cunt, Magnolia Blossom, Piece" and "Depressed? BUY, SHOP, STEAL, PUSH!") There was apparently general agreement that both economic and cultural revolutions were needed to ensure an end to women's oppression. Participants made plans to organize women on campuses and in communities and workplaces across the South. SSOC hired Rhonda Holland specifically to work on women's liberation, and Carol Hanisch from the Southern Conference Education Fund planned to travel throughout the South in the upcoming spring to explore the possibility of establishing a women's liberation project.[52]

50. Echols, *Daring to Be Bad,* 104–8, 369–77.
51. Braden, "Southern Women Talk Freedom," 6.
52. Webb, "Southern Women Get Together," 7; *Great Speckled Bird,* Feb-

Throughout the spring of 1969, despite the serious internal and external difficulties faced by the organization, SSOC women continued to press their concerns. For example, at its March 15 meeting in Georgia, SSOC took up the discussion of women's liberation. A male caucus discussed the implications of women's liberation for men and agreed that men should do "very little actively in response to women's liberation," perhaps out of the belief that women needed to organize autonomously. Some men discussed how male chauvinism had "narrowed their own personal and organizational possibilities." Others suggested that the movement could address the "institutional oppression of women" by creating alternative communities where "marriage was loose" and children could be educated communally. Despite such "enlightened" male sentiments, at least one male SSOC officer observed that "not a single male on the SSOC staff . . . did not express some reluctance about devoting SSOC resources to women's liberation."[53]

In April 1969, the First Annual Mississippi Youth Jubilee, organized by SSOC and *Kudzu,* a white radical Mississippi student newspaper, featured a workshop on women's liberation that in turn spurred the formation of a women's group. The group continued to meet in Jackson and organized protest actions at the Miss USA and Miss Universe beauty pageants.[54]

ruary 17, 1969, 4; The Southern Woman Conference Agenda, Southern Student Organizing Committee file, Wells Papers. An undated letter-flyer indicates that SSOC planned to issue a southwide women's newsletter, a handbook for women students, and a special women's issue of the *New South Student.* "Randa" to "Sisters," n.d., box 17, folder 6, Boyte Papers. Apparently, Carol Hanisch moved to Gainesville to organize women for the Southern Conference Education Fund and to work with Gainesville Women's Liberation, but the Southern Conference Education Fund newspaper, the *Southern Patriot,* carried no report of Hanisch's work in the South on women's liberation from 1969 to 1971. Echols, *Daring to Be Bad,* 140.

53. *Great Speckled Bird,* March 31, 1969, 7; Simon, "SSOC: A New Rebel Yell in Dixie," 96; Tom Gardiner, "Southern Student Organizing Committee," Charlottesville, Va., 1970, 31, quoted in Simon, "SSOC: A New Rebel Yell in Dixie," 96.

54. *Great Speckled Bird,* April 21, 1969, 2. One of the founders of *Kudzu* was SSOC member and Millsaps College student Cassell Carpenter, who was arrested as a "subversive" for handing out copies of the paper. Carpenter also was active in the women's liberation movement. See the biographical portrait of Carpenter by Robert Analavage, "Mississippi Belle Says 'Goodbye to All That,'" *Southern Patriot* 27 (March 1969): 4.

By early 1969, women's liberation activity was reported at campuses throughout the South. At the University of Arkansas, the University of Mississippi, the University of North Carolina campuses in Greensboro and Chapel Hill, the University of Virginia, and the University of South Carolina, women formed women's liberation groups and protested discriminatory practices and policies on their campuses and communities. In Durham, North Carolina, a women's liberation group began work with secretaries, laboratory technicians, and social workers at Duke University and the University of North Carolina at Chapel Hill, and with poor white women and girls in the community. In Tennessee, a Nashville group comprising campus women and working women planned to confront two insurance companies, the two largest employers in the city, for paying only minimum wage to secretaries. And in Florida, groups were formed in Sarasota, Gainesville, Tallahassee, St. Petersburg, and Miami.[55]

Despite such widespread activity, there could not have been a less propitious moment to advance the cause of women's liberation within SSOC, for by June the organization had self-destructed. Whatever gains the conference had made in solidifying the women's liberation movement in the South, the movement would continue without SSOC.

A month after the SSOC women's conference, Lyn Wells appeared at an SDS national council meeting in Austin. At the meeting, SDS broke its fraternal ties with SSOC and denounced the southern organization for its lack of radical politics, its racism, and its regional approach to organizing. Debate raged within SSOC over these issues and the charge that SSOC had "sold out" by accepting money from private foundations. At the April 1969 SSOC conference, Lyn Wells publicly confessed her "sins" of having "built on anti-Yankeeism" and admitted that she "used an individualist approach" to organizing southern students. A move to oust her from the organization was narrowly defeated by a 14–11 margin

55. Lyn Wells, "A Movement for Us," *Great Speckled Bird,* February 28, 1969, 2; January 20, 1969, 4; *Florida Free Newsletter,* February 25, 1969. Lyn Wells, *American Women: Their Use and Abuse* (SSOC: 1969), in box 17, folder 5, Boyte Papers. See also Sara Evans's untitled paper concerning work with white working-class women in Durham, box 1, Sara Evans folder, Boyte Papers.

(not for these "sins" but because her support for SDS and her intention to dissolve SSOC were seen as a betrayal of SSOC).[56]

The SSOC staff of forty, accused of having turned SSOC into a staff instead of a membership organization, agreed to resign on the first day of the upcoming June conference, where SSOC members would decide the organization's fate. SSOC changed to a staff organization in 1967, presumably to prevent a takeover by the Progressive Labor Party, which had deliberately sought a southern stronghold in order to provide a basis for strengthening its position within SDS. Some hold the Progressive Labor Party responsible for destroying SSOC, although the federal government, through the FBI's COINTELPRO, may also have played a role. As early as 1966, SSOC had come under government surveillance. The following year, Arkansas senator John McClellan held hearings to investigate several movement organizations including Southern Conference Education Fund, SSOC, SDS, and SNCC. Earlier that year, the House Un-American Activities Committee had initiated a probe of SSOC after the newsletter had called for an attack on "the system at its economic root." And FBI COINTELPRO files reveal that the FBI was involved in extensive surveillance of SSOC members and chapters throughout the South from at least 1968 and that FBI agents proposed numerous disinformation campaigns to disrupt the organization. FBI documents indicate that such campaigns were usually not approved, but it is not inconceivable that the FBI was involved in SSOC's dissolution. In any event, SSOC was unable to resolve its internal divisions regarding southern consciousness and SSOC's relationship to both the Black Power Movement and the national radical student movement. In June 1969, SSOC met at the Mount Beulah Center in Mississippi to discuss its internal problems and voted to disband the organization.[57]

56. Allen Young/LNS, "SDS National Council against SSOC," *Great Speckled Bird,* April 21, 1969, 6; Howard Romaine, "Movement South," *Great Speckled Bird,* April 28, 1969, 10–11. For a response to Romaine, see David Simpson, Jim Skillman, and Lyn Wells, "Dare to Struggle—Dare to Win," *Great Speckled Bird,* May 5, 1969, 6–7.

57. *Southern Patriot* 25 (April 1967): 1; U.S. Department of Justice, Federal Bureau of Investigation, Files No. 100–449698, COINTELPRO, New Left, Washington, D.C.; *Great Speckled Bird,* October 28, 1968, 2–3; *Southern Patriot* 25 (August 1967): 2; 27 (October 1969): 2; 28 (September 1970): 3. For several different viewpoints regarding the conflicts within SSOC and the causes of its

Despite SSOC's brief existence, the organization was a gadfly in the South for some of the most pressing social issues of the period. SSOC never resolved its internal problems concerning the organization's vision and mission. In part, these tensions reflected the state of the movement in 1964, when SSOC came into existence, especially the discussions regarding the role of whites in the black freedom movement. The passage of the Civil Rights and Voting Rights Acts in 1964 and 1965 finally ended legal segregation (although ingenious whites found numerous ways to circumvent the law), leading civil rights activists to shift their focus to the less blatant but more entrenched and intractable forms of racial injustice such as poverty and urban decay. These factors, together with the escalation of the Vietnam War, which provided an issue of immediate concern to whites, particularly young white men, at a time when whites were being urged to organize among themselves, all had an important impact on SSOC.

At first glance, it appears that SSOC's efforts to organize white southerners would have complemented the goals of the Black Power Movement. This seems especially true in light of SNCC's insistence that racism was a white problem and that whites could be most helpful to the black freedom movement, not by coming into SNCC or organizing in black communities, but by organizing whites. Yet SSOC never managed to overcome the perhaps irreconcilable contradiction of trying to organize whites without falling victim to charges of reinforcing racism and segregation.

Given the intransigence of racism and poverty, not only in the South but throughout the nation, perhaps SSOC's most enduring legacy rests in the southern women's liberation movement. This is indeed an ironic outcome, considering the organization's less than equal treatment of women. The gender politics within SSOC reveal another interesting contradiction. In the early period when women were most prominent, women's issues were least articulated, in

demise, see Sale, *SDS*, 537–39; David Simpson, Lyn Wells, and George Vlasits to "Dear Sisters and Brothers," May 26, 1969, box 17, folder 6, Boyte Papers; articles in the *Great Speckled Bird:* Steve Wise, "Southern Consciousness," March 17, 1969, 2; Nelson Blackstone, "Southern Consciousness: Consciousness . . . of What?," April 7, 1969, 11, 20; Bob Goodman, "SSOC Dissolves," June 16, 1969, 3, 19; Sue Thrasher, "SSOC Defended," June 30, 1969; Anne Braden, "SDS Action Divides SSOC Staff," *Southern Patriot* 27 (May 1969): 2, and "SSOC Dies," 27 (June 1969): 1.

part because of the absence of a women's movement. Later, as SSOC shifted its focus toward activities that tended to relegate women to the margins (that is, toward antiwar work and away from civil rights and community organizing), women were less visible, though women's issues were at least beginning to receive some, albeit minimal, attention. But if women were less visible within SSOC, they also provided the impetus within the organization to recognize the special problems faced by women, as SSOC chairman Tom Gardiner put it, "in spite of, not with, the men in SSOC." It may be that the women's position deteriorated within SSOC not simply because of the organization's sexism but because women who became social activists joined women's groups rather than organizations such as SSOC. The history of the southern women's liberation movement remains largely undocumented; but clearly, SSOC played an important, if thwarted, part in the emergence of the women's movement in the region.[58]

Like so many protest organizations of the 1960s, SSOC fell victim to ideological factionalism and government repression. Before SSOC's dissolution in 1969, the organization had grown to over three thousand members and had reached many more people throughout the South than simple mailing list numbers would suggest. As one SDS and SSOC member summarized the Southern Student Organizing Committee's accomplishments shortly after its demise: "During its five-year existence, SSOC accomplished a seemingly impossible task: the establishment of a white radical movement in this bastion of reactionary politics. Because of its efforts, many white southern students participated in civil rights action, student power struggles, community and labor organizing, and women's liberation and antidraft and antiwar work."[59]

58. Gardiner, "Southern Student Organizing Committee," 31, quoted in Simon, "SSOC: A New Rebel Yell in Dixie," 96; Sara Evans discusses a number of SSOC women who later became active in the women's liberation movement, including Cathy Cade, Cathy Barrett, and Peggy Dobbins. However, because her analysis of women's liberation shifts to a northern focus and ends in 1968, we still lack a full exploration of the links between civil rights and feminism in the South. Evans, *Personal Politics,* 46–47, 183. For a study of a local southern feminist newsletter-journal in the 1960s and 1970s, see Jennifer L. Gilbert, "Feminary of Durham–Chapel Hill: Building Community through a Feminist Press" (master's thesis, Duke University, 1993).

59. Harlon Joye, "Dixie's New Left," *Transaction* 7 (September 1970): 50.

In the 1960s, SSOC helped to create and sustain a generation of young white southern radicals, many of whom have continued the struggle to create a new South for both black and white southerners. However insensitive the SSOC logo and first newsletter title may have been to blacks, and however tainted their southern heritage concerning relations of race, class, and gender, these southern students were in a very real sense "new rebels."

"More Than a Lady"

Ruby Doris Smith Robinson and Black Women's Leadership in the Student Nonviolent Coordinating Committee

CYNTHIA GRIGGS FLEMING

Throughout the history of this country, countless African American activists have resisted racism and oppression in a wide variety of ways. A number of these activists were women, and a few of them became famous. Most Americans have at least heard of legendary black women like Harriet Tubman and Sojourner Truth, who were passionately committed to black freedom. There are many, however, who were never recognized for their achievements and their importance. One such woman was Ruby Doris Smith Robinson, who worked with the Student Nonviolent Coordinating Committee from its earliest days in 1960 until her death at age twenty-five in October of 1967.

Robinson was born in Atlanta, Georgia, on April 25, 1942, to Alice and J. T. Smith. She was the second of seven children; the oldest was a girl named Mary Ann, and then came Ruby, Catherine, Bobby, John, Willie, and Gregory.[1] The Smith family owned their own home in Summerhill, the oldest black neighborhood in Atlanta. While Summerhill had its share of crime, it also provided positive experiences for its residents. Mary Ann Smith Wilson, Robinson's oldest sister, described Summerhill as a "mosaic" that included all kinds of people. Middle-class families lived alongside those who were mired in abject poverty. Wilson also remembered

1. Mary Ann Smith Wilson, interview by author, Atlanta, Ga., November 19, 1989.

204

that the community provided a network of support for its young-sters. Schools, churches, and other institutions such as the YMCA sponsored activities and provided encouragement to neighbor-hood youth while they also protected community youngsters from the worst part of segregation.[2]

In such a warm and supportive atmosphere Ruby Doris Smith Robinson developed a keen sense of social and racial justice. She watched the events of the 1950s—the integration of Little Rock's Central High School, the Montgomery bus boycott—with a grow-ing sense of concern. When she entered Spelman College as a freshman in the fall of 1958, Robinson was excited about the pros-pect of change in the South's system of segregation. But, Robinson remembered, "I wasn't ready to act on my own." By the next academic year other idealistic black college students in the Atlanta University Center, which served Atlanta University, Gammon Theo-logical Seminary, and Spelman, Morehouse, Morris Brown, and Clark Colleges, created the Atlanta Committee on Appeal for Hu-man Rights. The group sponsored its first demonstration on March 15, 1960, at the state capitol building—a short distance from their campuses. This was just what Robinson had been waiting for. She enthusiastically joined the Atlanta committee and participated in that first demonstration.[3]

At the same time that Ruby Doris Smith Robinson and her col-leagues were protesting segregation in Atlanta, black college stu-dents all across the South were engaged in similar activities. It soon became obvious to some that all these student movements could benefit by establishing an organization to coordinate their activ-ities. Accordingly, in April of 1960 black student leaders from all over the South met and established the Student Nonviolent Coor-dinating Committee. By early 1961, even as Robinson continued her work with the Atlanta committee, she began to work with this new group, serving SNCC as an activist in the field as well as an administrator in the Atlanta central office.

In May of 1966 she succeeded Jim Forman as SNCC's executive secretary. She was the only woman ever to serve in this capacity.[4]

2. Wilson, interview.
3. Howard Zinn, *SNCC: The New Abolitionists* (Boston: Beacon Press, 1964), 17.
4. Clayborne Carson, *In Struggle: SNCC and the Black Awakening of the 1960's* (Cambridge: Harvard University Press, 1981), 203.

Robinson was elected during a particularly emotional and difficult staff meeting in Kingston Springs, Tennessee. The heated debates about strategies and goals that occupied the staff at that meeting were complicated by the serious splits that had developed within the ranks of the staff by this time. Splits based on gender, race, and status in the organization produced a great deal of suspicion and mistrust. Despite these problems, however, Robinson commanded the respect of the majority of her SNCC colleagues. They admired her unshakable commitment to the cause of civil rights in general and the Student Nonviolent Coordinating Committee in particular.

While Robinson had the practical experience and the firm commitment necessary to administer SNCC, she faced some unique problems and challenges because of her gender. Like some other female leaders in the organization, she found that her femininity was questioned because she exercised power over men. Furthermore, in the midst of her SNCC work Robinson was married in 1964 and had a child in 1965. This added dimension provoked a great deal of tension in her life as she sought to fulfill the traditional roles of wife and mother as well as the unusual role of female civil rights leader.

SNCC colleagues recognized Robinson's importance. One recalled, "You could feel her power in SNCC on a daily basis." Another insisted, "As a female, she was a pretty powerful person."[5] As SNCC's membership enlarged and its character changed over time, it became increasingly difficult to administer. But Robinson tried. SNCC had always had a flexible view of leadership. Most in the group believed that everyone could be a leader. Whereas this belief served to inspire broad participation by the membership, it also caused serious discipline problems. There were times when some members simply refused to follow orders. Regardless of the existence of such attitudes, Robinson demanded hard work and dedication from all those around her. Jack Minnis, a member of SNCC's research staff, insisted that it was almost impossible to fool Robinson; he had no doubt that she had "a 100 percent effective shit detector." Above all, she made sure that nobody abused the organization's limited financial resources. Stanley Wise, who would later succeed Robinson as executive secretary when she became

5. Matthew Jones, interview by author, Knoxville, Tenn., April 24, 1989; Mildred Forman, interview by author, Chicago, Ill., November 6, 1989.

ill, clearly recalled a particularly illustrative incident. It occurred when a group of field workers came to Atlanta for a meeting.

> She absolutely did not tolerate any nonsense. I remember some people came in there [the Atlanta central office] once from Mississippi. They had driven their car over there and they said they needed new tires. And she pulled out [a card] from her little file. She said, "Listen, I've given you sixteen tires in the last four months. . . . I've sent you four batteries, you had two motors in the car. You're not getting another thing. Now take that car out of here and go on back to Mississippi."[6]

Co-worker Reginald Robinson remembered that Robinson could be uncompromising about procedure. "When she became in charge of the payroll and you had reports to do—you had expense accounts to turn [in]. Well, if you didn't do what you were supposed to do, Big Mama [Robinson] would cut your money." Movement colleague Charles Jones succinctly summed up her no-nonsense approach. "You didn't run any games on her." As co-worker Worth Long declared, "The office would not have run except for her; and then the field would not have survived." Long recalled her as "a cantankerous person. . . . She's set in her ways, and she's mostly right. . . . She would take a principle[d] stand. . . . She'd argue, and she'd huff and puff too." In the freewheeling discussions that SNCC staff members had about organizational policy, Long remembered Robinson as "a formidable opponent. I wouldn't want to play poker with her."[7] There were indeed many sides to Ruby Doris Smith Robinson. Regardless of what colleagues thought of her administrative techniques and her office demeanor, all agreed that Robinson's actions were always guided by her sincere commitment to SNCC.

Despite her importance to SNCC, however, Robinson has received little attention from scholars and others who are now writing the civil rights movement's story. Has her gender consigned her to obscurity? That is part of the answer. Still another part of the answer, however, is rooted in Robinson's personality and her vision of her role in the movement. Even in childhood, Robinson had been an intensely private and independent person. Her older sister

6. Jack Minnis, interview by author, New Orleans, La., November 4, 1990; Stanley Wise, interview by author, Atlanta, Ga., November 11, 1990.

7. Reginald Robinson and Charles Jones, interview by author, McComb, Miss., June 28, 1991; Worth Long, interview by author, Atlanta, Ga., February 8, 1991.

remembered that their parents understood this and accepted it. They knew that "whatever she's going to do, she's going to do."[8] They never expected their daughter to consult them or even inform them of her activities; and she never did.

Robinson so guarded her privacy that she actively discouraged those who wanted to extend special recognition to her for her protest activities. While she understood that such activities themselves attracted a good deal of attention, she absolutely did not want any personal notoriety. Her attitude toward personal publicity became quite obvious in early 1961 when she became part of a SNCC delegation that was jailed in Rock Hill, South Carolina. The SNCC action in Rock Hill grew out of a decision that the group made at its February 1961 meeting. During that meeting, staff members expressed concern about the jail versus bail question. All over the South, thousands of black college students involved in protest activities were being arrested. In the majority of cases students posted bail and were released. Increasingly, however, some argued that there were compelling reasons why protestors should start refusing to post bail and should serve out their jail sentences instead.

Tactically, some insisted, those who protested segregation could do the movement a great service by remaining in jail. Clogging the jails with increasing numbers of protesters would put additional pressure on segregation by straining local resources. At the same time, others insisted that attempts to bail black students out of jail were placing a terrible financial burden on local black communities—a burden that could eventually interfere with their will and their ability to continue the fight against segregation. Finally, others argued that the protestors' presence in jail would provide powerful moral reinforcement of their position. The SNCC members attending that February meeting were aware that a group of South Carolina students had already taken a public stand on this issue. On February 1, just prior to the beginning of the meeting, students from Friendship College in Rock Hill, South Carolina, were convicted of trespassing after they had demonstrated in downtown variety stores and drugstores. The students refused to post bail, and they expressed a determination to serve out their full sentences. Participants in that February SNCC meeting unequivocally expressed their view of the stand taken by the Rock Hill students:

8. Wilson, interview.

Their sitting-in shows their belief in the immorality of racial segregation and their choice to serve the sentence shows their unwillingness to participate in any part of a system that perpetuates injustice.
Since we too share their beliefs and since many times during the
past year we too have sat-in at lunch counters, we feel that in good
conscience we have no alternative other than to join them.[9]

Robinson and the others who attended SNCC's February meeting were invigorated by their new stand. They excitedly debated
the question of which SNCC members should go to Rock Hill to
inaugurate this new policy. Finally the decision was made: Charles
Jones, Charles Sherrod, Diane Nash, and Mary Ann Smith, Robinson's older sister, were selected. But Smith remembered that after
she left the meeting she began to have some serious second thoughts
about going to jail in Rock Hill. "I started thinking about all the
little things I had in the making for next year, you know. Academ-
ically—fellowships and what have you." While Smith became increasingly uncertain, Robinson became increasingly excited. "So
what happened eventually is Ruby Doris talked it up, and I just
bowed out and let her go."[10]

After they protested segregation at Good's Drug Store in downtown Rock Hill, Robinson and the others were arrested. They served
thirty-day sentences in the York County jail. As the end of her jail
sentence approached, Robinson began to worry that she would be
the target of special recognition. She told her sister: "I think the
Rock Hillians are planning something for us when we get out. . . . I
don't care for the publicity that they'll probably give us when we
come out." Robinson clearly did not want any special recognition
from anyone. She did not even want family members and friends to
celebrate her achievements. "Please don't plan anything for me,"
she insisted. "I'm no celebrity and you know it."[11]

Despite Robinson's wishes, the *Atlanta Inquirer* had photogra-
phers on hand at the airport when she returned from serving her
jail time in South Carolina.[12] After her Rock Hill experience, Robinson participated in a number of protest activities over the next few
months in Atlanta and other Georgia cities and other states. Re-

9. *Student Voice* 2, February 1961.
10. Wilson, interview.
11. Ruby Doris Smith to Mary Ann Smith, February 25, 1961, in Mary Ann
Smith Wilson's private papers, Atlanta, Ga.
12. *Atlanta Inquirer,* March 18, 1961.

gardless of the media coverage that these protests attracted, Robinson continued to shun personal publicity.

Movement colleagues all agreed that Robinson was a team player. She did not want the movement to be affected by individual attitudes and aspirations. This conviction sometimes prompted Robinson to make pointed comments about civil rights veterans who seemed to enjoy the inevitable publicity and notoriety that accompanied their protest activities. She was particularly concerned that the media attention lavished on some could lead to serious distortions and dangerous misrepresentations. Her views of Stokely Carmichael's relationship to the press clearly indicate the depth of her concern. She charged that because of the media attention Carmichael attracted, he had become "the only consistent spokesman for the organization, and he has had the press not only available but seeking him out for whatever ammunition could be found— FOR OUR DESTRUCTION." Because of Carmichael's penchant for attracting press coverage, Robinson half-jokingly and half-seriously christened him "Stokely Starmichael."[13]

Robinson's attempts to stay in the background even in the face of her growing influence in SNCC clearly illustrate one of the conflicts that complicated her life as an activist. Indeed, her gender, race, personal convictions, personality, and position all meant that she would inevitably face conflicts in the environment of the civil rights movement of the sixties. Among the most painful of those conflicts was the issue of her own femininity—a problem that many of her African American female friends shared. Against the backdrop of the peculiar status of black women in American society, black female activist efforts have routinely been tied to a de-emphasis of black femininity. Such a linkage is entirely consistent with negative notions of black femininity that are firmly anchored in the nineteenth century and slavery. One scholar has identified the roots of this negative nineteenth-century notion.

> The slave system defined Black people as chattel. Since women, no less than men, were viewed as profitable labor-units, they might as well have been genderless as far as the slaveholders were concerned. . . . Judged by the evolving nineteenth century ideology of femininity, which emphasized women's roles as nurturing mothers and

13. Carson, *In Struggle,* 230; Mucasa (Willie Ricks), interview by author, Atlanta, Ga., April 8, 1990.

gentle companions and housekeepers for their husbands, Black women were practically anomalies.[14]

In the popular consciousness, notions of accepted female behavior are inconsistent with popularized views of the black female activist persona. Consequently, one does not think of the fierce "General" Tubman primping in front of a mirror, or the legendary Sojourner Truth worrying about which hat to wear. Of course, women in leadership roles, regardless of race, have often been vulnerable to attacks on their femininity. Yet the experience of black women activists is unique, since it is firmly based in the broader context of negative notions of black femininity in general.

Predictably, in Robinson's particular case, as she gained power and influence in SNCC, increasing numbers of her movement colleagues came to identify her by her role in the organization, not her gender. Some insist that part of the perception they have of her is rooted in their view of Robinson's physical appearance. Many remember her as a rather plain woman. She was five feet two inches tall with a stocky build. She had large hips, a small waist, and bowed legs. Because of her build she had a very distinctive walk. Her older sister Mary Ann remembered that this earned her the nickname "Duck." Robinson's skin color was medium, and she had a broad nose, relatively large lips, and kinky hair. Because she possessed these characteristics, Charles Jones described her as "practical and black" in terms of attitude and appearance. Co-worker Courtland Cox insisted that people in SNCC "didn't view her as a man or woman, they viewed her as a strength." Her friend and co-worker Joanne Grant remembered, "I think that everybody accepted her as one of the boys."[15]

A number of Robinson's colleagues were particularly impressed by her commanding voice. Constancia Romilly vividly recalled the impression Ruby's voice made on her. "Ruby . . . was as tough as the men, and as courageous, and her voice was as strong as any man's voice. . . . Yes, she had a—she had a carrying voice, and a very well defined [voice]. When she spoke, you could definitely

14. Angela Davis, *Women, Race, and Class* (New York: Random House, 1983), 5.

15. Wilson, interview; Robinson and Jones, interview; Courtland Cox, interview by author, Washington, D.C., December 16, 1988; Joanne Grant, interview by author, New Orleans, La., November 4, 1990.

hear what she had to say." Curtis Muhammad was also deeply impressed by Robinson's voice. He described it as authoritative, masculine, but not too heavy. In his words, "she didn't have a whiny female thing . . . none of that."[16]

Earlier acquaintances who observed Robinson before she began her movement work recalled a demeanor and behavior that were remarkably similar to those she would display as a mature activist. Fellow Spelman College student Norma June Davis remarked that "she [Robinson] seemed so atypical of Spelman, I mean at that point in time. It was amazing that she was even there. She didn't look like a Spelmanite, she didn't dress like a Spelmanite, she didn't act like one." Another early acquaintance, the Reverend Albert Brinson, explained that students at Spelman "were always taught to be a lady. A lady stood back and waited to be waited upon by a man." Brinson thought that Ruby did not fit too well in this atmosphere, since "she was not the lady-like kind. . . . She was rather aggressive."[17]

Robinson was indeed aggressive whenever issues of racial justice were at stake. It seemed to her that there was always so much to be done. When idealistic and enthusiastic students first organized the Student Nonviolent Coordinating Committee in April of 1960, they expected that their new committee would function as a coordinating body linking student protest movements in various communities. They soon recognized, though, that this was only the beginning. By February of 1961 the group became involved in plotting movement strategy when they made the decision to send the delegation to Rock Hill, South Carolina.

In May of 1961, shortly after Robinson and her colleagues finished serving their sentences in the York County jail, SNCC became involved in the freedom rides. Although the Congress of Racial Equality organized the rides, SNCC stepped in and provided the volunteers to continue when white resistance threatened to disrupt them. Robinson was one of those volunteers. She was later arrested and jailed for sixty days along with the other freedom riders. The riders served the first part of their sentence in the Hinds County jail

16. Constancia Romilly, interview by author, Atlanta, Ga., June 14, 1991; Curtis Muhammad (Curtis Hayes), interview by author, McComb, Miss., June 29, 1991.

17. Norma June Davis and Lana Taylor Sims, interview by author, Atlanta, Ga., November 11, 1990; Albert Brinson, interview by author, Atlanta, Ga., November 10, 1990.

in Jackson, Mississippi. They were later transferred to Parchman Penitentiary, a large state facility. Robinson's release came on August 11, 1961. By that time SNCC had decided to organize a voter registration campaign in McComb, Mississippi. Once again, Robinson was right there. She went door to door urging people in McComb to register.

It seemed that Robinson was always willing to volunteer for the most hazardous movement duty. Furthermore, in such circumstances colleagues could depend on her to be bold, daring, and frequently outrageous. Because of her attitude and her actions, Ruby Doris Smith Robinson soon became a legend—even among the bold and brave young people of the Student Nonviolent Coordinating Committee. Most people in early SNCC could recount at least one Robinson story. For example, Julian Bond remembered that when a delegation of SNCC staff members was preparing to board a plane for Africa in September of 1964, an airline representative told them that the plane was full, even though they had tickets for that flight. He wanted to know if they would wait and take a later flight. This angered Robinson so much that, without consulting the rest of the group, she went and sat down in the jetway, preventing passengers from boarding the plane, and refused to move. The group was given seats on that flight.[18]

Co-worker Michael Sayer particularly remembered Robinson's actions during an important SNCC staff meeting at Waveland, Mississippi, in November of 1964. The group confronted some very difficult and emotional issues at that meeting, but the conferees still managed to find time for recreation. After one especially intense and emotional day, "someone suggested we have a football game. And . . . we played tackle football with no equipment. . . . Ruby was quarterback. We played eleven on a side . . . and I was playing the line and she ran over me." Robinson's intensity generally affected everything she did. James Bond, who worked in the SNCC printshop, witnessed still another Robinson incident, which occurred when a group of SNCC staff members went to the airport to meet some of the organization's celebrity supporters in 1963.

So we went out there and met the first plane which was coming from California which had Marlon Brando and Tony Franciosa on it.

18. Julian Bond, interview by author, Washington, D.C., December 16, 1988.

And then we had to go meet a second plane which had Paul Newman on it. So we took them down to the other gate. . . . Ruby
Doris was with us. And as we stood out at the gate waiting . . . the
first person to come off the plane was Governor [George] Wallace.
And Ruby Doris went up to him and said, "How are you Governor?," and introduced herself and said, "I've spent time in your
jails." And he said, "Well, I hope they treated you well, and if
you're ever back, look me up."[19]

She never did.

Robinson's assertiveness, brashness, and courage were important, but they were not unique. Rather, her actions and her attitude
mirror the boldness displayed by many African American women
in the movement, and by many others over time. Consider the
example of Annelle Ponder. Ponder, a Southern Christian Leadership Conference voter education teacher, was arrested in Winona,
Mississippi, in 1963. Fannie Lou Hamer, who was arrested with her,
remembered hearing an exchange between Ponder and her white
prison guard. He demanded that she use a title of respect when
addressing him: "Cain't you say yessir, bitch?" Ponder answered,
"Yes, I can say yessir." The guard then demanded that she say it.
Ponder's reply: "I don't know you well enough." The guard was so
incensed that he beat her. Hamer remembered, "She kept screamin'
and they kept beatin' her . . . and finally she started prayin' for 'em,
and she asked God to have mercy on 'em because they didn't
know what they was doin'."[20]

Then there was the case of Annie Pearl Avery. During the course
of a demonstration in Montgomery, Alabama, in 1965, Avery came
face-to-face with a white policeman who had a billy club aimed
straight at her head. He had already beaten several others. Avery
"reached up, grabbed the club and said, 'Now what you going to
do, motherfucker?'" Then she slipped back into the crowd of dem-
onstrators. Another activist, Judy Richardson, had more than a
verbal confrontation with a policeman. During the course of a
demonstration, she kicked an Atlanta policeman in the groin. Richardson explained what prompted her to take such drastic action.

    19. Michael Sayer, interview by author, New Market, Tenn., May 5, 1990;
James Bond, interview by author, Atlanta, Ga., February 8, 1991.
    20. Paula Giddings, *When and Where I Enter: The Impact of Black Women
on Race and Sex in America* (New York: Morrow, 1984), 290.

"He was mistreating a Black demonstrator, and it forced me to do something."[21]

In an era when American women were regularly told that a woman's place was in the home, women like Ruby Doris Smith Robinson, Annie Pearl Avery, Judy Richardson, and Annelle Ponder definitely did not conform to contemporary notions of ladylike behavior. The advice offered by diplomat Adlai Stevenson in his commencement address to the class of 1955 at Smith College clearly illustrates contemporary expectations. "The assignment to you, as wives and mothers, you can do in the living room with a baby in your lap or in the kitchen with a can opener in your hand. If you are clever, maybe you can even practice your saving arts on that unsuspecting man while he's watching television. I think there is much you can do . . . in the humble role of housewife."[22]

Even though the behavior of black women activists did not always fit contemporary notions of proper female behavior, it did fit comfortably into an established tradition of black female assertiveness. Yet, because of the predominance of broader notions of a woman's place, the actions of Robinson and some of her African American movement sisters brought them face-to-face with many who questioned or ignored their femininity. Many, including Robinson, were troubled by this. Her colleague Cynthia Washington explained the frustration that many felt.

> I remember discussions with various women about our treatment as one of the boys and its impact on us as women. We did the same work as men—organizing around voter registration and community issues in rural areas—usually with men. But when we finally got back to some town where we could relax and go out, the men went out with other women. Our skills and abilities were recognized and respected, but that seemed to place us in some category other than female.[23]

The feminine side of their natures was a vital part of all of these women, including Robinson. Indeed, the feminine side of Robinson's nature dictated many of the choices she had made earlier in her life while she was growing up. A number of her SNCC col-

---

21. Ibid., 292.
22. Ibid., 243.
23. Cynthia Washington, "We Started from Different Ends of the Spectrum," *Southern Exposure* 5 (Winter 1977): 14.

leagues who knew her only as a legendary freedom fighter and hard-nosed administrator would have been surprised to know that she was a debutante in 1958. She was also one of the head majorettes with the Price High School marching band. Years later, her younger sister Catherine recalled how much Robinson cared about her appearance when she was in high school. She was very concerned about fashion and she had a keen sense of style. She liked wide skirts, wide belts, and sweaters. "She had very expensive tastes. *Very.* She wore nothing cheap. She couldn't stand cheap clothes, and cheap shoes she would not put on her feet." She was concerned that her clothes should flatter her figure.[24]

Her concern about her appearance did not end once Robinson entered the movement. Although she became less inclined to indulge her expensive tastes, she still took a great deal of care with her appearance, sometimes under very difficult circumstances. Movement colleague Connie Curry remembered one particularly illustrative incident that occurred when the SNCC delegation went to Rock Hill, South Carolina, in 1961.

> They all knew that they were going to be arrested and go to jail. And Rock Hill was a very tough and very scary place. We got up real, real early that morning. Everybody was ready to go. And Ruby Doris said, "Well everybody can just sort of sit down and do whatever because my hair is not right, and I'm rolling it, and I'm not leaving until it's curled." I thought, my God, this woman—she's going to be in jail within two hours. And she had these great big rollers . . . and everybody there just said, "Oh, okay."[25]

Robinson was not really "one of the boys" after all. What is clear is that Ruby Doris Smith Robinson was a woman whose existence called into question a whole range of stereotypes. Because she was an activist, she was not supposed to be "ladylike." Because she was an African American woman, she was not supposed to be feminine.

As she wrestled with the issue of femininity, Robinson was faced with a related problem: relationships between black and white women in SNCC. These relationships were the source of a great deal of tension within the organization at certain times. Part of this

24. Catherine Smith Robinson and Ruby O'Neal, interview by author, Atlanta, Ga., March 3, 1990.

25. Connie Curry, interview by author, Atlanta, Ga., November 10, 1990.

tension was rooted in the opposing perspectives of black and white women on some very fundamental issues. Cynthia Washington discussed some of those differences.

> During the fall of 1964, I had a conversation with Casey Hayden about the role of women in SNCC. She complained that all the women got to do was type, that their role was limited to office work no matter where they were. What she said didn't make any particular sense to me because, at the time, I had my own project in Bolivar County, Mississippi. A number of other black women also directed their own projects. What Casey and other white women seemed to want was an opportunity to prove they could do something other than office work. I assumed that if they could do something else, they'd probably be doing that.

Washington recognized how hard the work of a project director was, and besides that, "it wasn't much fun." Because of her insider's view, she was at a loss to understand why white women were complaining about their assignments. Their discontent over such issues only convinced Washington "how crazy they [white women] were."[26]

Even as they were conscious of the opposing perspectives of many of their white female colleagues, African American women in the movement were also painfully aware of the differences in the way society viewed them. One black female civil rights worker frankly discussed the resentment. "We've been getting beaten up for years trying to integrate lunch counters, movies, and so on, and nobody has ever paid us no attention or wrote about us. But these white girls come down here for a few months and get all the publicity. Everybody talks about how brave and courageous *they* are. What about us?" Another black female civil rights worker was both angered and amazed. When she was with a group demonstrating at a bus station, "a cop grabbed me by the arm and slapped my face. I don't know why I was surprised, but I really was." She decided to remind him of a basic tenet of southern etiquette. "I looked at him and I say, 'Listen Man, take another look at me. I'm a woman! You don't hit a woman! Didn't they teach you that?' He look kinda sorry, but he say, 'You're a niggah and that's all you are!'" Such a pervasive and negative view was bound to wound black women's sense of themselves. One black female civil rights

26. Washington, "We Started from Different Ends," 14.

worker clearly explained how deep those wounds were. White women, she said, did the less glamorous and domestic jobs "in a feminine kind of way, while [black women] . . . were out in the streets battling the cops. So it did something to what [our] femininity was about. We became amazons, less than and more than women at the same time."[27]

African American women's resentment about society's differential treatment of them was further complicated by the issue of physical appearance. Robinson and her African American colleagues came of age in a society that, from it earliest days, had judged African women by a European standard of beauty. Many women of African descent, including Robinson, had only to look in the mirror to see that they could never measure up physically. But many tried, and it was often quite painful.

Zohara Simmons, one of Robinson's SNCC colleagues and a fellow Spelman student, was keenly aware of the European standard of beauty that was idealized by so many. That awareness was born of Simmons's experience on the Spelman campus, a place famous for the "beauty" of its student body. Translation? A fairly high proportion of the students had light skin, keen features, and straight or nearly straight hair. Simmons explained the prevailing view at Spelman in the early sixties.

> First of all, the best of all possible worlds is that you are light as you can be, you have green eyes, or light brown, and you have long straight hair. They [Morehouse students] would be lined up outside your door, trying to get a date. Then you could be paper bag brown or above and have long hair that you have to straighten, you know, that's still real cool, right? Cause we were all straightening— tough—in those days. Then, of course, you could be darker and have straight hair, long straight hair. . . . Then the last, of the last category was that you were dark skinned and you had short hair or medium length hair, you know?[28]

Having physical features that did not measure up to the white standard of beauty could be painful for black women sometimes.

27. Alvin Poussaint, "The Stresses of the White Female Worker in the Civil Rights Movement in the South," *Journal of American Psychiatry* 123 (October 1966): 403; Josephine Carson, *Silent Voices* (New York: McGraw Hill, 1969), 60; Sara Evans, *Personal Politics: The Roots of Women's Liberation in the Civil Rights Movement and the New Left* (New York: Random House, 1979), 81.

28. Zohara Simmons, interview by author, Philadelphia, Pa., December 17, 1988.

Because she was dark skinned, Simmons learned that the pain was caused less by white reaction than by black rejection. She insisted, "Some of the Morehouse guys were so nasty to a person who looked like myself. *Overt.* I mean, straight up."[29] Appearance was important, but black women were powerless to change their appearance, at least permanently. Feelings of insecurity about their looks were a terrible burden that African American women were forced to bear. Ruby Doris Smith Robinson had to carry her share of this black women's burden because she was not particularly light skinned, she had broad features, and her hair was not naturally straight. Like so many African American women of her generation, she wrestled with negative views of who and what she was—views that were popularized by white society and then embraced, at least in part, by black society.

Thus the relationship between black female SNCC staffers and their white female activist colleagues was influenced by black female resentment about American society's history of negative perceptions and treatment of them. At the same time, however, the attitudes of white females also contributed to tension between black females and themselves. American white people, even sympathetic female activists, had all been touched to a greater or lesser extent by the negative black stereotypes so popular in their society. Psychiatrist Alvin Poussaint, in his evaluation of the adjustment of white women volunteers to the rigors of Freedom Summer, found that a number of these women were indeed struggling with racist stereotypes. In Poussaint's estimation, some of them lost that struggle. He identified a syndrome he labeled the White African Queen Complex.

> At the center of this "complex" is probably a tabooed and repressed fantasy of the intelligent, brave, and beautiful white woman leading the poor, downtrodden, and oppressed black man to freedom and salvation. One white female worker told me she sometimes felt like "the master's child come to free the slaves." Another confided, "What an electrifying feeling it is to be worshipped by the Negroes."[30]

Black women bitterly resented this attitude and the condescending behavior that accompanied it.

29. Ibid.
30. Poussaint, "The Stresses of the White Female Worker," 404.

A further complicating factor in this white female–black female conflict was the issue of class. Many of the white women who worked in the civil rights movement were middle class or even upper middle class. On the other hand, many of the African American activists, including Robinson, were from families with middle-class aspirations but only working-class incomes. Some of these black women had faced very difficult economic circumstances during their lives. Consequently, when middle-class white women doing office work began to complain about being oppressed, Robinson and other black women like her simply lost their patience. Joyce Ladner recalled tense times in the office.

> The impression Ruby conveyed was that . . . white women were always at kind of uneasy peace around her. She didn't mistreat them, but they sure didn't pull that . . . on her. She was the last person they would run to with some complaint about, "Oh we're poor oppressed, we're poor oppressed white women here. . . ." She'd been in jail and was from a poor background herself. So it was hard for her to have sympathy for a girl from Sarah Lawrence who felt put upon.[31]

Some in the movement charged that even though a preponderance of the white women on the permanent staff were limited to office work, they tried to exert too much influence. Regardless of its accuracy, this perception helped to intensify the conflict. Joyce Ladner clearly recalled this notion. "See, a lot of white women who came into SNCC even though they felt they were discriminated against, in quotes, . . . they still tried to dominate the office. I mean it was a matter of [not] being content anywhere—[even] if you put them in the field. They were white women: that's all that was necessary to know about them."[32] Because Robinson was such a critical part of the central office staff, she found herself in the middle of this complex of feelings and resentments plaguing both black and white women. In retrospect, at least one white female staff member in SNCC understood why Robinson and the other black women were so suspicious. "If I were to put myself in Ruby Doris's head what I would say is, you know, 'Here comes Dinky Romilly, here comes Mary King. Why are they here? They don't have any intrinsic interest in promoting the rights of black

31. Joyce Ladner, interview by the author, Washington, D.C., December 18, 1988.
32. Ibid.

people. They're middle class white women. . . .' And I can understand that . . . she would be very suspect of that."[33]

In such an atmosphere Robinson continued to exert her increasing authority. She had to cope with a variety of attitudes, resentments, and behaviors exhibited by white women staff members. At the same time, she had to balance these against the resentments and perceptions of the black women on the staff. In the midst of this she was still dragging around her share of the black woman's burden as she sought to cope with the historical and recent negative assessments of black female morality, femininity, physical appearance, and capabilities.

As Robinson wrestled with questions of femininity and black female–white female tensions, her life was complicated by still another factor. In addition to being a full-time freedom fighter, Ruby Doris Smith Robinson was also a wife and a mother. She married Clifford Robinson in 1964 and gave birth to a son, Kenneth Toure, in 1965. Even though she was totally committed to the movement, her family obligations were also important to her. One of her close movement friends, Mildred Forman, remembered that Robinson was "ecstatic over the baby and the husband." Even though Robinson was already extraordinarily busy with her work in SNCC, Forman felt that motherhood further enriched her life. "I think that was the best thing that could have happened to her, because she just . . . beamed and glowed with the baby." Although motherhood added a unique richness, it also added tasks to Robinson's already overburdened schedule. As she juggled motherhood and movement work, at times the frantic pace of her life caught up with her. Movement colleague and friend Freddie Greene Biddle clearly recalled an incident that graphically illustrated how overwhelming things sometimes became.

> I remember once Ruby came out [of her house] with all these bags
> and her pocket book and all this stuff, and we're going to the of-
> fice, and she's going to drop, uh, Toure . . . off. . . . Well she's back-
> ing out of the . . . driveway and I'm in the car. . . . She had all
> these bags and stuff and so then all of a sudden she said, "Oh shit!"
> [I] said "What's wrong?" She's forgotten the baby![34]

33. Romilly, interview.
34. Forman, interview; Freddie Greene Biddle, interview by author, McComb, Miss. June 29, 1991.

As Robinson settled into motherhood, she was still struggling to find a balance between her marital and her movement duties. Her husband, Clifford, was also a SNCC staff member. Despite his membership in the organization, however, Clifford's commitment paled in comparison to Ruby's. He freely admitted that he joined the movement only because of his wife's involvement. This differential commitment was sometimes the source of a certain amount of tension. Zohara Simmons recalled:

> I can just remember, you know, you run in the office and he's [Clifford] standing there waiting on her to go. And, you know, everybody's saying, "Ruby Doris, so and so and so." And he's saying, "Look, we got to go." And she's saying, "Cliff, wait a minute . . . I got to take care of this." And him stalking off mad. And her saying, "Oh, God . . . later for him, then." I imagine she caught hell when she got home.

But Clifford insisted that the volume of work Ruby did in SNCC did not cause a strain on their relationship, even though "it was going on all the time around the house." Clifford went on to explain, though, that when *he* thought Ruby was doing too much movement work after office hours, "I was there to stop it."[35]

Robinson tried very hard to balance her family relationships and her movement obligations. At the same time, she was confronted by enormous pressures and tensions in SNCC. Her determination and commitment had always given her the strength to cope with all these concerns. As a freedom rider Robinson faced down hostile white mobs. She confronted brutal southern sheriffs and assorted Klan representatives when she canvassed for voter registration. As a powerful leader, Robinson had confronted numerous and strident conflicts in SNCC. But when she was diagnosed with terminal cancer in April of 1967, even her strength and determination were not enough. She wanted to continue with the important things in her life: raising her son, caring for her husband, and guiding her beloved Student Nonviolent Coordinating Committee. But the cancer would not let her. Ruby Doris Smith Robinson died on October 9, 1967, at the age of twenty-five.

Many of her SNCC colleagues are convinced that it was not cancer but the frantic pace of her life that killed her. They all

35. Simmons, interview; Clifford Robinson, interview by author, Atlanta, Ga., March 17, 1989.

remember how Robinson always tried to do everything; her commitment to the civil rights movement did not stop her from trying to be a full-time wife and mother. Furthermore, according to some, the SNCC conflicts were exacerbated because of her gender. It was simply too much for one woman. Despite the conflicts and difficulties that faced her, however, Robinson would not have lived her life any other way. She was a woman who believed that she could and should do it all.

AFTERWORD

ELIZABETH FOX-GENOVESE

Emancipation, followed and confirmed by military defeat at Appomattox, destroyed the social system of slavery upon which the Old South had been grounded. In the event, the transformation of the formal status of southern blacks from enslaved to free people did not realize their dreams of freedom, but it did open a protracted period in which the relations among white and black southerners were gradually, and sometimes painfully, redefined. In this process of redefinition, the roles of women emerged as central to both black and white southerners as they sought to reconstruct their families and communities and to establish their place in a "free" biracial society. The struggles over the disposition of the labor of freedwomen captured in microcosm the essence of the struggles that informed Reconstruction and the initially halting construction of the New South. There can be no doubt that, for many if not most of the freedmen and freedwomen, freedom preeminently meant the ability to form their own households and, in the measure possible, to establish and defend their own conception of delineated male and female spheres. In this respect, as in surprisingly many others, they proved themselves heirs to many of the values on which white antebellum southerners had prided themselves, notably, the integrity of households and families, the right of men to represent both in the public sphere, and women's distinctly domestic identities and responsibilities.

Under these conditions, it would hardly have been surprising that the "woman question" emerged as central to the vicissitudes of Reconstruction and New South society and politics. Not least, former slave women's determination to realize the substance of the

224

formal claims to freedom with which emancipation had endowed them challenged white women's sense of their privileged status at every turn. The most obvious challenges were launched through such seeming trifles as the freedwomen's determination to dress and carry themselves, whenever their circumstances permitted, as ladies of quality.[1] The scarcely less obvious and no less provoking challenges concerned their determination to dispose of their own time, working for others only as their obligations to their own households and families permitted, and, to the extent possible, coming and going as they chose. Former slaveholding women found even these apparently small signs of independence almost unbearable because they served as constant reminders of the independence of those whom they had been accustomed to view (however preposterously) primarily as extensions of their own will.[2]

The more serious challenges, however, concerned the determination of freedwomen to establish themselves on an independent footing and, above all, to ensure the social and economic advancement of their children. A former slaveholder like Ella Gertrude Clanton Thomas did not miss the point. She raged at the idea that while her own sons worked in the fields, the sons of freedwomen attended school.[3] Gertrude Thomas was not alone in her resentment. Throughout the former slave states, whites moved steadily toward depriving freed people of as much of the economic mobility and independence normally associated with freedom as possible. Whether by attempting to bind laborers to plantations through tenancy, sharecropping, and the payment of annual (rather than weekly or monthly) wages, or by attempting to deny blacks such attributes of economic freedom as the free participation in

1. See, for example, Leon Litwack, *Been in the Storm So Long: The Aftermath of Slavery* (New York: Random House, 1979), and, on the antebellum antecedents of these attitudes, Eugene D. Genovese, *Roll, Jordan, Roll: The World the Slaves Made* (New York: Pantheon, 1974).

2. Mary Margaret Johnston-Miller, "Heirs to Paternalism: Elite White Women and Emancipation in Alabama and Georgia" (Ph.D. diss., Emory University, 1994).

3. Ella Gertrude Clanton Thomas Diary, Perkins Library, Duke University. See also *The Secret Eye: The Journal of Ella Gertrude Clanton Thomas, 1848–1889*, ed. Virginia Ingraham Burr (Chapel Hill: University of North Carolina Press, 1990).

markets, whites sought to ensure the economic marginalization and continuing impoverishment of blacks.[4]

Freedwomen responded to these and other assaults on their full disposition of their freedom in a myriad of ways. In general it is safe to say that notwithstanding, or even in the service of, their commitment to establishing and sustaining their families and households, they frequently acted with a vigorous independence that apparently had little to do with conventional notions of separate spheres. Yet their forceful claims to independence never meant that they simply embraced the vision of female individualism that was gradually gaining ground among northern defenders of woman suffrage.

The consequences of war and defeat also offered white women new opportunities for independence, though not always welcome ones. The absence or loss of husbands, fathers, brothers, and sons especially left rural white women to cope with problems of farm management to which most were unaccustomed and for which most were poorly prepared. The blows fell hard on the women of all classes, but elite women were especially prone to respond with a bitterness that embodied their knowledge that current hardships might portend a permanent change in their social and economic status. Under these conditions, the response of a Gertrude Thomas, although far from admirable, was painfully understandable. The corrosive sense of her own family's loss fueled her resentment of her former slaves' gain. Nor were her responses unique. Throughout the South, elite women experienced emancipation as their own and their families' loss of property that had legally been theirs. Thus even those who had enjoyed what they considered warm personal relations with their slaves—and we know that the slaves frequently viewed those relations differently—registered emancipation as a trauma that, however paradoxically, transformed intimates into threatening rivals or even enemies.

Even at the worst, most elite women were able to employ one or more female servants to do, or at least help with, the housework, which elite women notoriously disliked. And in many cases, as those relations were reestablished on the new footing of wage labor, elite women appear to have attempted to infuse them with a

4. Mary Ellen Curtin, "The 'Human World' of Black Women in Alabama Prisons," in this volume.

personal dimension that defied wage labor's logic of contractual relations among formal equals. Freedwomen, for their part, seem to have had their own reasons for complying in this effort, with a view to retaining some semblance of elite women's traditional obligations to them. Thus a freedwoman, working for wages, would expect her employer to provide a "servant's pan" of food for her family or other goods and would expect more flexibility in the hours she worked than, say, an Irish maid in Boston or New York. Elite women, for their part, would expect to treat their female servants more as dependents than as employees and would never hesitate to ask them to work longer than the stipulated hours.[5]

Both groups of women, in other words, concurred that the relation between mistress and maid should have a personal dimension that transcended the contractual relations of wage labor. But they differed in their understanding of what the appropriate personal dimension should be. In this respect their struggles to define a "free" model of household labor mirrored the struggles between planters and field hands in areas like the sugar parishes of Louisiana, in which wage labor rather than sharecropping predominated. Both sides in these struggles had their own reasons to wish a reconstruction of aspects of their former relations, even as both sides had distinct ideas of how a "New" South should differ from the Old.[6]

These struggles, which lay at the core of the southern experience of Reconstruction, cast a long shadow over the emergence of the New South. They shaped the fabric of the lives of both white and black women, but they have remained largely hidden stories, not so much because of the blindness of historians, although that has had its say, but because these struggles occurred within the interstices of families and households. And although the destruction of slavery included the destruction of the distinctly independent foundations of southern households, the nature of Reconstruction in a tensely biracial, rural society mightily contributed to

5. Johnston-Miller, "Heirs to Paternalism"; Voloria Mack-Williams, "Hard Workin' Women: Class Divisions and African-American Women's Work in Orangeburg, South Carolina, 1880–1940" (Ph.D. diss., State University of New York at Binghamton, 1991).

6. John Rodrigue, "Raising Cain: From Slavery to Free Labor in Louisiana's Sugar Parishes, 1862–1880" (Ph.D. diss., Emory University, 1993).

a resurrection of households as the fundamental units of southern society, albeit on a new basis.[7]

As Jacquelyn Dowd Hall and her colleagues have pointed out, the metaphor of family that had enjoyed such a powerful sway in the Old South reemerged in the New to capture and humanize the relations among laborers and employers.[8] The textile mills of the New South had their immediate roots in the sharecropping and tenancy of the Reconstruction and post-Reconstruction periods. Most laborers clung to their own rural households, even when they and the households were enmeshed in the tentacles of landlords' control. Unlike the slaves of the antebellum South, these laborers did not, as a rule, regard themselves as members of the landlord's household, but even as they worked to establish the fragile independence of their own households they retained a commitment to reciprocity, although more often than not it worked to their disadvantage.

In fiercely defending the integrity of households and families, black and white southerners collaborated in the creation of a world in which the life of individuals was, at least rhetorically, subordinated to and contained within the life of the immediate groups to which they belonged. Thus even if black southerners recognized the relics of paternalism and the myth of family in the relations between employers and workers as more mythical than substantive, they perfectly understood that aspects of the myth facilitated their creation and defense of families and households of their own. The harsh realities of postbellum racism ensured that black southerners could only be most fully themselves within the security of their own households and, by extension, churches and such other institutions as they managed to build.

Postbellum racism, aided and abetted by subsequent (including antiracist) historians, focused the spotlight of public attention on what, in the end, may well have been the least significant aspect of the relations between blacks and whites—sexuality. The infinitely complex, continuing struggles between blacks and whites of all classes over the possibility of establishing economic independence

7. For a discussion of the distinct nature of antebellum southern households, see Elizabeth Fox-Genovese, *Within the Plantation Household: Black and White Women of the Old South* (Chapel Hill: University of North Carolina Press, 1988).

8. Jacquelyn Dowd Hall et al., *Like a Family: The Making of a Southern Cotton Mill World* (Chapel Hill: University of North Carolina Press, 1987).

in the one case and securing economic domination in the other were cloaked in an imagery of sexuality that then, and sometimes since, served to distract attention from what the struggles were really about. The imagery especially played upon the sexuality of white women and black men, painting lurid pictures of the predatory aspirations of the latter and no less lurid pictures of the vulnerability of the former. And by so doing, it reinforced the predisposition of southerners to believe that only at great risk could women venture upon the public space.

The preference to restrict women to the private sphere had also prevailed in the North, where even after the Civil War it retained a strong ideological grip. But the rapid progress of industrialization and urbanization had in practice pushed or pulled innumerable women at least partially into the public sphere, and after the war it was increasingly pushing or pulling them in as individuals. Cities, among their other advantages, offered women a range of employments and made it much easier than rural areas for women to live independently. By the end of the nineteenth century, northern and midwestern women in particular were establishing a public presence that fully justified the demand of growing numbers that their right to vote be acknowledged.

The accelerating urbanization and atomization of northern society further gave substance to women reformers' claims that public spaces required public housekeeping, including adequate lighting of streets, sewage, safe drinking water, and various protections of the interests of unsuspecting consumers. The causes with which women associated themselves and the issue of suffrage were ever more likely to intertwine as growing numbers of women insisted that they must themselves be able to defend their interests and the interests of women less fortunate or independent than they. Their rhetoric in pursuing their goals figuratively destroyed the walls of households by insisting that the public sphere should be understood as a household writ large and be safe for each of its individual members. Thus even though most northern and midwestern women remained primarily identified with the families that supported and concealed them, women's lives had decisively moved into the public gaze.

As the nineteenth century drew to a close, the South also began to experience some of the urbanization and industrialization that dominated other parts of the country. But the acceleration of urbanization did not, overnight, lead southerners to abandon their assumptions about the primacy of households. Dallas business leaders, for example, held progressive views on some urban issues, but tended, with respect to urban social policies, to rely upon rural assumptions about household responsibility and self-sufficiency. Confronted with the problem of planning for their growing city, they maintained that families should make their own arrangements for water, fuel, and waste disposal. In their view, according to Elizabeth Enstam (in this volume), "matters of health . . . lay within the private sphere, with each separate household." And when Dallas women challenged the city's reluctance to provide for the public sphere, they justified their efforts in the name of motherhood.

The tendency to justify women's public efforts by reference to their private identities was not unique to the South; but because the South came to these problems later than other regions and, especially, because it came to them with a distinct social legacy, the tendency persisted longer in the South than elsewhere. And its persistence in turn perpetuated rather than challenged the rhetoric of family, even as the specific policies were gradually undermining the rugged independence of households. Women reformers' adoption of a familial language, with its echoes of the older paternalism, also underscored an emphasis upon the responsibilities of the elite rather than upon the rights of the poor.

In Atlanta and Birmingham, where, even more than in Dallas, racial relations decisively dominated any move toward enlightened public policies, the tension between elite responsibilities and popular rights assumed central importance, and both drew attention to women's appropriate public roles. As Atlanta grew and its urban problems grew with it, elite white women typically directed their efforts toward the Woman's Christian Temperance Union and a host of other reform activities such as the needs of "wayward" girls. By the early decades of the twentieth century, their efforts had created a charitable web, which Darlene Roth has called a system of "matronage."[9]

Most of these women reformers continued to work from the

9. Darlene Roth, "Matronage: Patterns in Women's Organizations, Atlanta, Georgia, 1890–1940" (Ph.D. diss., George Washington University, 1978). See also Megan Seaholm, "'Earnest Women': The White Woman's Club Movement in Progressive Era Texas, 1880–1920" (Ph.D. diss., Rice University, 1988).

basis of their families and, like the women of Dallas, to underscore their sense of maternal responsibility for those less privileged than they. But in the world of Jim Crow that the South had become, their public maternal instincts did not extend to the unfortunate of the black community. In Atlanta, which by the turn of the century was the most segregated city in the South, elite black women like Lugenia Burns Hope, drawing upon the resources of their own community, undertook those responsibilities themselves.[10]

Segregation weighed heavily upon southern urbanization with its attendant problems of raising and allocating public resources for general welfare. And as segregation shaped the experience of white and black women, so it shaped southern attitudes toward woman suffrage. Widespread southern hostility to woman suffrage derived in no small part from white concerns that granting white women the vote would once again raise the question of universal suffrage, forcing white voters to compete with black. But it also derived from the persisting conviction that women belonged within families and households, not in public affairs. The white women who supported suffrage disagreed, insisting that in a rapidly chang-ing world women had a necessary role in public affairs, if only to protect their own and their children's interests. As a rule, however, they did not countenance black suffrage, whether for women or men. They thus, in effect, argued that southern society could af-ford a significant measure of individualism for white women with-out disturbing the biracial caste system.

Throughout the rural South, opposition to woman suffrage far outweighed support for it, in part out of concern to retain a white monopoly of political power, but in part out of commitment to traditional household values. Southern antisuffrage rhetoric, which remained closely tied to antebellum patterns, "flourished on the plantation, in the Black Belt, and in the country town." Product of rural conservatism that it might be, southern antisuffragism espe-cially expressed the values of plantation-based economic elites, many of which were profiting from national and, increasingly, regional industrial development. According to Elna Green (in this volume), the leaders spoke for big agriculture and big textile inter-ests, and the fundamental unit of their worldview was the family,

10. Jacqueline Anne Rouse, *Lugenia Burns Hope: Black Southern Re-former* (Athens: University of Georgia Press, 1989).

not the individual.[11] Eugene Anderson, a convinced antisuffragist, attacked the suffrage movement explicitly as "an attempt at individualism and an attack on the home." Anderson angrily refused to countenance the setting up of individualism "in place of the family unit." According to a Kentucky newspaper editor who shared his views, "Votes for women means that the individual and not the family is to be the unit of the State."[12]

The antisuffragists were right that American society was moving from an emphasis on the family to one on the individual, but tinkering with the electorate could not stop the trend, which was resulting from economic and demographic forces that politics could not reverse. And although in the South families still remained stronger and individualism weaker than in the more industrialized sections of the nation, by the early twentieth century the South was following the national path. Enfranchisement of women acknowledged and articulated those changes but did not produce them. Nor would denying women the vote arrest them.

For white antisuffragists, the determination to restrain the progress of individualism could not be divorced from the determination to forestall any change in the relations between the races. Not content with white supremacy, the antisuffragists wanted a white monopoly. Indeed the very economic and demographic changes that seemed to invite woman suffrage were also drawing more blacks and whites into cities, where they had to share the public space. Jim Crow and *Plessy v. Ferguson* had ensured the institutional segregation of the public space, and white antisuffragists resisted any concessions that might jeopardize it. Seeing relations of gender, race, and class as inextricably entwined, they opposed any change in any element of the fragile balance.

White southerners were not alone in their opposition to suffrage, which significant numbers of blacks shared, also because of concerns about gender and race. Some blacks feared unleashing white hostility. Others, like Annie Blackwell, a black temperance leader in North Carolina, feared that it would result in votes for

11. See also Marjorie Spruill Wheeler, *New Women of the New South: The Leaders of the Woman Suffrage Movement in the Southern States* (New York: Oxford University Press, 1993).

12. Eugene Anderson, *Unchaining the Demons of the Lower World, or A Petition of Ninety-Nine Per Cent against Suffrage* (Macon, Ga.: n.p., [1918?]); *Berea (Ky.) Citizen,* April 1, 1920; quoted in *Woman Patriot,* April 24, 1920.

white women only and, accordingly, would not help and might even hurt the black community. And some opposed woman suffrage because of their commitment to the notion of separate spheres. Like southern whites, southern blacks could not judge woman suffrage on its merits as a natural right or a question of simple justice. They had always to think about its impact upon southern blacks as a group.[13]

Woman suffrage, which passed despite widespread southern opposition, did not immediately threaten the racial segregation that white southerners so fiercely sought to preserve. Nor did it apparently bring serious dissension into the white southern families, since, for many decades, white southern women overwhelmingly voted the same as the men of their families. Yet the passage of suffrage did confirm that the times were changing, and it especially confirmed women's emerging claim upon a variety of public roles. Southern women in growing numbers, though at a slower pace than women in other parts of the country, were entering the labor force and a variety of public organizations. For most, like the black and white female teachers of the Georgia up-country, these new activities do not seem to have threatened women's strong ties to their families. Many teachers, indeed, appear to have brought the values of an older paternalism into their work with students.[14]

Black southern women, who were no less concerned than white women with strengthening their own families and communities, were also beginning to find new opportunities. Always more likely to work outside their own households than white women, black women were less likely to find paid labor a novel experience. And at least until World War II, the vast majority continued to be restricted to domestic service of various kinds. A small but growing number, however, were beginning to join the ranks of teachers, nurses, and other low-level professionals.[15] Their progress in these

13. Elna Green, "'Ideals of Government, of Home, and of Women': The Ideology of Southern White Antisuffragism," in this volume.

14. Ann Short Chirhart, "'It Strains Your Charity beyond Endurance': African-American and White Female Teachers of the Georgia Upcountry, 1920–1970" (Ph.D. diss., Emory University, in progress).

15. Mack-Williams, "Hard Workin' Women"; Stephanie Shaw, "Black Women in White Collars: A Social History of Lower-Level Professional Black Women Workers" 2 vols. (Ph. D. diss., Ohio State University, 1986); Chirhart, "'It Strains Your Charity Beyond Endurance'"; Rose Cannon and Jackie Zalumas, "South-

areas did not challenge segregation, for their training and exercise of their professions normally occurred under segregated conditions, and they received constant reminders of the restrictions under which they labored. Black nurses had to live with being addressed as "nurse" while white nurses were addressed as "Miss"; black women, like black men, could not safely travel unless they had a friend, relative, or contact with whom to stay for every lap of the journey; black teachers, especially in rural areas, worked with even fewer resources than white.

Segregation exposed southern black women to countless pervasive indignities, but it never crippled them. And, as we are slowly beginning to learn, in many instances it also afforded them a wall of privacy behind which to build and strengthen their families and communities with minimal white interference. Black teachers, for example, treated black students not as second-class citizens but as the heirs to the kingdom, and they may even have been more willing than white teachers to insist that they perform to the best of their abilities. Black women also had their own struggles with the men of their families and communities, not least to secure support for the causes and projects they especially valued. Among black women and men, as among white, sexual tensions, frequently (but not exclusively) over male philandering abounded.

Black and white women, notwithstanding the innumerable differences in their situations, shared many of the liabilities of women within a strictly male-dominated society for which that domination articulated and anchored inequalities of class and race. Yet the vulnerabilities and obstacles they shared did not lead them to make common cause with one another. For both groups, the gradual move from the seclusion of households into the public arena occurred within the context of their communities and, more often than not, depended at least in part upon alliances with and support from the men of their own race. Both also confronted a public sphere that was perceived to be especially dangerous precisely because of the pervasive tensions between the races. Thus even as women emerged from the seclusion of families and even as the

ern Nursing in the Age of Segregation: Visions in Black and White" and Peggy Bell, "Birthed in the Shadows: The Influence of the Tuskegee School of Nurse-Midwifery for Colored Nurses on the Health Status of Southern Blacks in the 1940s," in *Servants or Professionals? Thoughts on Nursing and the Politics of Caring* (forthcoming).

independence of households was eroded by the progress of industrialization and urbanization, women's lives and accomplishments remained shadowed, if not hidden, by the high walls that continued to enclose their respective races.

By the end of World War II, it was becoming clear that even those walls would not stand. In Georgia, for example, mobilization for combat and industrial production during the war pulled innumerable black and white women off farms into cities and factories. One after another of the women openly expressed the satisfaction she took with her work and the pleasure she derived from a newfound sense of competence and independence. Notwithstanding segregation, blacks and whites increasingly worked together in massive factories such as the Bell Plant in Marietta, Georgia, and, working together, rediscovered what those who had lived and worked together in rural households had always known, namely, that people of the other race were people.[16]

No more than in the past did the recognition of one another's humanity lead most white southerners to embrace integration. But the wave of postwar prosperity that was rapidly transforming the South from a backwater into the Sun Belt ensured that southerners would increasingly have to share the public space of cities, including a variety of workplaces. And the same forces that brought blacks and whites together did, as the antisuffragists had fearfully predicted, increasingly release women from the control of families. By the 1960s, the civil rights movement was drawing progressive southern white women into the struggle for integration, which many were beginning to see as a matter of justice and morality; and for some, work in the movement led naturally into a commitment to a resurgent feminism. As the social relations that had limited the freedom and opportunities of white women and black people began to crumble, a new wave of individualism, frequently expressed as a concern for individual rights, made its mark on many parts of the South, especially some college and university campuses, some of the larger cities, and regions such as North Carolina that seemed to have longer progressive traditions.

As is well known, not all southerners embraced the new spirit of individualism with equal enthusiasm, and some bitterly op-

16. Interviews for Georgia Public Television's documentary, *War Abroad, Changes at Home,* on women in Georgia during World War II.

posed it. Nor, even after the initial dust had settled and the basic gains been achieved, did black southerners move easily into full equality with whites. The long history of economic and educational deprivation ensured that formal equality of opportunity, in the measure that it emerged, would not alone guarantee anything that resembled equality of social and economic condition. Under these conditions the needs and aspirations of black and white women inevitably diverged as much or more than they converged. The temptation for black women, in the South as throughout the rest of the country, to view the woman's movement as a white woman's movement remained justifiably strong. But even stronger than black women's sense of exclusion was their sense that now, as in the past, their first commitment must be to the men, women, and children of their own community.

By the 1980s, it was abundantly clear that women of both races, but especially black women, were gaining freedom from men at an extraordinary rate. As the rates of single women, single mothers, and never-married mothers soared, women struggled with the burdens as well as the opportunities of their new independence. Released from the seclusion as well as the protection of households and families, women, by choice or necessity, assumed a still frequently tenuous place in the public sphere. Women's emergence from the shadows of privacy signaled the South's coming full participation in the nation and, thus, however paradoxically, confirmed the centrality of their roles to the dynamics and character of southern society.

From antebellum times through Reconstruction and beyond, southerners, especially white southern men, had been wont to insist upon (white) womanhood as the highest embodiment of southern culture and values. Woman's "purity" had justified white men's domination over her and over all black people. Her purported vulnerability to rape by predatory black men justified and masked the exclusion of black people from virtually all forms of economic opportunity. Upon her remaining hidden, it was claimed, depended the "well-being of society" (read, an entire system of social and economic stratification). Black men were never in a position to claim the same position for the black woman in society at large, but there is good reason to believe that they harbored a similar vision of her importance within their own community. Certainly many held black women to high standards of domesticity and resisted women's independence as destructive to the prospects of "the race."

If the Civil War had, in large measure, been fought to decide the fate of slavery within the United States, it had no less been fought to determine the political and economic future of the country. In retrospect, we may see that the southern defeat at Appomattox signaled the unfettering of the country's industrial forces and the triumph of a consolidated, rather than confederated, conception of government. It released individualism from the lingering traces of corporatism that had—especially in the South—bound women to households dominated by men. The inescapable consequences of this individualism included new and rapidly changing roles for women and African Americans.

But in time and place, these implications of victory were less than clear to many Americans on both sides. For many Americans, independent of their position on slavery or states' rights, had emerged from the war as they had entered it—attached to the dream of independent farm households. The majority of freedmen and freedwomen assuredly assumed that "forty acres and a mule" constituted the substance of freedom. But their vision, which was doomed to swift disappointment, was shared by untold numbers of others, northern as well as southern, who were loath to accept that wage labor, crowded cities, and capitalist agriculture epitomized the good life for which so many had fought and died. Southerners were especially reluctant to relinquish the vision, all the more because they believed that much of its substance had been wrested from them by the Union armies and the Federal government. The signs of the times may have been there to be read by those who chose to do so, but many did not so choose.

But where northerners could focus upon getting back to the lives that the war had disrupted, black and white southerners could hardly escape the knowledge that their lives had changed beyond recognition. As white southerners set about pulling together the remnants of their lives and their region, many clung the more fiercely to the values and habits they could salvage. Facing the economic devastation of their region, they also faced a revolution in the relations between black and white people. Determined to enforce a hierarchical separation between whites and blacks, they pulled a newly punitive racism from the ashes of slavery. For however debilitating the racism that had permeated slavery, the destruction of slavery as a social system unleashed a racism of an altogether more virulent order. No less portentously, it unleashed what would eventually prove the irreversible forces of an individualism that implied the emergence of women as independent beings from the constraints (and protections) of families and households.

Postbellum southern racism, which had more in common with pervasive northern racism than is commonly acknowledged, embodied the fears and tensions of a world in which whites and blacks competed directly for scarce resources.[17] That the war, emancipation, and defeat had seriously debilitated the economic resources of many elite families only made the situation worse. Struggles between planters and freed people took somewhat different forms in different parts of the South, but were ubiquitous. And at the heart of many of those struggles lay the resistance of freedwomen to return to work in the fields, or indeed in the houses, of whites on the old terms—or frequently on any terms at all.

As the essays in this volume suggest, the virtually simultaneous emergence of black and white women from their previously "hidden" history resulted from the decisive weakening of the structures of family and household within which they had previously been contained. And, notwithstanding persistent inequalities of economic resources among women themselves, it resulted in growing similarities in women's social position. Thus while the differences between white and black men continue to widen, those between white and black women as individuals are beginning, however marginally, to decline. It would appear that now, as in the past, women's situation indeed embodies the essential values of southern society, and that, more than in the past, women hold the core of the future in their hands.

17. On nineteenth-century black women's bitterness about northern racism, we may consider the verdict of Harriet E. Wilson, *Our Nig; or, Sketches from the Life of a Free Black, in a Two-Story White House, North. Showing That Slavery's Shadows Fall Even There,* ed. Henry Louis Gates, Jr. (New York: Vintage Books, 1983).

NOTES ON THE CONTRIBUTORS

Mary Ellen Curtin received her doctoral degree from Duke University. She taught at the University of South Florida and is currently on the faculty of Georgia Southern University.

Elizabeth York Enstam, who received her Ph.D. from Duke University, is an independent historian in Dallas, Texas. She is completing a manuscript, "Women and the Creation of Urban Life, Dallas, Texas, 1843–1920."

Cynthia Griggs Fleming, who received her Ph.D. from Duke University, is director of African-American Studies at the University of Tennessee, Knoxville, where she holds a joint appointment with the Department of History.

Glenda Elizabeth Gilmore completed her Ph.D. degree at the University of North Carolina at Chapel Hill and is an assistant professor at Queens College, Charlotte, North Carolina. Her dissertation won the 1993 Lerner-Scott Prize, awarded by the Organization of American Historians for the best dissertation in U.S. women's history.

Elna Green has joined the faculty of Sweet Briar College in Virginia following the completion of her doctoral program at Tulane University.

Christina Greene is project director of the Duke University–University of North Carolina Center for Research on Women and is completing a doctoral dissertation at Duke University on black and white women's activism.

Kathleen C. Hilton is an assistant professor of history at Pembroke State University in North Carolina. She received her Ph.D. in social history from Carnegie Mellon University.

Marianne Leung teaches part-time in the Department of History at Memphis State University, where she is completing her doctoral studies on the grass-roots birth control movement.

Steven Noll teaches part-time in the Department of History at the University of Florida, where he received his doctoral degree.

Lynne A. Rieff is part-time assistant professor of history at Judson College. She is completing her Ph.D. at Auburn University. Her research is a comparative study of home demonstration work in five southern states.

INDEX

business progressivism, 148–49; in Dallas, 85, 230; and institutionalization movement, 37, 43; race, class, and gender divisions in southern progressivism, 109, 135–36, 149; rural focus of, in South, 134–35; and USDA Extension Service, 6, 114, 115, 134–49

Prohibition of alcohol. *See* Temperance movement

Prostitution, and mental retardation, 41–43, 42n, 45–46

Public School Art League, 71

Pure Food and Drug Act, 83

Pure food and drug ordinance, in Dallas, 83–84

Race. *See* Black men; Black women; Civil rights movement; Discrimination

Racism. *See* Discrimination

Radical Southern History Conference, 188

Rafter, Nicole, 33

Ransom, Roger L., 17

Ray, Mrs. J. E., 167n

Reagon, Bernice, 196

Reconstruction, 224–28, 236, 237–38

Red Cross, 46, 93, 148

Reed, James, 60n

Religion, 131, 165

Republican party, 158, 170

Richardson, Judy, 214–15

Robinson, Clifford, 221–22

Robinson, Kenneth Toure, 221

Robinson, Reginald, 207

Robinson, Ruby Doris Smith: administrative style of, 206–7; and black femininity, 210–12, 215–21; boldness and courage of, 213–14; cancer of, 207–8; early life of, 204–5, 216; as executive secretary of SNCC, 205–6; physical appearance of, 211, 216, 219; privacy sought by, 207–10; protest activities of, 209–10, 212–13, 222; and relationships between black and white women in SNCC, 216–21; in

SNCC, 7, 204–23; as team player, 210; voice of, 211–12; as wife and mother, 206, 221–23

Rodrique, Jessie M., 67

Rogers, P. J., 22

Romaine, Anne, 192

Romaine, Howard, 183, 186–87, 188n

Romilly, Constancia, 211–12

Roosevelt, Theodore, 83

Roth, Darlene, 230

Rowe, Nancy, 17

Rural areas. *See* Extension Service

Russett, Cynthia, 33

Salt of the Earth, 197

San Antonio Express, 96

Sanders, Rabbi Ira, 52, 58, 64

Sandy, T. O., 126n

Sanger, Margaret, 4, 53, 54, 60, 60n, 63, 68

Sanger, Stuart, 53

Savage, Mary, 18–19

Sayer, Michael, 213

Scarritt College, 175–76

Schools: black teachers in, 139–40, 233–34; compulsory education law in Texas, 78, 79; election of women to Dallas school board, 87–89; improvement of, in Dallas, 71, 72, 73–74, 78, 86, 91n; southern Progressives' view of, 135; southern women's roles in, 88, 233

SCLC. *See* Southern Christian Leadership Conference (SCLC)

Scotia Seminary, 159, 161, 165

SDS. *See* Students for a Democratic Society (SDS)

Segregation. *See* Discrimination

Separate spheres of women, 74, 103–5, 226, 229, 231

Sexual assault, 25–26, 236

Sexuality: among male and female prisoners, 22–26; of feebleminded women, 34–35, 39, 41–43, 45–48, 51; of white women and black men in postbellum South, 228–29, 236